The Economic Crisis and European Integration

The Economic Crisis and European Integration

Edited by

Wim Meeusen

Professor of Economics, Universiteit Antwerpen, Belgium

Edward Elgar

Cheltenham, UK • Northampton, MA, USA

Published by
Edward Elgar Publishing Limited
The Lypiatts
15 Lansdown Road
Cheltenham
Glos GL50 2JA
UK

Edward Elgar Publishing, Inc.
William Pratt House
9 Dewey Court
Northampton
Massachusetts 01060
USA

A catalogue record for this book
is available from the British Library

Library of Congress Control Number: 2011924194

ISBN 978 1 84980 420 2

Printed and bound by MPG Books Group, UK

Contents

List of Contributors

Fabio C. Bagliano
Università di Torino
Dipartimento di Scienze Economiche
e Finanziarie
Torino, Italy
fabio.bagliano@unito.it

Helge Berger
Freie Universität Berlin and IMF
Berlin, Germany
hberger@imf.org

Nicola D. Coniglio
Università degli Studi di Bari 'Aldo
Moro'
Department of Economics and Mathematics
Bari, Italy
mconiglio@yahoo.com

Paul De Grauwe
Katholieke Universiteit Leuven
Centre for Economic Studies
Leuven, Belgium
Paul.DeGrauwe@econ.kuleuven.be

Sorin Dumitrescu
Academy of Economic Studies
Bucharest, Romania
sorin.dumitrescu@rei.ase.ro

Martin Heipertz
Federal Ministry of Finance
Minister's Office
Berlin, Germany
Martin.Heipertz@bmf.bund.de

Alexandra Horobet
Academy of Economic Studies
Bucharest, Romania
alexandra.horobet@rei.ase.ro

Demosthenes Ioannou
European Central Bank
DG International and European
Relations
Frankfurt-am-Main, Germany
Demosthenes.Ioannou@ecb.int

Kang-Soek Lee
Negocia, Paris Chamber of
Commerce and Industry (France) and
Université d'Orléans, France
Kang-soek.lee@univ-orleans.fr

Arjan M. Lejour
CPB, Netherlands Bureau for
Economic Policy Analysis
The Hague, The Netherlands
arjan.lejour@cpb.nl

John Lewis
De Nederlandsche Bank
Economics and Research Division
Amsterdam, The Netherlands
j.m.lewis@dnb.nl

Jasper Lukkezen
CPB, Netherlands Bureau for
Economic Policy Analysis
The Hague, The Netherlands
jasper.lukkezen@cpb.nl

Wim Meeusen
Universiteit Antwerpen
Department of Economics
Antwerpen, Belgium
wim.meeusen@ua.ac.be

Claudio Morana
Università del Piemonte Orientale
Dipartimento di Scienze Economiche
e Metodi Quantitativi and ICER
(Torino)
Novara, Italy
claudio.morana@eco.unipmn.it

Volker Nitsch
Technische Universität Darmstadt
Darmstadt, Germany
nitsch@vwl.tu-darmstadt.de

Mara Pirovano
Universiteit Antwerpen
Department of Economics
Antwerpen, Belgium
mara.pirovano@ua.ac.be

Francesco Prota
Università degli Studi di Bari 'Aldo
Moro'
Department of Economics and Math-
ematics
Bari, Italy
prota.francesco@tin.it

Zongxin Qian
Tilburg University
CentER and EBC
Tilburg, The Netherlands
qzx1983@hotmail.com

Selen Sarisoy Guerin
Vrije Universiteit Brussel
Institute for European Studies
Brussels, Belgium
sguerin@vub.ac.be

Jacques Vanneste
Universiteit Antwerpen
Department of Economics
Antwerpen, Belgium
jacques.vanneste@ua.ac.be

André Van Poeck
Universiteit Antwerpen
Department of Economics
Antwerpen, Belgium
andre.vanpoeck@ua.ac.be

Paul Veenendaal
CPB, Netherlands Bureau for
Economic Policy Analysis
The Hague, The Netherlands
paul.veenendaal@cpb.nl

1. Introduction and Outline

Wim Meeusen

The credit crunch and the ensuing financial and economic crisis of 2007-2009 did not only strike hard at the economy in the Western world itself, but also at its policy-makers, many of whom lost their bearings, at economics as a scientific discipline and, specifically, at the process of European integration itself. The latter aspect of the crisis was the theme of a conference held at the European Parliament on 2 June 2010 in Brussels, under the title 'The Economic Crisis and the Process of European Integration'. Obviously, the other aspects mentioned were never far away. The papers in this volume are a selection of the keynote addresses and of the contributions to this conference.

In Part I European governance issues are discussed. *De Grauwe*, in Chapter 2, argues convincingly that the present sovereign debt crisis in a number of Western economies finds its origin in unsustainable debt accumulation in the private sector and the operation of automatic stabilisers set in motion by the economic crisis. A tightening of the parameters of the Stability and Growth Pact of the European Monetary Union (EMU), regardless of the fact that this pact did not work well in the past, is therefore not the right answer. De Grauwe subsequently asks the question why there is presently such a high degree of macroeconomic divergence in the eurozone. After having dismissed a number of alternative explanations, like structural rigidities on labour markets, he concludes that 'idiosyncratic' (i.e. national) credit-fuelled 'animal spirits' must lie at the source of the crisis and the divergence across countries it created. The European Central Bank (ECB), being responsible not only for price stability but also for financial stability, is in his view the right instrument to deal with this. Its ability to apply differential minimum reserve requirements and to impose anti-cyclical capital ratios should be used to the full, and it should follow up its presidency of the recently created European Systemic Risk Board (ESRB) by action, and not only by issuing warnings.

Ioannou and Heipertz, in Chapter 3, write in the same vein. They forcefully advocate more political integration in the EU. Their thesis is that, more than being desirable as a matter of principle or from a normative, federalist point of view, increased political integration, in the face of the economic crisis and the divergence it caused across EU member states, should be seen as a necessary pre-condition for improving socio-economic performance in the EU. They argue that a 'quantum leap' in the political governance of the EU is necessary to continue to be able to provide 'SEES' ('stability, equity, efficiency and security' (Padoa-Schioppa et al., 1987)), in a period when the crisis has incited nation states to retreat behind their own borders, possibly endangering the long-term survival of the eurozone itself.

While the sovereign debt lapse is indeed a consequence rather than a cause of the present difficulties in the EU and the EMU, it became at the same time of course also a problem in itself. In Chapter 4, *Lejour, Lukkezen and Veenendaal* therefore examine in a technical way the sustainability of government debt in Europe. They carefully provide results for a number of alternative but related key indicators of debt sustainability under a few scenarios. The 'usual suspects' surely come out, but there are also some surprises. When the extra costs related to an ageing population are taken into account, Germany, France, the Netherlands, Spain, Italy and Portugal have to make larger efforts than the present ones to maintain sustainability of debt. Surely, in Greece and Ireland these efforts should be even more considerable.

In Chapter 5, *Coniglio and Prota* look into intra-country regional convergence/divergence and the role of economic and financial crises herein. They note that current growth theory does not yield consistent answers, and they therefore come up with a challenging hypothesis that would explain the observed 'accordion effect', i.e. the succession over time of increases and decreases of the movement towards convergence in many EU member states. The clue would be that less developed regions are hit by the negative shocks more severely than rich regions because existing firms localised in central regions are on average more modern and technologically more advanced, and thus better able to adjust their production to the shocks. Moreover, in the lagging areas spells of unemployment in the workforce induced by adverse shocks will with a higher probability lead to a permanent loss of skills and to a faster obsolescence of the stock of equipment and infrastructure (hysteresis).

In Chapter 6, *Sarisoy Guerin* deals with a more specific question of European governance. She examines empirically whether Bilateral Investment Treaties (BITs) have the desired positive effect on FDI inflows and outflows. She also addresses the question whether the transfer of competences from the member states to the EU for the conclusion of new BITs and the 'grandfathering' of existing BITs by the EU is expected to be beneficial.

Part II of the book is devoted to the effect of the crisis on global economic imbalances. *Bagliano and Morana*, in Chapter 7, ask the question whether economic and financial crises in the US have had an influence upon economic convergence in the euro area. They use a factor vector autoregressive (F-VAR) econometric methodology. They convincingly show that the interaction between US and Euro Area (EA) real and financial markets are complex and involve not only first, but also second and third moments. One of their results is that there is no evidence for a linkage between the state of the US business cycle and inflation dynamics in Europe. This result is, however, less striking than it may seem, in the light of Leijonhufvud's argument that (in spite of the new-classical and new-Keynesian inflation-targeting rhetoric of the Fed and also of the ECB) the inflation rate in both regions, in reality, is determined by not much more than massive and cheap but highly price-elastic imports from China (Leijonhufvud, 2008).

Lee, in Chapter 8, also uses a VAR econometric methodology, the S-VAR (structural vector autoregression) method popularised by Blanchard and Quah (1989), but in a context in which he examines whether a US dollar peg or, alternatively, a euro peg system for the Chinese yuan would be warranted in the light of sufficient symmetry between these entities of aggregate demand and supply shocks. His conclusions are mixed. His relatively positive evaluation of the euro peg alternative is not derived from any observed tendency to greater symmetry between macroeconomic shocks in Europe and China, but rather from the longer-term convergence one might expect on the basis of the endogeneity argument of Frankel and Rose (1998).

In Chapter 9, *Berger and Nitsch* examine the source of the observed increase in trade imbalances between countries (EU, EMU and non-EU), and more in particular the role of inflexibilities, both on labour, exchange and goods markets. Their empirical econometric approach is a neat and transparent one. Their conclusion is, not surprisingly, that all three of these inflexibility types matter to explain the persistence and sometimes increasing degree of trade imbalance, but that this should not lead us to doubt the efficiency of a monetary union if at the same time one tries to introduce more flexibility on national labour and goods markets.

Qian, in Chapter 10, goes in great detail into the issue of the supposed excess liquidity in China and its possible relation to financial risk. He questions the results obtained by Zhang and Pang (2008) and Zhang (2009). With the help of a careful econometric study he finds that excess liquidity has not significantly affected China's CPI inflation rate. Rather, a large amount of the over-supply of money has entered the real estate market through direct FDI and other channels. That in itself is, however, sufficient to conclude that the risk of a Chinese real estate bubble is not to be taken lightly.

In Part III of the book we have collected papers that deal with the euro perspectives and financial perspectives in Central and East European countries (CEEC) after the crisis. In Chapter 11, *Lewis*, in a sweeping empirical study of the main indicators, demonstrates that it is mainly the Maastricht deficit criterion that creates a problem. What seemed, before crisis, to be a cyclical issue, now turns out to have a structural character. But also the problems with the exchange rate, inflation and interest rate criteria seem to be challenging. Overall the euro prospect is receding in CEEC, at least in the medium run.

Pirovano, Vanneste and Van Poeck, in Chapter 12, examine empirically the patterns and determinants of the inflow of portfolio and short-term capital in the new and potential EU countries. They differentiate explicitly between 'push' and 'pull' factors. New and potential member countries show a clearly different pattern. All in all, they observe that the potential member countries are on average less exposed to short-term capital inflows, while many of the new member countries rely heavily on this form of financing. It also appeared that portfolio and other investment flows (bank loans, trade credits, transactions in currency and deposits and other short-term capital) are very different in nature and can hardly be grouped under the same heading.

Chapter 13, by *Horobet and Dumitrescu*, focuses on the role of diversification in investment behaviour in old and new EU member states and in a few important non-EU countries. More in particular the authors consider the possible, but theoretically ambiguous, benefits for eurozone investors of holding internationally diversified portfolios, as compared to other investors. It would seem that diversification benefits are still high for a eurozone investor and they have slightly increased after 2004. In times of financial crisis international diversification may bring attractive benefits in the form of low portfolio volatility, although these benefits are smaller than in normal times.

REFERENCES

Blanchard, O.J. and D. Quah (1989), 'The Dynamic Effects of Aggregate Demand and Supply Disturbances', *American Economic Review*, **79**, 655-73.

Frankel, J.A. and A.K. Rose (1998), 'The Endogeneity of the Optimum Currency Area Criteria', *Economic Journal*, **108**, 1009-25.

Leijonhufvud, A. (2008), 'Keynes and the Crisis', *CEPR Policy Insight*, no. 23, London: Centre for Economic Policy.

Padoa-Schioppa, T., M. Emerson, M. King, J.C. Milleron, J.H.P. Paelinck, L.D. Papademos, A. Pastor and F.W. Scharpf (1987), *Efficiency, Stability and Equity: a Strategy for the Evolution of the Economic System of the European Community*, Oxford: Oxford University Press.

Zhang, C. (2009), 'Excess Liquidity, Inflation and the Yuan Appreciation: What can China Learn from Recent History?', *The World Economy*, **32**, 998-1018.

Zhang, C. and H. Pang (2008), 'Excess Liquidity and Inflation Dynamics in China: 1997-2007', *China and the World Economy*, **16**, 1-15.

PART I

Global European Governance after the Crisis

2. What Kind of Governance for the Eurozone?

Paul De Grauwe

---

1. INTRODUCTION

The survival of the eurozone hinges on the capacity of its leaders to improve the eurozone's governance. This has become very clear since the eruption of the government debt crisis in the eurozone in 2009, which can be said to result from a failure of economic governance. In order to answer the question of how the economic governance of the eurozone should be reformed, we should first make a diagnosis of the crisis in which the eurozone has been thrown since 2009.

2. DIAGNOSIS

A consensus seems to building up in Europe identifying the failure of the Stability and Growth Pact (SGP) to keep a lid on national budget deficits and debts as the root cause of the government debt crises in the eurozone. I want to argue that, with the exception of Greece, the reason why countries got into a sovereign debt crisis has little to do with the poor performance of the SGP. The root cause of the debt problems in the eurozone is to be found in the unsustainable debt accumulation of the private sectors in many eurozone countries. I show the evidence in Figures 2.1 and 2.2. It can be seen that household and bank debt were increasing very fast prior to the debt crisis. Surprisingly, the only sector that did not experience an increase in its debt level (as a percentage of GDP) was the government sector.

The private debt accumulation in the eurozone then triggered the well-known debt deflation dynamics (analysed by Irving Fisher (1933) and later by Minsky (1986)) forcing the governments of the eurozone countries to allow their own debt levels to increase. This was achieved through two chan-

nels. The first one consisted in governments actually taking over private debt
(mostly bank debt). The second one operated through the automatic stabilisers set in motion by the recession-induced decline in government revenues.
As a result, the government debt/GDI ratio started increasing very fast after
the eruption of the financial crisis. In Figure 2.3 we show the government
debt to GDP ratios before and after the crisis for the eurozone countries. The
most surprising feature of Figure 2.3 is that except for Germany and Portugal,
the government debt ratios of the other eurozone countries were all declining
prior to 2008. Even more striking is to find that in two countries that have
experienced severe government debt problems recently, Ireland and Spain,
the government debt ratios were declining spectacularly prior to the crisis.
These were also the countries where the private debt accumulation has been
the strongest.

   From this evidence it is clear that it is difficult to maintain that the cause
of the government debt crisis in the eurozone is due to government profligacy
prior to the crisis. The only country where this can be said to be true is
Greece. It does not apply to the other countries, where the fundamental cause
of the crisis is to be found in unsustainable private debt accumulation forcing
governments to step in to help out (in some cases to save) large segments of
the private sector.

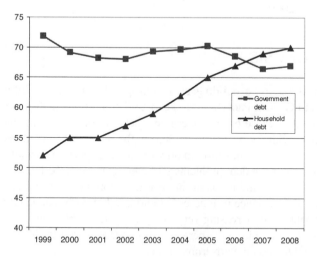

Source: European Commission, AMECO database and CEPS.

Figure 2.1   *Household and government liabilities in the eurozone*
                (percent of GDP)

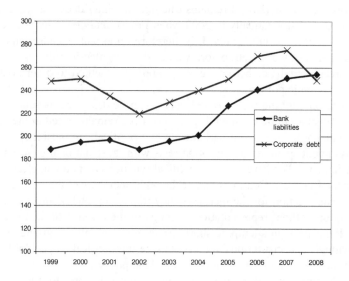

Figure 2.2   Bank and corporate liabilities in the eurozone (percent of GDP)

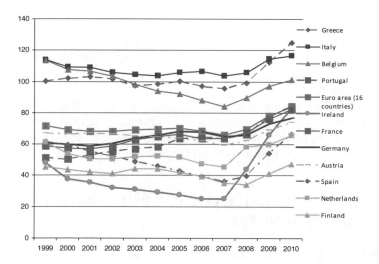

Source: European Commission, AMECO database.

Figure 2.3   Government debt in the eurozone countries (percent of GDP)

Although the cause of the government debt crisis is not to be found in the poor workings of the SGP, it remains true that the latter does not work well. This was shown dramatically in 2003 when France and Germany decided to waive the SGP rules unilaterally. It is therefore important to understand why the SGP does not work well, before we decide to tighten its rules and to impose more sanctions, or before we try to apply its method to other areas of national economic policies.

The reason why the SGP worked poorly can be described as follows. As long as budgetary policies (spending and taxation) remain vested in the hands of national governments and parliaments, the political responsibility for the decisions about spending and taxation rests with these national governments and parliaments. The latter face the political sanctions by national electorates. Neither the European Commission nor the other members of the Council face the political sanction for the measures they impose on one member country. 'No taxation without representation' belongs to the essence of democracies. The SGP has been an attempt to short-circuit this principle, by giving powers to individuals and institutions that do not face the political responsibility for their actions. Such an attempt had to fail and happily so.

The Commission has proposed to tighten the rules and to apply stiffer sanctions in the SGP. It is unclear how stiffer rules and sanctions will help to salvage the SGP that is deeply flawed because it disregards elementary principles of political economy. It looks increasingly likely that the Task Force presided over by the President of the European Council will propose a similar tightening of the SGP rules.

The previous analysis leads to the following two conclusions. First, the crisis in the eurozone is mainly the result of the divergent developments in private debt. The latter have much to do with macroeconomic divergences in general. So, something must be done about these divergences. The question is what, exactly.

Second, the method of convergence implicit in the SGP should not be the model used to impose convergence in other areas of national economic policies. This method has not worked well in imposing convergence in the budgetary field; it is unlikely to do so in other fields.

3. HOW TO DEAL WITH MACROECONOMIC DIVERGENCES?

Here also we need the right diagnosis. Where do these macroeconomic divergences come from? I think we do not have a very good answer today. We do not understand very well how these macroeconomic divergences in the eurozone have come about.

It is often said that the source of the boom and bust dynamics in countries like Spain, Greece and Ireland is due to the fact that thanks to the entry into the eurozone these countries enjoyed a strong decline in their real interest rate. This decline in the real interest rates then triggered a boom in consumption and a bubble in the housing markets. Fair enough, but this does not explain everything. Italy similarly enjoyed an unprecedented decline in its real interest rate when it entered the eurozone, yet it did not experience a boom and a bubble.

This leads me to bring in another explanatory variable: animal spirits, i.e. waves of optimism and pessimism that in a self-fulfilling way drive economic activity (see Akerlof and Shiller, 2009; Leijonhufvud, 1973; Minsky, 1986). My hypothesis is that as far as animal spirits are concerned, the eurozone is far from being integrated. Remember just a few years ago when 'angst' prevailed in Germany while bursts of optimism exploded in Spain and Ireland. Today optimism drives the German recovery and pessimism prevails in the once booming countries. Thus, member states of the eurozone are still very much independent nations creating their own animal spirits.

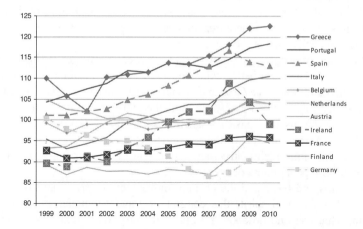

Note: I take the average of the relative unit labour costs over the period 1970-2010 to be a close approximation of the equilibrium values and set this average equal to 100. The divergent movements in unit labour costs are less pronounced than when 1999 is selected. Nevertheless there is upward divergence in Greece, Portugal, Spain, Italy and until 2008 also Ireland.

Source: European Commission, AMECO database.

Figure 2.4   Relative unit labour costs in the eurozone
(average 1970-2010 = 100)

The existence of idiosyncratic animal spirits is at the core of the divergences in competitiveness observed during the last decade. The optimism prevailing in peripheral countries led to booms in economic activities which in turn triggered wage and price increases in these countries. A few years of such booming activity was enough to bring prices and wage costs out of line with the rest of the eurozone, as is shown in Figure 2.4, where I present the evolution of the relative unit labour costs in the eurozone since 1999. Note that, contrary to what is usually done, I do not take 1999 as the base year. This tends to exaggerate the degree of divergence because it assumes that 1999 was a year in which relative competitiveness was in equilibrium (see Gros and Alcidi (2010) on this). Instead I selected the average over the period 1970-2010 to better represent the equilibrium values.

There is a tendency in Europe to blame 'structural rigidities' for the divergent movements in competitiveness in the eurozone, and that thus 'structural reforms' should be instituted. While undoubtedly the European Union exhibits lots of rigidities, these have probably little to do with the divergent movements in competitiveness. I show some evidence in Figure 2.5. This presents the OECD index of employment protection (on the horizontal axis) and relative change in unit labour costs from 1999 to 2010 (on the vertical axis). It can be seen that there is no relationship between the OECD index of rigidities in the labour markets of the eurozone countries and the changes in competitiveness since the start of the eurozone.

Structural reforms are therefore not the answer to divergences in competitiveness. The latter are better explained by divergent movements in macroeconomic conditions (see Gros and Alcidi, 2010), that in turn are very much influenced by national animal spirits. It is therefore surprising to find that the European Commission considers sanctioning countries that do not introduce structural reforms to improve their competitive position. There is simply no evidence that introducing structural reforms in the labour markets will improve the competitiveness of countries.

If booms and busts and the ensuing movements in prices and wages are the results of animal spirits that continue to have a national, not European origin, what can one do about it? Put differently, do national governments have the tools to deal with this?

They surely have some. Budget policies for example can in principle be used as an anti-cyclical instrument. The use of these policies, however, is very much constrained, mainly because the decision-making process underlying these policies makes them less than flexible instruments.

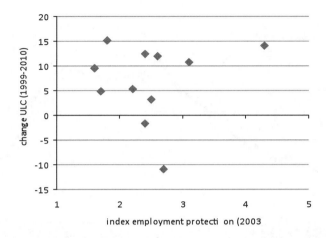

Source: OECD for Employment Protection index and AMECO for ULC.

Figure 2.5 Change in unit labour costs and employment protection

There is another aspect that tends to reduce the capacity of national governments to deal with local booms and busts. Booms and bubbles achieve
dangerous intensities when they are fuelled by credit expansion. It is the
combination of bubbles and credit expansion that makes bubbles potentially
lethal. Figure 2.6 shows the evolution of bank credit in the eurozone together
with the movements in the stock prices. It is striking to find how correlated
these two series are. It is also striking to see that the ECB did not act when
prior to the crash of 2008 bank credit was growing at more than 10% per year
helping to fuel a bubble in the stock market and a boom in economic activity.

Thus, any policy aimed at stabilising local economic activity must also be
able to control local credit creation. It is clear that because the member states
of the eurozone have entered a monetary union they lack the instruments to
deal with this. Put differently, if the movements of economic activity are
driven by credit-fuelled animal spirits the only instruments that can effectively deal with this are monetary instruments. Members of a monetary
union, however, have relinquished these instruments to the European monetary authorities.

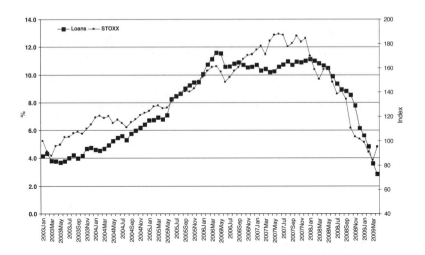

Source: ECB for growth rate of bank loans.

Figure 2.6   Growth rate of total bank loans (left) and STOXX-50 index (right) in the eurozone

The next question then becomes: can the European monetary authorities, in particular the ECB, help out national governments? We have been told that this is impossible because the ECB should only be concerned by system-wide aggregates. It cannot be made responsible for national economic conditions. The reason is that it has one objective, which is the maintenance of price stability in the eurozone as a whole, and because it has only one instrument to achieve this goal.

This I believe is too cheap an answer. The ECB is not only responsible for price stability but also for financial stability. The financial crisis that erupted in the eurozone last year clearly had its origin in a limited number of countries. It is therefore important that the ECB focuses not only on system-wide aggregates but also on what happens in individual countries. Excessive bank credit creation in a number of member countries should also appear on the radar screens of the ECB in Frankfurt upon which the ECB should act.

One may object that the ECB does not have the instruments to deal with excessive bank credit in parts of the eurozone. This, however, is not so. The Eurosystem has the technical ability to restrict bank credit in some countries more than in others by applying differential minimum reserve requirements, or by imposing anti-cyclical capital ratios. These can and should be used as stabilising instruments at the national level.

Another objection is that it is the responsibility of the financial supervisors to deal with excessive risk taking by banks. When banks extend too much credit and thereby increase the risk of their balance sheets, national supervisors should intervene. This is undoubtedly so. At the same time it does not absolve the Eurosystem from its responsibility in maintaining financial stability. When a credit-fuelled boom emerges in some member states, it is also the responsibility of the Eurosystem to act. The Eurosystem also has the most powerful toolkit in controlling the macroeconomic consequences of booms and busts.

The recent reforms in the supervisory landscape in the eurozone increase the scope for action by the Eurosystem. As will be remembered, the European Systemic Risk Board (ESRB) was created. Very pointedly, the president of the ECB will also preside over the ESRB. Thus the creators of the ESRB have clearly understood that the ECB is at the centre of the monitoring of emerging systemic risks in the eurozone. It would be quite paradoxical that the president of the ESRB (ECB) would emit warning signals about systemic risk and would then not follow-up this warning by action to reduce the risks, leaving it to the national supervisors to act alone.

4. CONCLUSION

Much of the discussion about how to impose more convergence among member states of the eurozone has focused on what national governments should do to avoid divergent developments in a number of macroeconomic variables (competitiveness, current account imbalances). Without denying that national governments have their part of responsibilities, the role of these governments has been overemphasised. Conversely the role of the monetary authorities, in particular the ECB, has been underemphasised.

This conclusion is based on the diagnostic of the causes or the present crisis. This is that the divergences between member-states of the eurozone have been driven mainly by what I have called 'national animal spirits', i.e. waves of optimism and pessimism that continue to have a strong national basis in the eurozone. There are as yet no animal spirits gripping the eurozone as a whole. These national animal spirits endogenously trigger credit expansion and contraction. It is this link between credit and animal spirits that make the latter so powerful in shaping movements in output and investment. It follows that the key to the control of the national divergences in macroeconomic variables lies in the control over the movements of credit at the national level. The key institutions in the eurozone that can influence national credit movements are the monetary authorities, including the ECB.

The official EU-proposals (from the Commission and the Task Force) to deal with national divergences in the eurozone should therefore not concentrate almost exclusively on what governments of the member-states should do, but also on the responsibilities of the eurozone monetary authorities. Some hard thinking about the role of these monetary authorities will be necessary to come to grips with endemic macroeconomic divergences in the eurozone.

Finally we also stressed that the European Commission's proposals to strengthen the stability and growth pact by adding more sanctions is ill conceived. The fundamental cause of the debt crisis in the eurozone is to be found in the unsustainable expansion of private debt prior to the crisis. The strong expansion of government debt levels in the eurozone started after the financial crisis erupted and was necessary first to save large parts of the private sector and second to prevent a downward spiral in economic activity. The Commission proposals suggest that future governments that intervene to save the private sector should be punished for such wickedness.

REFERENCES

Akerlof, G. and R. Shiller (2009), *Animal Spirits: How Human Psychology Drives the Economy and Why It Matters for Global Capitalism*, Princeton: Princeton University Press.
Fisher, I. (1933), 'The Debt-Deflation Theory of Great Depressions', *Econometrica*, **1**, 337-57.
Gros, D. and C. Alcidi (2010), 'Fiscal Policy Coordination and Competitiveness Surveillance: What Solutions to What Problems?', *CEPS Policy Briefs*, 7 September 2010, Brussels: Centre for European Policy Studies.
Leijonhufvud, A. (1973), 'Effective Demand Failures', *Swedish Journal of Economics*, **75**, 27-48.
Minsky, H. (1986), *Stabilizing an Unstable Economy*, New York: McGraw Hill.

3. EMU, Political Union and Economic Performance: Lessons from the Stability and Growth Pact and the Lisbon Strategy

Demosthenes Ioannou and Martin Heipertz[1]

1. INTRODUCTION

We argue that bold progress in political integration has become a necessary condition for substantially improving the institutional preconditions for the economic performance of the European Union (EU) as a whole. While the Economic and Monetary Union (EMU) has in its short existence shown that it can function even in times of crisis without a fully-fledged political union, we hold that a greater level of political integration would, ceteris paribus, enhance the EMU's performance by improving the institutional framework conditions of the European economy. We develop a conceptual framework that explains the links between political integration and economic performance in the EU context. We look for an empirical confirmation of our proposition in the functioning of the Stability and Growth Pact and the Lisbon Strategy during the first eleven years of EMU.

What should be the 'finalité' of the European integration process? The United States of Europe, a confederation of sovereign nation states, a free trade area or some unfinished sui generis form of governance structure, continuously in the making? The normative debate between pro-integrationist federalists and opposing defenders of national sovereignty is as old as the process of integration itself. Recently, it has re-emerged in the context of how the economic governance framework should be adapted to ensure a smooth functioning even at times of crisis.

Beyond the ideological dispute between integrationists and defenders of national sovereignty, there are sober and objective practical arguments that speak in favour of further integration towards a deeper political union. Al-

17

ready during the negotiations over the blueprint of monetary union, that is, of the Treaty of Maastricht in the early 1990s, the Deutsche Bundesbank, for example, had advocated political union as a necessary complement to EMU in the long run (e.g. Deutsche Bundesbank, 1990). A number of observers and policy makers have argued the same over the years before as well as after the introduction of the euro (De Grauwe, 2005, and in this volume). But why is it precisely that EMU should require further political integration and, by extension, a much deeper political union?

Avoiding a normative discussion on the intrinsic desirability of further political integration, we argue that a deeper political union should be seen as a precondition for improving socio-economic performance in the EU, given that the degree of political integration is central in shaping economic governance in the EU. This argument is based on extending the central theme of economic institutionalism to European integration, namely, that institutions in the long run are the main determining factors of economic performance.

In the European context, the economic performance of the EU member states and the EU as a whole depends on the process of integration because, by definition, national and European political and economic institutions are shaped by that process of integration (Jones, 2002). Therefore, if the current level of political integration can be shown to be leading to suboptimal institutional solutions (which in turn lead to suboptimal economic outcomes), then the present institutional framework of the EU can be seen as placing a cap or premium on the EU's economic performance. If a higher level of political integration led to a better institutional framework, economic performance would, ceteris paribus, improve.

More precisely in our argument, a higher degree of political integration (meaning a further pooling of national sovereignty) would enable adapting and innovating the institutional framework for EMU so that, over time, more effective solutions could be found that currently remain simply 'out of reach' for the EU polity. A stronger form of political union would allow for more adaptation and thereby entail a much wider solution space than the currently, limited level of integration. Political union is thus raised not as a sufficient but rather as a necessary condition for improved governance and economic performance.

The above set of causal relationships is summarised in the flow chart of Figure 3.1. Apart from the variables already mentioned, the chart includes the notions of input and output legitimacy. These two forms of legitimacy create a conceptual link between deeper political integration and economic performance. Input legitimacy in any democratic political system is a *sine qua non* condition for its long-run survival, reflecting popular assent. In the case of the EU, it is also a necessary condition for deeper political integration. Input legitimacy is also the possible result of political integration in the sense that the process of integration can provide for better participation and democratic accountability of European institutions. Output legitimacy in turn is ensured when, broadly speaking, the provision of socio-economic performance is deemed to be adequate by those participating in the political process.

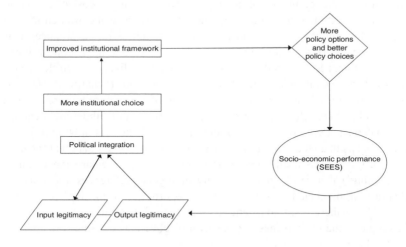

Figure 3.1   Causal relationships between political and institutional integration and economic performance

As an example of how these causal relationships may play out in reality, one can view the Lisbon Treaty as a step towards deeper political integration. The new Treaty provides some, albeit incremental, institutional solutions for solving policy problems more effectively. These institutional solutions allow for better policy choices which in turn should lead to improved socio-economic outcomes. Such outcomes legitimise the authorities that provide them (output legitimacy) and may thereby give an impetus to further political integration. The new treaty may also be viewed as increasing the degree of input legitimacy, having given significant new powers to the European Parliament.

The parameters presented in Figure 3.1 can be both dependent and independent variables. Higher levels of legitimacy, for example, can be the cause as well as the result of better institutional solutions and policy choices. Moreover, each causal relationship also implies a potential constraint from one variable to the next.

2. THE CONCEPTUAL FRAMEWORK

We argue that the EU finds itself in a 'half-way house situation' in terms of institutional development and governance effectiveness. The metaphor of a 'half-way house' points to the incomplete nature of the process of European integration.[2] At the start of the integration process, one can expect an inverse relationship between integration and the effectiveness of governance. This occurs because of developments both at the national and the European level. At the national level, a reduction in effectiveness is likely due to the asymmetric degree of integration in different policy domains (Scharpf, 1997a).[3] At the European level, the creation of a new form of governance requires time to take hold and consolidate. Moreover, it is the product of suboptimal negotiation outcomes (Scharpf, 1997a; Moravcsik, 2002), and it is moving in incremental steps that entail uncertainty, arguably also due to the fact that the end-state of the process itself remains undefined and due to enlargement rounds ('widening') that result in increasingly divergent preferences and interests that are not paralleled by sufficient and proportional 'deepening' of governance. Under these conditions, and as long as the integration process remains incomplete, the effectiveness of the overall governance framework may be affected adversely.

We define 'effectiveness of governance' as the capacity of a polity's institutional structure and political processes to deliver highest-order policy goals as summarised under the quartet of stability, equity, efficiency and security (SEES), a concept adopted by the report of Padoa-Schioppa et al. (1987) and used here to denote a formalised and idealised set of socio-economic outcomes. For the sake of completeness, we define 'stability' as sustainable, non-inflationary economic growth in the absence of volatility and financial or economic crises, 'equity' as the absence of extreme inequalities and a reasonable degree of social cohesion, not least through equality of opportunity, 'efficiency' as the optimal relationship between policy inputs (usually in the form of financial resources) and policy outputs and, finally, 'security' as the containment of external and internal threats to the peaceful existence of a polity.

One can depict this evolution over time in the stylised representation of Figure 3.2. Under the 'half-way house' metaphor, the governance of the unitary nation state within the international order of the 1950s (Scharpf, 1997b) is eventually transformed through the integration process: SEES is now to be provided by the interplay of integrated nation states within the European framework of multi-level governance (MLG). However, this cooperative and federalist[4] framework needs to ensure that it safeguards SEES and delivers not only by historical standards but also in line with citizens' increasing expectations and in an environment of increasingly tough international competition. A shortfall in any one of these dimensions may thus be explained as the discrepancy between the concrete, institutional and policy-induced assignment of competences and the ideal assignment of competence according to the theoretical principles of collective action and public goods (e.g. Olson, 1971).[5]

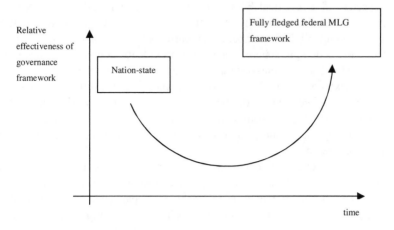

Figure 3.2   European integration and governance effectiveness

Centrally to our proposition, we argue that there is a link between the effectiveness of the EU governance framework and the polity's ability to provide SEES. The suboptimal governance framework due to incomplete integration is seen as the principal cause of a certain, endogenous component of SEES shortfall. This is in line with the findings of the institutional economics literature which broadly defines institutions as 'the rules of the game in a society or [...] the humanly devised constraints that shape human interaction (and) [...] structure incentives in human exchange, whether political, social or economic' (North, 1990, p. 3). Economic outcomes are in the long run determined by the institutional set-up and the policies that this set-up enables (e.g. Matthews, 1986; North, 1990). In the extreme, as Olson (1996, p. 20) has put it, 'the great differences in the wealth of nations are mainly due to differences in the quality of their institutions and economic policies'.[6]

Applying this perspective to European integration suggests that an institutional set-up at a 'half-way house' state is suboptimal when compared to a more complete institutional structure that is capable of adapting to changing circumstances and of designing and implementing more efficient and more effective policy. A point to be stressed in this context is that, within the politico-economic institutional framework that has resulted from the current

level of European integration, the economic outcomes may be (close to) optimal. However, with greater political integration, a higher provision of SEES
could *ceteris paribus* be possible. In the case of economic governance under
EMU, while it may be perceived as providing the most advanced governance
solutions given the current level of integration, it appears suboptimal from a
perspective of a 'political EMU', that is, a much more politically integrated
structure for members of the euro area, or more broadly, a deep 'political
union' among all EU members that participate in monetary union, much
beyond the economic sphere. Such a 'quantum leap' in the governance of the
euro area holds the potential for a much higher provision of SEES.[7]

The next conceptual step in our argument is 'legitimacy' as the link
between the effectiveness of the EU governance framework and political
integration. The EU's institutional and policy effectiveness is defined by the
degree of input and output legitimacy, in turn dependent on the level and
quality of integration.

Legitimacy can be understood to exist in two forms, following Scharpf
(1997a). First, 'input legitimacy' is the acceptance of governance and political choices by the citizens of a polity thanks to participation in the political
process, ranging from the selection of political leadership to the shaping of
political decisions and socio-economic outcomes. As Lenaerts and Gerard
(2004) explain, input legitimacy addresses the question of direct legitimis-
ation of political power through the democratic participation of the citizens or
their elected representatives in transparent decision-making and constitution-
making procedures (see also Stein, 2001).

Second, 'output legitimacy' is defined as the problem-solving capacity of
a polity and its institutional framework, or the legitimacy acquired through
effectiveness. Output legitimacy measures the extent to which citizens see
their interests and desires mirrored in the outcomes of political processes and
therefore accept and support the political order as 'effective' (as opposed to
'right', which would relate to input legitimacy and the process of policy
rather than its outcome). Output legitimacy can therefore be seen as the type
of legitimacy that is associated with an adequate provision of SEES as developed above. Provided that the EU manages to provide its citizens as a whole
with adequate levels of SEES, it is likely to enjoy a certain level of output
legitimacy even if it does not enjoy enough input legitimacy.

Whether one form of legitimacy is more important than the other in the
EU context is an important part of the debate. Collignon (2005), for example,
suggests that in a context of deep economic integration, input legitimacy
grows in importance. At the same time, some observers (e.g. Pisani-Ferry,
2005) have held that the rejection of the Constitutional Treaty was the outcome of inadequate output legitimacy. In a fully integrated political system,
both forms of legitimacy are necessary but can, up to a point, be complemen-

tary. At the same time, providing one form of legitimacy depends on the other; output legitimacy in particular is conditioned by the degree of input legitimacy (cf. Scharpf, 1997a). Moreover, perceptions of output and input legitimacy of the EU level of governance is also very strongly conditioned (and often mixed up with) the output and input legitimacy of the national level of governance. In sum, the processes that deliver input legitimacy are not disconnected from the achievement of output legitimacy, and the realisation of one of the two interconnected notions of legitimacy depends mutually on the fulfilment of the other. Additionally, both forms of legitimacy are necessary for enhancing equity and efficiency.[viii]

Against this background, European integration can be viewed as a process which furthers the attainment of input and output legitimacy. To the extent that input legitimacy is found lacking, the process of integration is incomplete and fulfils only partially those 'structural preconditions on which authentic democratic processes depend: European political parties, European political leaders, and European-wide media of political communication' (Scharpf, 1997a).

The above string of arguments may be presented in a stylised fashion as in Figure 3.3. In the context of the EU integration process, the EU political structure is associated with a 'frontier' of input and output legitimacy. The effectiveness of the governance structures determines the maximum level of SEES that citizens can enjoy, constrained at the same time by the degree of input legitimacy of those structures.[ix] The frontier between output (SEES) and input legitimacy determines all possible socio-economic outcomes, denoted here as the 'frontier of socio-economic outcomes' or FSEO, and represented by the line AA'. AA' thus engulfs all outcomes that are possible under the current parameters set by the level of political integration in EMU/EU. One may formally say that the two forms of legitimacy are the (political) inputs, the combinations of which determine the frontier of possible (socio-economic) outputs. We depict the shape of this frontier in stylised fashion, acknowledging that only empirical research could identify the mix of input and output legitimacy that would allow for and support specific institutional set-ups and thereby socio-economic outcomes in the EU.

For the sake of demonstration, one may represent the current position of EMU in terms of political integration by point X. With incremental changes within the current political-economic framework, EMU may marginally optimise its functioning and move onto the frontier AA' at point X'. In institutional terms, such an incremental improvement could take the form of making use of currently unused provisions in the Lisbon Treaty. However, only considerable progress in political integration would push the possibility frontier of socio-economic outcomes outwards to BB'. At the same time, according to Collignon (2005), such an integration 'leap' would need to satisfy input legitimacy concerns, i.e. popular acceptance for and participation in deeper integration.

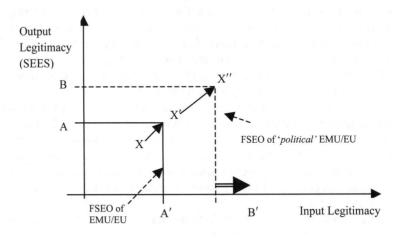

Figure 3.3   The constraint of EU political integration on the provision of SEES

Once significant progress in political integration has occurred, the current optimum (X') becomes suboptimal compared to the new optimal point denoted here by point X" on the possibility frontier BB'. Therefore, only from a perspective of deeper political integration can one argue that the current functioning of EMU is suboptimal and that 'there can be little doubt that the absence of a political union is a serious design flaw in the European monetary union that will have to be remedied to guarantee the long-run survival of the eurozone' (De Grauwe, 2006). By contrast, within the current parameters set by the present level of political integration, EMU is functioning (close to) the feasible optimal level (X or X'). At the same time, the issue has important implications, not least if indeed the SEES premium on the present, relatively suboptimal state of affairs is so large that lacking governance effectiveness undermines the (output) legitimacy of the existing institutional set-up.

Although we focus here on political EMU, the interdependencies between economy and polity imply that further political integration not only in the economic domain but also in non-economic fields, such as defence/security, foreign policy or justice and home affairs, would contribute to an overall improvement.[x] However, a thorough analysis in such other, non-EMU policy areas would transgress the scope of the present analysis, which restricts itself to the empirical investigation of the extent and quality of political integration in the internal dimension of economic governance.

3. LESSONS FROM THE SGP AND THE LISBON STRATEGY

To validate the above conceptual framework and to illustrate the constraining impact of the current, limited depth of political union, we turn to empirical evidence in the functioning of the Stability and Growth Pact (SGP) and the Lisbon Strategy in the first 11 years of EMU. The current economic governance framework has failed to deliver fiscal consolidation and structural reform and insufficiently addresses spillovers and imbalances existent in monetary union. The EU and its constitution of EMU importantly lack the capability of effective, thorough and swift institutional adaptation in times of crisis and in the face of growing geopolitical competition, beyond the implementation of mere short-term emergency back-stops.

3.1. The Stability and Growth Pact

The EU's rules-based fiscal policy framework as enshrined in the present Treaty is built on national institutions and decision-making. The purpose of the very limited European component to this framework is to counter perverse incentives at the national level that cause or enhance a 'deficit bias' of public finance, i.e. a predisposition of national governments in favour of conducting imprudent, unsustainable fiscal policies.[11] The SGP's 'excessive deficit procedure' defines the conditions under which a general government deficit ratio above the reference value of 3% of GDP is considered 'excessive' and prescribes procedural steps by which the EU Council of Ministers of Finance and Economy (ECOFIN) deals with that situation – ultimately, by issuing financial sanctions to the country in question. Besides this 'corrective arm' of the Pact, a 'preventive arm' prescribes a rudimentary form of budgetary co-ordination and surveillance, centred on the annual submission of so-called 'Stability and Convergence Programmes' by Member States who define their own 'medium-term budgetary objectives' (MTOs) in structural terms to achieve sound budgetary positions over the economic cycle.

In practice, the SGP can be said to suffer from a 'dilemma of self-commitment' (Heipertz, 2005). As Member States commit to budgetary targets and deficit ceilings, they inevitably agree to limit their budgetary room of manoeuvre. A Member State, in order to respect the 3% of GDP reference value, accepts a potentially very significant loss of sovereignty over fiscal policy. While such commitments can be taken at low cost ex ante, their actual implementation has in practice been seen to be frequently overridden by the political economy of public budget-making as well as the complexity and unpredictability surrounding outcomes and domestic political requirements of national fiscal policies.

At the frustration of the European Commission and the ECB, fiscal policy-makers have in the past often seemed unable or unwilling to live up to fiscal commitments for their intrinsic value, sometimes also at comparatively low political cost. By consequence, the dilemma of self-commitment consists of choosing between, on the one hand, accepting and living up to the voluntary reduction of fiscal discretion through credible commitments (which would have to be attained also at high political costs) and, on the other hand, retaining de facto fiscal discretion and a politically desirable 'marge de manoeuvre' at a minimum degree of externally imposable fiscal discipline at the cost of, whenever necessary, violating previous commitments, which would be bound to undermine their credibility over time. Experience has shown that, in most cases, policy-makers confronted with the dilemma have opted for the latter option, in the light of domestic priorities. This also means, however, that the EU fiscal framework entails a governance gap. Notably, since market forces imposing fiscal discipline may be augmented under EMU, governance needs to ensure an equivalent disciplining structure through appropriate coordination. The adverse effect of failing to close this gap can be felt very strongly at times of financial and economic stress. Therefore, transferring some 'guidance' role for fiscal policy-making to the European level, as part of a more mature form of political union, could represent an institutional arrangement that delivers more effective co-ordination of fiscal policies than the status quo, which evidently has been unable to prevent excessive fiscal laxity.

Regardless of the precise form of such more extensive fiscal policy coordination, the crucial advantage of deeper political union – rather than cornering the EU into one single and permanent institutional solution such as the present SGP – would be the option to adapt different policy solutions and institutional designs through decision-making that depends on performance and legitimacy. By contrast, the absence of deeper political union automatically rules out a thorough adaptation and improvement of the institutional framework and leads the EU to be 'stuck' with an arrangement that is the path-dependent, petrified outcome of a drawn-out genesis of political compromise brokering in the 1990s (Heipertz and Verdun, 2010).

Experience up to now, and the extreme tensions in debt markets revealed during the crisis, do not seem to support the view that the SGP in its present form can effectively address the persistent problem of fiscal imbalances in the EU and implement a structural adjustment of public finances. Consequently, the present level of integration not only does not allow for fiscal synergies at the European level through a selective and gradual replacement of national spending items through an appropriately sized federal budget responsible for areas of common concern (e.g. security), but also does not even represent a sufficient external lever against national deficit bias and the danger of free-riding, up to the fact that the fiscal situation in some EU countries has become untenable without external stabilisation.

The opportunity cost of the present framework might be considerable. While EMU continues to function even in times of crisis thanks to considerable emergency measures, one cannot ignore the possibility that a continued, unsustainable course of fiscal policy could still damage the edifice beyond repair. Importantly, as said before, economic governance without deeper political union remains 'stuck' within the boundaries of the present institutional framework, regardless of its performance under increasingly complex and challenging conditions.

3.2. The Lisbon Strategy

Between 2000 and 2010, the Lisbon Strategy was at the centre of socio-economic discourse in the EU. In the end, it proved unsuccessful in meeting by 2010 its extremely ambitious overarching goal of making the EU 'the most competitive and dynamic, knowledge-based economy in the world'.

The goals, functioning and impact of the Lisbon Strategy – as well as its successor, the EU 2020 strategy, which entails a number of the former goals and objectives while also having to take into account the implications of the global financial crisis – illustrates both the policy ambitions of the EU as well as the shortcomings in terms of governance for achieving them. In analytical terms, the Lisbon Strategy reflected very much the SEES quartet of the approach used in the conceptual section above: the original goal of the Strategy indicated that the EU seeks not only efficiency (i.e. the optimal relationship between policy inputs and outputs through higher levels of competitiveness, productivity and employment) but also social cohesion, or more broadly, 'equity'. As explicitly stated in the European Council conclusions of 2000 that set up the Lisbon Strategy, achieving efficiency and equity requires macroeconomic stability. Finally, the Lisbon Strategy ambitions implicitly acknowledged the need for security as a necessary basis for achieving efficiency, equity and stability. But did the EU multi-level governance structure have the necessary policy tools and enjoy adequate input legitimacy to achieve such ambitious, output-oriented, goals?

Following some years of learning-by-doing in the first half of the 2000s, the Lisbon Strategy underwent a mid-term review in 2005, at the same time as the SGP review. This medium-term review illustrated the legitimacy constraint problem that confines the number, as well as quality, of possible institutional solutions to problems of economic governance in the EU. More specifically, in 2005, several recommendations of the so-called Kok and Sapir Reports for strengthening EU economic governance were in the end not taken up.[12] Similar to some of the most constructive Commission proposals on strengthening the SGP framework, these recommendations for improving the framework were ignored and the Lisbon mid-term review was essentially limited to a streamlining of the multilateral surveillance procedures. And while such a streamlining was much needed at the time, it was a solution that had to remain within the existing boundaries of political integration. The mid-term review did not tackle therefore the more fundamental coordination problems at the EU level. It did not, for example, seek to strengthen benchmarking and peer-pressure, let alone introduce additional and more effective ways of policy-making. Instead, and again similar to the SGP reform, the mid-term review focused on ways to enhance the so-called 'national ownership' of the strategy, which meant a greater focus on the national aspects of governance of the Lisbon strategy.

However, contrary to original expectations, it appears that stronger forms of coordination in the structural reform area are not much less important than those for fiscal policies for the stability of the EU economy. While in the first years of EMU it was felt that the economic case for supply side coordination was 'weak'[13], persistent national divergences especially in competitiveness positions, the importance of cross country policy spillovers and inadequate single market integration proved to be a major challenge for the EU economy in times of crisis. Consequently, the calls in 2005 by observers to increase the Commission's powers, and/or the setting up of independent agencies with the power to enforce already existing rules, to deepen the single market and increase its efficiency were not heeded. Independent agencies would have avoided, for example, the reproduction at the EU level of the 'capture' of national governments by national interest groups. Instead, as suggested at the time, 'the European level of government does not have the political legitimacy needed to arbitrate among opposing interests'.[14]

The direction taken in the 2005 reform to focus on increasing national ownership while failing to provide for governance solutions at the EU level, reflects the proposition that the lack of possible institutional arrangements at the European level resulted in a form of 're-nationalisation' of the structural reform agendas of Member States. Consequently, the Kok Group's recommendation to construct 'league tables' and praise good performance while castigating bad, was in the end not taken up. Policy-makers did not seek to 'benchmark member states' performance and preferred avoiding the political consequences of too apparent non-delivery.[15] The mid-term review also ignored recommendations linked to the allocation of the EU budget's resources.[16] This, too, however, would seem to go beyond the 'legitimacy frontier' of the governance status quo. Finally, it is hardly surprising that any more ambitious suggestions, such as upward delegation to independent agencies, were also put aside.

To sum up, instead of seeking ways to improve governance effectiveness also at the EU level, the SGP and Lisbon Strategy reviews of 2005 largely sought to increase 'national ownership' and to employ the legitimacy of national actors in order to implement the necessary fiscal consolidation and structural reforms. As the Commission staff put it at the time concerning the Lisbon Strategy: 'There is a lack of legitimacy and political support to the whole Lisbon strategy.'[17]

In the case of the Lisbon Strategy, increasing legitimacy and support for reform was sought through an attempt to increase the involvement of national stakeholders in the structural reform process; in the case of the SGP, by placing all hopes on improved national fiscal rules and institutions. Such an approach may have been the only possible solution within the existing level of political integration. In other words, input and output legitimacy constraints appear to have placed a cap on the alternatives for governance reform, assuming that this could only occur through empowering the Member States to act individually – even in cases where EU-wide solutions, also in the form of a stronger coordination at the European level, would have been preferable. However, compared to a political setting of deeper integration, the 're-nationalisation' of fiscal and structural policy was largely suboptimal and a second-best solution.

As for the proposals of the European Commission (2010) for strengthening the economic governance framework in response to the financial crisis that started in 2007, these reforms are constrained by the boundaries set by the current level of political integration; boundaries that may prevent necessary institutional steps that have become even more urgent in the light of the crisis itself. As shown in this section, an estimation of this 'political premium' on economic performance is difficult to derive precisely, but can be significant, as the Greek sovereign debt crisis of May 2010 illustrated.

4.   CONCLUSION

Our conceptual framework illustrates that further integration towards a deep political union in the EU is linked to economic performance. While marginal improvements in the EU's and euro area's economic performance can take place within the existing institutional framework, further political integration is presented as a condition for facilitating the appropriate institutional frameworks and policy choices which would allow, ceteris paribus, for better economic performance and an overall enhanced provision of SEES for Europe in a globalised world.

The conceptual framework is based on the economic institutionalist account of the process of European integration. Institutions determine (economic) performance in the long run. The process of EU integration is about the evolution of EU and national institutions. Through the ways in which input and output legitimacy are centrally linked to the process of integration, the degree of political integration sets limits on the form of economic and political institutions as well as on the overall quality of governance and, thereby, on the attainability of better policy outcomes. Deeper political union would allow to adapt and innovate European governance so that over time more effective solutions would be found that currently remain 'out of reach' for the EU polity.

Empirical grounding for our proposition and conceptual framework is provided through an assessment of the functioning of the two main pillars of EU economic governance, the SGP and the Lisbon Strategy. Both examples show that deeper political integration would allow adaptation and improvement of the institutional design of economic governance. This is required in a context of global complexity and change driven by technological innovation and not least in times of crisis and in the light of geopolitical changes to which Europe will need to stand up. Our expectation with regard to political union is not that favourable adaptation would immediately occur, but that at least the possibility for institutional change would exist and ultimately be put to good use.

The conceptual links advanced herein point to the need for further European integration at the level of the EU, or among an avant-garde of Member States, in order to improve European socio-economic performance. This assessment suggests that any shortfall in economic performance, in conjunction with the perceived legitimacy of the European level of governance, relates to the opportunity cost of leaving integration incomplete. Facing major challenges such as the latest crisis, continued globalisation, climate change, demographic ageing, and relative shifts in geopolitical power, the EU should no longer be viewing deep political union as some kind of federalist ideal but rather as an economic imperative.

NOTES

1. The opinions expressed in this paper are those of the authors and do not necessarily reflect those of the European Central Bank or of the German Federal Ministry of Finance. Earlier versions of this paper were presented at the International Conference on 'The Economic Crisis and the Process of European Integration', organised by the University of Antwerpen and the Institute of European Studies of the Free University of Brussels (Brussels, 2 June 2010); at the International Conference on 'The Political and Economic Consequences of European Monetary Integration' (University of Victoria, B.C. Canada, 18-19 August 2005), as well as at the VIII Villa Mondragone International Economic Seminar on 'Europe – a new

economic agenda?' (Rome, 26-27 June 2006). The authors would like to thank participants at all three events for their comments.

2. On the metaphor of the half-way house, see Ian Begg (1995) who uses the concept in the context of a regional integration project that finds itself in a semi-integrated institutional and market framework.

3. Additionally, there might be external reasons for reduced state effectiveness (related to globalisation, for example). To the extent that this is true, the effectiveness that is regained at the European level could even be seen as turning integration into the 'rescue of the nation state' (Milward, 1992).

4. See Börzel (2004) who suggests that the EU corresponds rather closely to the model of cooperative federalism and finds itself in a double legitimacy trap in which declining problem solving capacity (output legitimacy) can no longer compensate for the lack of democratic participation and accountability (input legitimacy); on the two types of legitimacy, see below.

5. See also the application of these principles in the European context by Collignon (2003).

6. See also Persson and Tabellini (1992) who provide empirical evidence that the most promising explanation of why policy choices differ systematically across countries (which explains why countries grow at different rates), is different political incentives and different political institutions.

7. The discourse focuses on the euro area because political union seems unthinkable for countries that prefer not to (or are themselves not yet able to) join monetary union as a first step.

8. See, for example, Begg et al. (1993) who make this point about accountability in particular. Accountability in turn is part of the broader concept of input legitimacy.

9. Along these lines, see Collignon (2003) who shows that legitimacy and efficiency may both depend on the scope of the institutional framework. Cf. also the argumentation by Ioannou and Niemann (2004) with reference to the economic policy coordination framework in general, and Enderlein et al. (2005) who make a similar argument with regard to the legitimacy constraints on the possible institutional reform of the EU budget.

10. In the area of international economic relations see, for example, Bini-Smaghi (2006) and Sapir (2007).

11. The concept of a politically caused 'deficit bias' was developed by Buchanan and Wagner (1977). Beetsma (1999), among others, has argued that this deficit bias is enhanced in a monetary union due to externality effects.

12. See European Commission (COM (2005) 24, SEC (2005) 192 and SEC (2005) 193), and European Council (2005).

13. As Tabellini and Wyplosz suggested in 2004, 'all in all, the case for the centralisation of supply side policies is weak'.

14. Tabellini and Wyplosz (2004, p. 39).

15. Kok et al. (2004, pp. 42-43); own italics emphasising the political dimension in national public debate of the EU governance framework for structural reform.

16. The Sapir report of 2003, for example, had called for a much higher concentration of EU budget resources on Research and Development (R&D).

17. European Commission, SEC (2005) 160, of 28 January 2005, p. 49.

REFERENCES

Beetsma, R.M.W.J. (1999), 'The Stability and Growth Pact in a Model with Politically Induced Deficit Biases', in A. Hughes Hallett, M.M. Hutchison and S.E.H. Jensen (eds), *Fiscal Aspects of European Monetary Integration*, New York: Cambridge University Press, 1999, pp. 189-215.

Begg, D. et al. (1993), *Making Sense of Subsidiarity. How Much Centralisation for Europe – Monitoring European Integration 4*, London: CEPR.

Begg, I. (1995), 'Factor Mobility and Regional Disparities in the EU', *Oxford Review of Economic Policy*, **11**, 96-112.

Bini-Smaghi, L. (2006), 'Powerless Europe: Why is the Euro Area Still a Political Dwarf?', *International Finance*, **9**, 261-279.

Börzel, T. (2004), 'What can Federalism Teach us About the European Union? The German Experience', *Regional and Federal Studies*, **15**, 245-257.

Buchanan, J.M. and R. Wagner (1977), *Democracy in Deficit: the Political Legacy of Lord Keynes*, New York: Academic Press.

Collignon, S. (2003), *The European Republic*, London: Federal Trust.

Collignon, S. (2005), 'The "New" Lisbon Strategy, the Stability and Growth Pact and European Democracy', published in Italian in *Italianieuropei*, No. 2.

De Grauwe, P. (2005), 'On Monetary and Political Union', mimeo, preliminary draft, University of Leuven.

De Grauwe, P. (2006), 'Flaws in the Design of the Eurosystem?', *International Finance*, **9**, 137–144.

Deutsche Bundesbank (1990), 'Statement by the Deutsche Bundesbank on the Establishment of an Economic and Monetary Union in Europe', Monthly Report of the Deutsche Bundesbank, October 1990, pp. 40-44.

Enderlein, H., J. Lindner, O. Calvo-Gonzalez and R. Ritter (2005), 'The EU Budget – How Much Scope for Institutional Reform?', *ECB Occasional Paper Series*, No. 27, Frankfurt: European Central Bank.

European Commission (2005), 'Working Together for Growth and Jobs: a New Start for the Lisbon Strategy', COM (2005) 24, 2 February 2005.

European Commission (2005), Commission Staff Working Document in Support of the Report from the Commission to the Spring European Council, 22-23 March 2005, on the Lisbon Strategy of Economic, Social and Environmental Renewal (COM (2005) 24), SEC (2005) 160, of 28 January 2005.

European Commission (2005), 'Lisbon Action Plan Incorporating EU Lisbon Programme and Recommendations for Actions to Member States for Inclusion in their National Lisbon Programmes. Companion Document to the Communication to the Spring European Council 2005', COM (2005) 24, SEC (2005) 192, 3 February 2005.

European Commission (2005), 'Delivering on Growth and Jobs: a New and Integrated Economic and Employment Co-ordination Cycle in the EU. Companion Document to the Communication to the Spring European Council 2005', COM (2005) 24, SEC (2005) 193, 3 February 2005.

European Commission (2010), 'A New EU Economic Governance: A Comprehensive Commission Package of Proposals', comprising COMs (2010) 522, 523, 526, 527, of 29 September.

European Council (2005), Presidency Conclusions, 22-23 March 2005.

Heipertz, M. (2005), *Der Europäische Stabilitäts- und Wachstumspakt – Institutionendesign im Selbstbindungsdilemma*, Dissertation, Universität zu Köln.

Heipertz, M. and A. Verdun (2010), *Ruling Europe: The Politics of the Stability and Growth Pact*, Cambridge, UK: Cambridge University Press.

Ioannou, D. and A. Niemann (2004), 'European Economic Governance: Towards a Conceptual Framework and the Way Ahead', *Journal of European Affairs*, **2**, 25-30.

Jones, E. (2002), *The Politics of Economic and Monetary Union: Integration and Idiosyncrasy*, Lanham: Rowman & Littlefield.

Kok, W. et al. (2004), 'Facing the Challenge – the Lisbon Strategy for Growth and Employment', Report of the High Level Group chaired by Wim Kok, November 2004.

Lenaerts, K. and D. Gerard (2004), 'The Structure of the Union According to the Constitution for Europe: the Emperor is Getting Dressed', *European Law Review*, **29**, 289-298.

Matthews, R.C.O. (1986), 'The Economics of Institutions and the Sources of Growth', *Economic Journal*, **96**, 903-918.

Milward, A.S. (1992), *The European Rescue of the Nation-State*, London: Routledge.

Moravcsik, A. (2002), 'In Defence of the "Democratic Deficit": Reassessing Legitimacy in the European Union', *Journal of Common Market Studies*, **40**, 603-624.

North, D.C. (1990), *Institutions, Institutional Change and Economic Performance*, Cambridge, UK: Cambridge University Press.

Olson, M. (1971), *The Logic of Collective Action. Public Goods and the Theory of Groups*, Cambridge, MA: Harvard University Press.

Olson, M. (1996), 'Big Bills Left on the Sidewalk: Why Some Nations are Rich, and Others Poor', *Journal of Economic Perspectives*, **10**, 3-24.

Padoa-Schioppa, T., M. Emerson, M. King, J.C. Milleron, J.H.P. Paelinck, L.D. Papademos, A. Pastor and F.W. Scharpf (1987), *Efficiency, Stability and Equity: a Strategy for the Evolution of the Economic System of the European Community*, Oxford: Oxford University Press.

Persson, T. and G. Tabellini (1992), 'Growth, Distribution and Politics', *European Economic Review*, **36**, 593-602.

Pisani-Ferry, J. (2005), 'What's Wrong with Lisbon?', paper presented at the Aspen Brainstorming Session on 'Restarting Europe', Aspen Institute Italia, Rome, 22 July 2005.

Sapir, A. (ed.) (2007), *Fragmented Power: Europe and the Global Economy*, Brussels: Bruegel.

Scharpf, F.W. (1997a), 'Economic Integration, Democracy and the Welfare State', *Journal of European Public Policy*, **4**, 18-36.

Scharpf, F.W. (1997b), 'Introduction: the Problem Solving Capacity of Multi-level Governance', *Journal of European Public Policy*, **4**, 520-538.

Stein, E. (2001), 'International Integration and Democracy: No Love at First Sight', *American Journal of International Law*, **95**, 489-534.

Tabellini, G. and C. Wyplosz (2004), 'Supply Side Coordination in the European Union', Report prepared for the Conseil de l'Activité Economique, May 2004.

4. Sustainability of Government Debt in the EMU

Arjan M. Lejour, Jasper Lukkezen and Paul Veenendaal

1. INTRODUCTION

Government debts have surged in Europe and other western countries in response to the worldwide financial crisis which forced several EU member states to support financial institutions and to stimulate the economy while tax revenues dwindled. On average debt increased from 66.0%, end of 2007, to 78.7% of GDP, end of 2009 in the European Economic and Monetary Union (EMU). Debt increases as a percentage of GDP were most pronounced in Ireland, Greece and Spain (see Figure 4.1).

Apart from rising debt levels, sovereign bonds have experienced unprecedented volatility. In 2009 sovereign bond spreads between the most default-free German Bund and less default-free government bonds of other eurozone member states have risen and fallen again. Recently some southern eurozone member states, in particular Greece, Spain and Portugal, have experienced additional volatility again and are dealing with much higher bond spreads. Greek 10-year government bonds even peaked at about 900 basis points over German Bunds. The rising and volatile sovereign bonds spreads urged the EU and IMF to take drastic action in supporting Greece and other threatened member states.

These developments lead to several questions. First, are government debts in Europe indeed unsustainable and – if they are – for which countries is this the case? Second, why and how do developments in one member state affect the situation in other countries? To answer these questions we first survey the literature on sustainable government debt in section 2 and then give an overview of the literature on cross-border spillovers of government debt in section 3. The theoretical literature provides insights in the determinants of government debt and spillovers. We use the empirical literature to judge the relevance of these determinants and derive four indicators that appear to be useful for assessing sovereign debt sustainability.

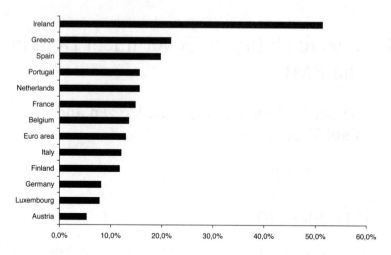

Source: Eurostat.

Figure 4.1 *Change in government debt as a percentage of GDP (first quarter 2008 to first quarter 2010, selected EMU countries)*

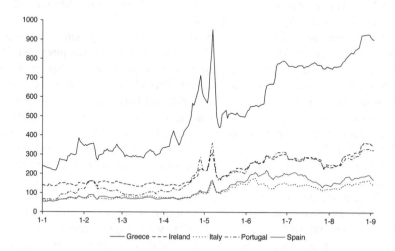

Source: Datastream.

Figure 4.2 *Sovereign euro bond spreads in basis points, January 1 to September 6 2010, selected EMU countries*

In section 4 we develop a sustainable debt model based on van Wijnbergen and Budina (2008). This model allows us to assess the expected development of government debts based on historic inputs. The stochastic simulations provide some indications on the possible bandwidth of outcomes due to uncertainty. We apply an OECD baseline and consider two OECD variants that reflect extra consolidation of government budgets (raising primary surpluses) and the additional costs of ageing (reducing primary surpluses). Moreover, we apply two stress tests on the baseline projection. Using the four indicators for sustainability we derived in section 2, we conclude that a wide variety of scenarios is conceivable in which, in the baseline scenario with consolidation, only a few of the member states considered are in a difficult sovereign debt position, while in other cases (baseline + ageing, prolonged recession) most countries under consideration are potentially heading for unsustainable debts.

Thus, our assessment of the sustainability of sovereign debts within EMU provides an important background for judging current policy actions by the EU and the Member States to raise primary surpluses. From this perspective we indicate that it is vitally important to strengthen the Stability and Growth Pact (SGP) and to put other mechanisms in place that can serve as guidelines for crisis management. EMU definitely should become prepared to prevent future sovereign debt crises.

2. SUSTAINABLE DEBT LEVELS IN THE LITERATURE

In this section we derive four indicators that appear useful in assessing sovereign debt sustainability: a backward and a forward looking sustainability gap indicator, that describe the gap between primary surplus and the primary surplus needed for a stable debt to GDP ratio, and two empirically motivated indicators. Before we do so, however, we will first examine the sustainability requirements from a theoretical perspective.

2.1. No Ponzi-finance Scheme

From the literature (e.g. Buiter, 2009; van Wijnbergen and Budina, 2008) we know that the basic requirement for the sustainability of public debt, is that governments should not engage in a Ponzi-finance scheme. In such a scheme existing debt is serviced forever by issuing additional debt to cover both interest payments and principal repayments. Instead governments should stay within their intertemporal budget constraints. This implies that the discounted value of current and future income plus initial wealth should at least be equal to the discounted value of all current and future non-interest expenditure (van Wijnbergen and Budina, 2008). Formally this comes down to

$$\sum_{i=t+1}^{\infty} \frac{g_i}{(1+r)^{i-t}} \leq -b_t + \sum_{i=t+1}^{\infty} \frac{t_i + s_i}{(1+r)^{i-t}} \quad . \tag{4.1}$$

Equation (4.1) states that the discounted value of all non-interest expenditure g_i should at most equal initial sovereign wealth (which is negative due to government debt) plus the discounted value of all public sector non-interest income, here summarised as the sum of tax revenues t_i and seigniorage revenues s_i. Seigniorage is the net income the public sector derives from issuing money. Note that b_t represents government debt at the end of year t. We assume the nominal interest rate r to be constant over time, merely to simplify the equations. Defining the net receipts of the government as the augmented primary surplus $p_i = t_i - g_i + s_i$ (where the augmentation refers to the addition of seigniorage to the primary surplus) we obtain

$$b_t \leq \sum_{i=t+1}^{\infty} \frac{p_i}{(1+r)^{i-t}} \quad , \tag{4.2}$$

or: initial (net) debt should at most equal the discounted value of all future augmented primary surpluses. In what follows we will often for simplicity call p_i the primary surplus although it also includes seigniorage.

To understand the implications of (4.2), it is useful to write down the period budget constraint

$$b_t = b_{t-1}(1+r) - p_t \quad , \tag{4.3}$$

which states that the new level of debt equals initial debt plus interest payments minus primary surplus. It shows that government policy will only affect the debt level in as far as it influences the primary surplus p_t and possibly the interest rate r via the adjustment of the primary surplus. We can rewrite the flow budget constraint and substitute it repeatedly in itself from $t+1$ onwards to obtain:

$$b_t = \sum_{i=t+1}^{\infty} \frac{p_i}{(1+r)^{i-t}} + \lim_{i \to \infty} \frac{b_i}{(1+r)^{i-t}} \quad . \tag{4.4}$$

Equation (4.4) indicates that initial debt equals the present value of future primary surpluses if and only if discounted future debt converges to zero or the growth of debt should ultimately be smaller than the rate of interest.

2.2. Sustainability Gap Indicators

Many authors have focused on indicators of how far fiscal policy departs from sustainability (e.g. Chalk and Hemming, 2000). It should be noted that such indicators are not formally backed by a definition of sustainability. Instead, they rely on a more intuitive notion of what distinguishes sustainable from unsustainable fiscal policy.

If the government wants to prevent debt (as a percentage of GDP) from growing, a lower bound on the augmented primary surplus is implied:

$$\tilde{p}_t \geq (r - \gamma)\tilde{b}_t \ , \tag{4.5}$$

where $\tilde{b}_t$ denotes end of period government debt as a share of GDP, γ the nominal GDP growth rate and $\tilde{p}_t$ the augmented primary surplus as a share of GDP. Note that in (4.5) we have approximated the term $(1+r)/(1+\gamma)$ with $1 + r - \gamma$. This is merely done to shorten the notation. In our calculations we always use the precise expressions.

From (4.5) it follows immediately why it may be impossible to stabilise the debt ratio if a country is heading towards a sovereign debt crisis. First, in such a situation γ is likely to be small or negative. Second, the interest rate on new roll-over debt may rise quite substantially. Thus, a target for primary surplus that would stabilise the debt ratio may easily become infeasible, in particular – as within EMU – if simply expanding the money supply is not an option.

Buiter (2009) argues that the permanent share of the state's augmented primary surplus in GDP should not fall short of the outstanding stock of sovereign net debt as a share of GDP times the difference of the long-term real interest rate on sovereign debt and the long-term growth rate of real GDP. Deviations of the actual augmented primary surplus and its target value would then indicate how sustainable the fiscal policy is. However, appropriate assessments of sovereign net debt and the long-term development of the real interest and GDP growth rates may be difficult to arrive at. Hence, this indicator may not be a very practical approach for the assessment of sustainability.

Blanchard (1990) proposes to start from (4.5) and to evaluate sustainability with the gap indicator

$$\tilde{p}_t - (r - \gamma)\tilde{b}_t \ . \tag{4.6}$$

The sustainability gap indicator shows the distance in terms of primary surplus as a percentage of GDP from a stable debt ratio. A negative value indicates a shortfall from the primary surplus that would stabilise the debt ratio and a positive value indicates an excess over primary surplus that would stabilise relative debt. This sustainability gap indicator is forward looking as it uses projections of primary surplus, interest rate and GDP growth. We will present the indicator for the average projected development between 2010 and 2019 and the end year 2019 (criterion 1).

Callen et al. (2003) propose the so-called 'overborrowing ratio' as an indicator of fiscal sustainability. This indicator expresses the current debt-to-GDP ratio as a fraction of the debt-to-GDP ratio that would emerge from past averages in primary surpluses, real interest rates and real GDP growth rates. The information of the over-borrowing ratio can also be written in terms of a backward-looking sustainability gap, as in

$$\widetilde{p}_{av} - (r_{av} - \gamma_{av})\widetilde{b}_t \quad . \tag{4.7}$$

A negative value of this indicator shows that the current debt ratio could not be maintained at past values of the primary surplus, interest rates and growth rates, while a positive value implies an over-borrowing ratio that is less than unity. The difference between equations (4.6) and (4.7) is that the first considers only the end-of-the-period variables, while the latter averages variables over a number of years. We calculate these averages for the period 1995-2009 (criterion 2).

2.3. Other Benchmark Indicators for Default

Another approach would be to construct a benchmark of defaulting countries analogous to what one finds in an IMF study by Callen et al. (2003). The IMF compared the characteristics of emerging market economies that defaulted since 1998 with the characteristics of non-defaulting countries. In general, defaulting countries had higher debt-to-GDP ratios, a higher share of foreign government debt funding, a higher debt to government receipts ratio and a smaller ratio of the broad money base to GDP than non-defaulting countries.

This benchmark would likely consist of parameters as (debt/GDP, debt/government revenue, foreign debt/total debt, broad money base on GDP, etc.). From these characteristics we might construct a range that could be considered to indicate fiscal non-sustainability. Any member state venturing towards this range might be heading for default. Callen et al. (2003) show that for defaulting emerging market economies the average debt-to-government revenue indicator was 350% and 250% for non-defaulting countries.

Limitations of this method are that they are dependent on historical data and that no OECD country has defaulted since the Second World War. It might therefore not be appropriate to use these criteria as the current circumstances originate from other factors than the historical circumstances in countries leading to default. A different debt level might therefore be acceptable. However, for the EMU countries we consider a ratio below 350% as sustainable (criterion 3).

Yet another approach would be to examine the effects of a high debt burden on the real economy. Reinhart and Rogoff (2010) show for example that countries with a debt/GDP level higher than 90% have a median GPD growth that is 1% lower. The effect is stronger for countries with a lot of external public debt. The main characteristic of this threshold is that it indicates the effects on the economy of a country as a whole. It links debt (a potential problem in a part of the economy) to the functioning of the economy as a whole. Hence, it is likely that maintaining debt ratios around 90% or higher is more difficult and less sustainable than debt ratios at a more modest level (criterion 4).[1]

3. THE SPILLOVERS OF GOVERNMENT DEBT IN EMU

This section discusses the international dimensions of government debt, in particular in the EMU countries. Many of the spillover channels between countries are also apparent between countries outside the eurozone, but they are more intensive in a common currency area. We review the theoretical and empirical arguments pro and contra coordination.

The issue of coordination was already raised in preparing the establishment of EMU and triggered an extensive debate on the relevance of the Maastricht (1991) criteria that define the entry conditions to EMU and of the SGP that addresses budgetary discipline. We do not review this debate.[2] We concentrate on the possible spillovers from the steep rise in government deficits and debt in some EMU countries on the economic performance and on the sustainability of government debt in other countries.[3] The literature discusses various cross-border spillovers[4] and other arguments for coordinating fiscal policies.

The first externality is higher inflation expectations in the eurozone. High debt in one country could be recovered with inflation, provided the European Central Bank would allow inflation to rise in the union, thereby affecting price stability in other EMU countries. Fischer et al. (2002) show that larger budget deficits exert an upward pressure on inflation in developing countries, but these effects are insignificant in developed countries. Canzoneri et al. (2001) confirm these results by showing that government debt in Europe and the US is not a significant determinant of the price level. We conclude that the spillovers of national budget deficits on the inflation rates are negligible because the EMU countries are low inflation countries with a targeted inflation rate of the ECB of at most 2%.

The second externality is a higher long-term interest rate on government debt. Every eurozone country issues its own bonds with a national rate of interest. However, the high interest rate of a particular country could exert an upward pressure on the interest rates in other countries (perceptions of investors). This could even be the case for non-EMU countries, in particular if they have plans to join. This is closely connected to contagion and reputation issues which played a role in the Latino debt crisis and the Asia crisis. Ardagna et al. (2007) estimate for 16 OECD countries the effect of primary deficits and government debt on the nominal interest rate on 10-year government bonds in the period 1960 to 2002. In their preferred specification a one percentage point increase in the primary deficit to GDP ratio leads to a 10 basis point rise in the nominal interest rate. In the longer run a permanent increase in the primary deficit ratio could raise the interest rate by 70 basis points after five years.

Faini (2006) focuses exclusively on the EMU countries between 1979 and 2002 and distinguishes an EMU and national interest rates. An increase in the budget surplus of the EMU lowers the EMU interest rate with 41 basis points. The analogous effect at the country level is much smaller, only 3 basis points. Faini (2006) concludes that there are substantial spillovers of national fiscal policies on the interest rate but budget deficits are not permanent and most EMU countries are relatively small. The effect of higher government debt (as a ratio of GDP) on the interest rate is nonlinear. Ardagna et al. (2007) conclude that if government debt is higher than (about) 60% of GDP an increase in debt could exert an upward pressure on the interest rate. If government debt is 141% (maximum in the sample) the interest rate increases by 114 basis points if debt increases by one standard deviation (which amounts to 26% government debt). This is considerable, but a 26% increase in debt/GDP is also quite dramatic (see Figure 4.1). On the other hand, Faini (2006) does not find strong evidence that the spillover effects of high debts on the interest rate and the country spread are larger than for low debts.

A third externality is that many European financial institutions hold bonds of other EU members. The data of the Bank of International Settlement (BIS) show that banks hold a significant share of eurozone debt and it is uncertain whether a breach in bank balance sheets caused by sovereign default will lead to a chain reaction in the form of another banking crisis. Assessing the impact of such an event is crucial in determining whether such a spillover is significant. The formation of the EMU has probably stimulated the cross holdings of government bonds, because the exchange rate risk is eliminated, but these relations do also exist between countries with national currencies.

A fourth externality is the stability of the euro vis-à-vis non-euro countries. Exporters benefit from a weaker euro, but imports become more expensive. The net economic effect is not always clear and depends on the economic structure of a country. A deterioration of the euro in response to high debts in one or two member states has certainly an effect on the trading behaviour of euro members with non-members.[5] Moreover, financial markets interpret depreciation of currencies often as a sign of weakness of the economic development with adverse effects on stocks markets.

A fifth externality is the transmission via the real economy due to budgetary decisions on the economies in other countries. As an example, Giuliodori and Beetsma (2005) estimate that a net tax reduction of 1% of GDP in Germany leads to a maximum 0.7% GDP increase in the Netherlands after seven quarters. After about four years the effect dies out. That is not only the case for the Netherlands, but often also for other countries. The size of the spillovers depends on the bilateral trade relations, which are very tight between Germany and the Netherlands, but much looser between other EMU countries. We conclude that the long-term effects are small although the short-term effects are larger.

We conclude that the magnitudes of most of these spillovers are weak. There are no empirical indications that inflation expectations are affected or economic performance in other countries via trade, FDI etc. in the longer term. There are modest effects on the interest rates from high budget deficits and high government debts but these are not overwhelming.

Only the case of contagion via financial markets has shown large spillovers. Contagion may even endanger financial stability, especially if cross ownership of government bonds holdings is important. With a weak and fragile banking system, the contagion mechanism could lead to disruptive effects on the economy in the form of higher interest rates or banks getting into trouble in case of a (partial) government default. This is the main argument for coordinating fiscal policies to some extent. Therefore the prevention of contagion can be seen as the main objective of fiscal policy coordination.

Solidarity between member states and economies of scale of euro bond systems can be additional reasons for intervention. In euro bond systems the liquidity of the sovereign bond market would increase, making it easier to attract money. In particular smaller EMU member states would benefit from a liquidity premium resulting in a lower rate of interest.[6] Yet, these additional motives seem less compelling for coordinated action than the wish to prevent the potentially disruptive effects of contagion via financial markets. These disruptive effects could be so strong that a sovereign debt crisis in even a small country could endanger the future of EMU.

4. MEDIUM-TERM SUSTAINABILITY ANALYSIS

We assess the sustainability of government debt in the EMU countries using the Fiscal Sustainability Simulation model (FSS) as an analytical tool. The FSS model generates a stochastic forecast for the development of government debt/GDP ratio. Our approach closely follows van Wijnbergen's approach for the assessment of sovereign debt sustainability. Van Wijnbergen and Budina (2008) apply the central flow budget equation for the development of government debt as a percentage of GDP, including debt denominated in foreign currency and seigniorage revenue. Within the eurozone most government debt is euro-denominated and we assume that the exchange rate risk of the non euro-denominated part of government debt is hedged. Therefore we drop the foreign currency part. Furthermore we consider monetary policy to be an externality within the eurozone (set by the ECB) and take seigniorage revenue as part of the primary surplus. This simplifies our central equation to:

$$\widetilde{b}_t = (1 + r_t - \gamma_t)\widetilde{b}_{t-1} - \widetilde{p}_t + OF \quad . \tag{4.8}$$

Here $\widetilde{b}_t$ is government debt as a percentage of GDP at the end of year t, $\widetilde{p}_t$ the augmented primary surplus as a percentage of GDP, r_t the nominal interest rate and γ_t the nominal GDP growth rate. Finally, OF stands for other exogenous factors that influence the debt ratio.

To obtain a debt path we need a forecast for the development of the primary surplus and for the long-term interest and GDP growth rates. Note that we can take either both r_t and γ_t real or nominal for small levels of inflation. To obtain a stochastic debt forecast we must make either some or all of the forecast variables stochastic.

We obtain a quarterly projection for the primary surplus, the long-term interest rate and nominal GDP growth rate from the OECD (OECD, 2010). Table 4.1 presents the projections on the primary surplus. We use OECD projections as a baseline because they are available for all eurozone member states and follow the same methodology for all countries.

Stochastic features are added to these projections in the following way. For the primary surplus we calculate the variance of the primary surplus at the country level from historical data from Eurostat. We use annual figures from 2001 until 2008 and convert the annual variance into a quarterly variance. In this way we avoid large seasonal fluctuations. For GDP growth and the interest rates we take the inter-country dependencies or spillover effects into account in the stochastic part by using a covariance matrix obtained by the following Vector Auto Regression.

$$\Phi_t = C + A\Phi_{t-1} + \varepsilon_t \,, \quad \text{var}(\varepsilon_t) = \mathbf{\Omega} \quad . \tag{4.9}$$

Here Φ is a vector containing GDP growth and interest rates per country. We use quarterly historical data from Eurostat from 2000.2 until 2009.3 to estimate C, A and $\mathbf{\Omega}$.

The stochastic parts are generated by a multivariate normal distribution using the variance of the primary surplus and the covariance matrix of GDP growth and long-term interest rates. These results are added to the OECD projections of the primary surplus, GDP growth and long-term interest rates and used to calculate next period's debt ratio. We discuss the main features of these projections in this section.

The OECD projections assume that the output gap is closed over the period 2012-2015 (Table 4.1 presents the outputs gaps in 2011). Hence, GDP growth rates will be relatively high during this time period. Inflation is assumed to be lower than the ECB target of 2% until 2015 due to the current economic crisis. Except for Ireland this will, however, not lead to deflation. After 2015 inflation is expected to be at the ECB target. After 2011 the primary surplus is expected to improve automatically because of the closure of the output gap. In a fiscal consolidation variant the OECD assumes from 2012 onwards extra fiscal consolidation measures in all countries where the debt ratio does not stabilise. In these countries primary surplus is raised by 0.5% of GDP per year, starting in 2012. The number of years with extra consolidation vary from zero years for Belgium, four years for the Netherlands and Germany to 14 years for Ireland.

We use the simplifying assumption that the entire debt will be rolled over to the next period with equal parts being redeemed in every period. This may imply that interest rate volatility is extended over a longer time period than actually might be the case. Furthermore we also assume that all debt is financed against average maturity and that the interest rate due is the long-term interest rate. For the countries under consideration the average maturity of the government debt ranges between 6 and 8 years.

The OECD expects the long-term interest rates to rise from the historic low rates of the 2000s to their historical average of 4.4% for the eurozone. Inter-country differences are explained by an interest rate premium of 4 basis points for every 1% debt/GDP above 75%. This is consistent with OECD estimates (Egert, 2010).

Table 4.1   *Primary surplus, output gap, EMU debt and government revenue in % GDP in OECD baseline*

	Primary surplus			Output gap	EMU debt	Gov. revenue
	2009	2010	2011	2011	2009	2009
Belgium	-2.4	-1.4	-0.5	-3.5	98	48
Germany	-1.0	-3.1	-2.1	-1.6	73	44
Ireland	-13.8	-10.6	-9.0	-3.0	64	34
Greece	-8.8	-2.8	-1.3	-5.0	115	37
Spain	-9.9	-8.0	-5.5	-2.2	55	35
France	-5.3	-5.5	-4.3	-2.0	76	48
Italy	-0.8	-0.7	-0.1	-2.0	115	47
Netherlands	-3.7	-4.7	-3.6	-2.2	61	46
Portugal	-6.6	-4.2	-1.8	-1.2	77	42

We assume a budget-neutral effect of the current and possible future bailouts of the banking sector. This means we neglect externalities of this type. The ageing of the European population will add considerable cost to eurozone primary surpluses. The increase in costs due to ageing assumes unchanged policy arrangements and structural trends. In a separate ageing variant we assume that the additional costs of ageing are included in the primary surplus projections from 2012 onwards.

We have run the stochastic simulation model for four OECD scenarios: with and without additional consolidation and with and without additional ageing costs. In Figure 4.3 we plot the results of the baseline scenario with additional consolidation for illustrative purposes. The results of all four scenarios are summarised in Table 4.2. We present the results for nine EMU countries: Belgium, Germany, Ireland, Greece, Spain, France, Italy, the Netherlands and Portugal. We did not consider some small countries and new EMU members.[7] The results are plotted for each quarter.

In our model we repeat the calculations 5000 times, such that we obtain 5000 debt paths. The expected debt path and its expected standard deviation are then calculated and plotted. The vertical axis presents the sovereign debt to GDP ratio. The line in the middle represents the average debt development according to the FSS model. The other lines reflect the uncertainty with one or two standard deviations above or below the average debt development per country. The results are summarised in Table 4.2.

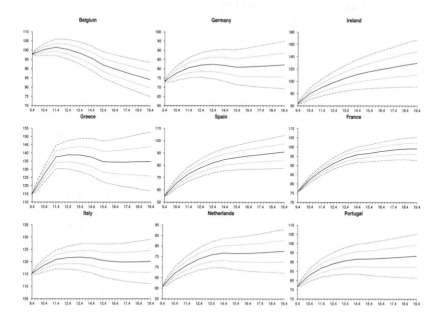

Figure 4.3   OECD baseline forecasts with additional consolidation and without ageing costs

Table 4.2   EMU government debt (% of GDP) in OECD projections, 2009.4 to 2019.4

| | 2009.4 | 2019.4 | | | | 2019 std dev. |
		Base-line	Consoli-date	Ageing costs	Cons. & ageing	
Belgium	97.9	84.2	84.2	91.8	91.8	4.5
Germany	73.3	93.2	82.1	97.8	86.8	6.7
Ireland	64.0	148.1	129.8	155.3	136.9	16.3
Greece	115.1	139.1	134.7	149.6	145.2	7.8
Spain	55.0	107.8	90.9	113.7	96.8	6.7
France	75.7	117.9	99.1	121.3	102.5	3.5
Italy	115.4	124.6	120.3	129.3	125.0	5.0
Netherlands	60.9	91.0	77.5	97.9	84.4	5.2
Portugal	76.8	107.1	93.3	111.6	97.8	6.5
Weighted average	80.4	108.5	96.4	113.5	101.5	

A first conclusion from the projections is that government debt will continue to rise almost everywhere in the medium term. Without additional consolidation the average government debt ratio rises by 28.1 percent-points. Additional budget consolidation reduces debt to GDP by 5.1 percent-points on average. The burden of ageing on the government budget worsens the budgetary positions of all EMU countries. The average effect of ageing is an increase of the debt ratio with 5.0% of GDP. This demonstrates that a significant rise in primary surplus is required in most member states in order to offset the additional costs of ageing, even when these only pertain to the projection period. Including the additional costs of ageing and of extra debt consolidation, sovereign debt only stabilises in Belgium due to a sturdy primary surplus and closure of the output gap. We therefore conclude, in line with other studies, that structural reforms will be necessary to address the ageing issue in the projection period and further beyond.

Only with additional consolidation does debt also stabilise in Germany and the Netherlands at levels that exceed the debt ratio of 2009.4 by 8.8 percentage points (Germany) or 16.6 percentage points (Netherlands). This is no longer true, however, if the additional costs of ageing are also taken into account. In Italy government debt is more or less stabilised at a higher level of 4.9 percentage points after consolidation; however the ageing issue needs to be addressed in order to obtain a stable debt to GDP ratio. Furthermore the level at which government debt is stabilised is relatively high. In Spain, France and Portugal government debt is stabilised only in case of additional consolidation and without taking additional ageing related costs into account. Even then debt levels stabilise only after an increase of 16.5 percentage points (Portugal), 23.4 percentage points (France) or 35.9 percentage points (Spain). Again the levels of government debt at which stabilisation occurs are relatively high.

Debt levels in Ireland have not stabilised after 8 years of fiscal consolidation, even without addressing the ageing issue. In the time frame under consideration they rise by 65.8 percentage points to relatively high levels. In Greece government debt ratios stabilise after a significant increase in 2010 and 2011 due to a closure of the output gap. However, if the ageing issue is dealt with, debt levels will rise again and become unstable. In Greece, too, debt levels remain high throughout the projection period.

Two stress-test scenarios are developed on top of the baseline consolidation scenario. In stress-test scenario 1 (S1) the eurozone is not able to win back the trust of financial markets and Portugal, Italy, Ireland, Spain and Greece have to pay 250 basis points additional interest premium on their debt in 2011 and 2012. This leads to higher interest payments in 2011 until 2018 due to the assumed maturity structure of debt. The precise end date is country-dependent.

In stress-test scenario 2 (S2) we assume that the current economic recession turns into a Japan-style lost decade. Here the output gap persists, resulting in lower real GDP growth in the period 2012-2015 and lower improvement of the primary surplus from 2012 onwards (the member states have permanent lower tax revenue and higher social security expenditures).

We show the values of the criteria described in section 2 for the OECD projections and the stress tests in Table 4.3. It is to be noted that we do not present the results of the criterion on the debt government revenue test because they turned out not to be very informative. In all cases Greece and Ireland do not meet this criterion while the other countries always do so.

Table 4.3   *Values of sustainability criteria in OECD projections and stress tests*

		Baseline			Ageing costs			Consolidation		
	SGhs	SGav	SG19	/GDP	SGav	SG19	/GDP	SGav	SG19	/GDP
Belgium	-8.0	0.9	1.5	Y	0.1	-0.2	N	0.9	1.5	Y
Germany	-5.9	-2.3	-2.2	N	-2.8	-3.2	N	-1.2	-0.5	Y
Ireland	-20.7	-9.2	-7.6	N	-10.0	-9.2	N	-7.4	-3.4	N
Greece	-14.3	-3.7	-1.1	N	-4.8	-3.6	N	-3.3	-0.4	N
Spain	-13.0	-5.6	-4.4	N	-6.2	-5.7	N	-3.9	-1.2	N
France	-8.7	-4.7	-4.7	N	-5.1	-5.5	N	-2.8	-0.3	N
Italy	-8.7	-1.6	-1.2	N	-2.1	-2.3	N	-1.2	-0.6	N
Netherlands	-7.8	-3.3	-2.6	N	-4.0	-4.2	N	-1.9	-0.4	Y
Portugal	-10.7	-3.4	-2.9	N	-3.9	-3.9	N	-2.0	-0.6	N

	Ageing and consolidation			S1: higher interest			S2: output gap		
	SGav	SG19	/GDP	SGav	SG19	/GDP	SGav	SG19	/GDP
Belgium	0.1	-0.2	N	0.9	1.5	Y	-2.1	-2.5	N
Germany	-1.7	-1.5	Y	-1.2	-0.5	Y	-2.7	-2.3	N
Ireland	-8.1	-5.0	N	-9.3	-5.1	N	-9.3	-6.6	N
Greece	-4.3	-2.9	N	-5.8	-2.6	N	-8.0	-7.0	N
Spain	-4.5	-2.5	N	-5.4	-2.4	N	-5.5	-3.6	N
France	-3.2	-1.1	N	-2.8	-0.3	N	-4.5	-2.6	N
Italy	-1.7	-1.7	N	-3.4	-2.4	N	-2.7	-3.0	N
Netherlands	-2.6	-2.0	Y	-1.9	-0.4	Y	-3.5	-2.9	N
Portugal	-2.5	-1.6	N	-3.7	-2.0	N	-2.9	-2.0	N

Here 'SGav' denotes the average sustainability gap in the simulation period 2010-2019, 'SG19' denotes the sustainability gap at the end of the period. A positive number indicates an improvement of the debt position. The average sustainability gap being negative in almost all scenarios for all countries implies that average debt levels must be rising in the projection period. Furthermore a negative sustainability gap in 2019 implies government debt to be unsustainable if left unattended. If the gap is smaller than –1% we interpret this as a relatively stable situation, otherwise more action is required. If the sustainability gap falls below –3% we consider this as an alarming situation. '/GDP' is the outcome of the debt/GDP test and 'N' is the worrying sign that debt exceeds 90% of GDP. These test outcomes clarify the conclusions based on visual inspection of the FSS debt path. We will now interpret the test outcomes in order to conclude.

Only Belgium shows a solid debt development in the baseline scenario. Action is required in Germany, Italy, the Netherlands and Portugal (the sustainability gap is between –3% and –1% of GDP).[8] Other countries need significant additional fiscal consolidation or structural reforms to prevent their debt from spiralling out of control.

With fiscal consolidation Belgium has no debt issues, Germany, the Netherlands, France, Italy and Portugal have a stable debt outlook, because SG19 is smaller than –1% in 2019, and Greece and Spain still need to take additional action. For Ireland debt is still not under control and additional measures must be taken.

When the extra costs of ageing are added to the fiscal consolidation scenario, debt developments worsen for all countries. Belgian debt is still relatively stable. Additional action is needed in Germany, France, the Netherlands, Spain, Italy and Portugal. In Greece and Ireland larger efforts are needed to maintain debt sustainability.

When applying a 250 basis points interest shock to Italy, Ireland, Greece, Spain and Portugal (compared to the consolidation scenario), Greece's debt sustainability becomes potentially dangerous, as is also the case for Irish debt. Portugal, Spain and Italy have to take action compared to the consolidation case. The fact that the sustainability gap of Greece and Italy deteriorates more by an interest rate shock than the gap of Portugal and Spain is caused by their higher initial debt and thus higher interest rate payments.

In the most severe stress-test – which is essentially a lasting depression – Belgium, the Netherlands, Germany, France and Portugal need to undertake additional action to stabilise debt, whereas the other member states need to make structural adjustments and fiscal consolidation.

Concluding on a country basis for the 'consolidation' scenario, which implies additional fiscal consolidation for most member states, it turns out that extra measures over and above the OECD consolidation scenario are required in Greece, Ireland and Spain.

5. CONCLUSIONS

Government debt in the EMU countries has increased by about 13 percentage points in 2008 and 2009 and is expected to rise further in 2010 and 2011. There are worries that government debts may not be sustainable, at least not in some countries. This paper discusses the sustainability of government debt in selected EMU countries (Germany, France, Italy, Spain, the Netherlands, Belgium, Ireland, Greece and Portugal). Using a stochastic sustainability model and OECD projections, we assess the development of government debt until 2019. The stochastic simulations provide a bandwidth of outcomes reflecting uncertainty. Moreover, we have performed various stress tests to address the robustness of the results.

Without consolidation of the budget, and taking into account the public costs of ageing until the end of the projection period, budget deficits in all EMU countries will rise and sovereign debt is not sustainable, apart from Belgium. Even ignoring the cost of ageing, in nearly all EMU countries consolidation of sovereign debt is necessary. Consolidation would eliminate doubts on the sustainability of Belgium, Dutch, French, Italian, Portuguese and German sovereign debts. For Greece, Spain and Ireland additional actions are required on top of the consolidation in the OECD projections. If the costs of ageing are included extra efforts to improve government finances are required for all countries except Belgium. If the current output cap cannot be closed (the recession is turning into a depression), government debts will reach dangerously high levels by the end of 2019.

Our assessments indicate mixed results under miscellaneous assumptions. Thus, recurrent sovereign debt crises within EMU are not at all inconceivable in the coming decade. This calls for a quick realignment of policy rules and institutions that would enable to prevent crisis development and would install an authority with the capacity to manage crisis situations (if they nevertheless occur) efficiently and proficiently. In order to prevent contagion this authority should oversee fiscal consolidation programs of member states that are in trouble, organise a bail-out when necessary and a structured default when inevitable.

If anything, the results of our sustainability assessments point to an undiminished necessity to quickly make progress in preventing and managing government debt crisis situations. After all, our analysis shows that the possibility of sovereign debt crises in Europe is not behind us yet at all. Even if the growth of government debt in Europe due to the current economic crisis can be reversed, new fiscal challenges are ahead, in particular covering the public cost of ageing beyond the projection period.

NOTES

1. Another possibility would be the use of empirically estimated feedback rules from government debt on primary surplus. Examples are Bohn (1998) for the US over the period 1916 to 1995 and Lukkezen et al. (2011) for the Netherlands over the period 1814-2005. It was, however, beyond the framework of this chapter to estimate these feedback relations for all EMU countries and to implement them in the model.
2. Recently, Beetsma and Giuliodori (2011) provided a survey of the cost and benefits of the EMU based on this literature. The European Commission (2008) has presented an extensive overview on ten years of EMU including the successes and challenges ahead.
3. Note that we ignore private debts here.
4. Other potential spillovers are labour mobility and fiscal transfers. These spillover channels are often discussed with the US in mind and do not apply for the EU due to the low mobility of labour and very limited fiscal transfers.
5. Outside a currency union, a country can simply depreciate its currency in response to difficult economic circumstances. Beetsma and Giuliodori (2011) describe some examples. These depreciations may have serious negative effects on other countries due to fewer exports and more imports. This externality is eliminated by introducing a common currency. The fourth externality is probably much weaker than the eliminated one.
6. See De Grauwe and Moesen (2009) and Depla and von Weizsäcker (2010).
7. The results for Austria, Finland and Luxembourg are available upon request. The outcomes are not presented due to space limitations. In all scenarios these countries do not seem to have any sustainability problem.
8. Superficially, Greece also belongs in the class of countries, but it does not meet the government revenue debt target.

REFERENCES

Ardagna, S., F. Caselli and T. Lane (2007), 'Fiscal Discipline and the Cost of Public Debt Service: Some Estimates for OECD Countries', *B.E. Journal of Macroeconomics*, **7**(1), article 28.

Beetsma, R. and M. Giuliodori (2011), 'The Macroeconomic Costs and Benefits of the EMU and other Monetary Unions: an Overview of Recent Research', *Journal of Economic Literature* (forthcoming).

Blanchard, O.J. (1990), 'Suggestions for a New Set of Fiscal Indicators', *OECD Economics Department Working Paper*, no. 79.

Bohn, H. (1998), 'The Behavior of U.S. Public Debt and Deficits', *Quarterly Journal of Economics*, **113**, 949-63.

Buiter, W. (2009), 'The Limits to Fiscal Stimulus', *CEPR Discussion Paper*, 7607, London: Centre for Economic Policy Research.

Callen, T. et al. (2003), 'Public Debt in Emerging Markets: is it Too High?', *IMF World Economic Outlook* 2003, Washington D.C.: International Monetary Fund.

Canzoneri, M., R. Cumby and B. Diba (2001), 'Is the Price Level Determined by the Needs of Fiscal Solvency?', *American Economic Review*, **91**, 1221-38.

Chalk, N. and R. Hemming (2000), 'Assessing Fiscal Sustainability in Theory and Practice', *IMF Working Paper*, WP/00/81, Washington D.C.: International Monetary Fund.

De Grauwe, P. and W. Moesen (2009), 'Gains for All: a Proposal for a Common Eurobond', *Intereconomics*, May/June.

Depla, J. and J. von Weizsäcker (2010), 'The Blue Bonds Proposal', *Bruegel Policy Brief*.

Egert, B. (2010), 'Fiscal Policy Reaction to the Cycle in the OECD: Pro- or Counter-cyclical?', *OECD Economic Department Working Paper*, no. 763.

European Commission (2008), 'EMU@10: Successes and Challenges after 10 Years of Economic and Monetary Union', *European Economy*.

Faini, R. (2006), 'Fiscal Policy and Interest Rates in Europe', *Economic Policy* (July 2006), pp. 443-489.

Fischer, S., R. Sahay and C.A. Végh (2002), 'Modern Hyper- and High Inflations', *Journal of Economic Literature*, **40**, 837-880.

Giuliodori, M. and R. Beetsma (2005), 'What are the Trade Spillovers from Fiscal Shocks in Europe? An Empirical Analysis', *De Economist*, **153**, 167-197.

Lukkezen, J., A. France, S. van Wijnbergen and P. Veenendaal (2011), 'The Response of Primary Surplus to Sovereign Debt: an Analysis of Two Centuries of Fiscal Behavior in the Netherlands', *CPB discussion paper*, forthcoming.

OECD (2010), *OECD Economic Outlook*, no. 87, volume 2010/1.

Reinhart, C. and K. Rogoff (2010), 'Growth in a Time of Debt', *CEPR Discussion Paper*, 7661.

van Wijnbergen, S. and N. Budina (2008), 'Quantitative Approaches to Fiscal Sustainability Analysis: a Case Study of Turkey since the Crisis of 2001', *World Bank Economic Review*, **23**, 119-140.

5. Economic Crises and Regional Convergence in the EU: an Exploration of Facts, Theories and Policy Implications

Nicola D. Coniglio and Francesco Prota

1. INTRODUCTION

Looking from a historical perspective at the evolution of the economic performances of European regions, there is strong evidence of persistence of disparities in terms of per capita GDP within countries: the regional rankings of per capita GDP in Spain, Italy and other EU Member States in the last decade look more or less identical to those observed at the beginning of last century. Within this framework of long-term inertia, with few success and failure stories, we can observe an accordion-like effect where periods of convergence – for instance between the 1950s and 1970s (Barro and Sala-i-Martín, 1991; Tondl, 2001) – are followed by periods of divergence – as from the mid-1970s until 1985-86 (Cuadrado-Roura, 2001).

The theoretical prediction of the neoclassical growth models of higher growth rates in lagging regions contrasts with these stylised facts. At the same time the discontinuity in convergence patterns does not fit well either with those theories that predict regional divergence, such as some new endogenous growth theories and new economic geography. The discontinuity in regional convergence implies that those economic forces that were working toward a reduction (widening) of regional inequalities are reverted at some point in time.

Why? Our hypothesis is that strong exogenous shocks, such as the current financial crisis that started in 2007, might play an important role in explaining the discontinuity in regional convergence, since they affect core and peripheral regions in a highly heterogeneous way.

The aim of this chapter is to shed light on the impact of strong exogenous shocks on the pattern of regional convergence. For this reason we discuss how previous economic shocks of a different nature – such as the oil crises in the early 1970s or the 1992-93 economic crises – have affected within-countries regional performances. Despite a wide number of studies on regional convergence, to our knowledge, there are few attempts in the literature to provide such an analysis. The paper concludes with policy implications for the present EU cohesion policies.

2. THE PERSISTENCE OF REGIONAL DISPARITIES WITHIN EUROPEAN COUNTRIES: SOME STYLISED FACTS

The policy interest in the regional disparities in economic development and standards of living goes back to the post-war period (United Nations, 1955) and, in some countries such as the United Kingdom, even before that.[1] A seminal study of Williamson (1965) investigates the nature of spatial inequality within national borders in a large sample of countries at different levels of development and the pattern of change in regional inequality between the 1930s and the post-war period. The study shows a high degree of regional economic disparities and their relation with the national development process. Williamson argues the existence of an inverted U-shaped relationship between the development of countries and inequalities within its regions.

A map that would show the degree of economic development between different regions within Western European countries in the 1950s (see e.g. United Nations, op. cit.) would learn that the poor regions in individual countries are generally those situated at the periphery of Europe. The similarity of this map with the actual geography of regional disparities would be striking. Over the last six decades disparities in per capita income have diminished between European countries, but at the regional level, the intra-national inequalities (both within rich and poor countries) are still significant and in many cases even increasing (OECD, 2009). Indeed, there is a growing role of within-countries inequality in explaining total European spatial inequality. The breakdown of inequality into between-country and within-country components suggests that most of interregional inequality occurs within countries rather than between countries.

The importance of the within-country component has increased over time, notably since the mid-1990s (Table 5.1). Looking at regional inequalities in a historical perspective, we can infer therefore that there is strong evidence of persistence of regional disparities within countries.

Another important stylised fact is the high degree of immobility of intra-country regional rankings in terms of GDP per capita (or similar measures). They are quite stable over a long period of time in most countries. In other words only few regions change their positions in the ranking.

The historical territorial distribution of wealth is stable in Europe, despite the economic evolutions and the deep socio-economic and political transformations of the last decades (technological advances, regional economic integration, modification in social class structure, etc.): old core regions are still the core, while few peripheral regions have converged to the club of rich regions.

Table 5.1   *Regional disparities in per capita GDP within and between countries and regions (coefficient of variation, PPS)*

	1995 (a)	2006 (b)	b – a
EU-15 (between regions)	28.5	28.8	+ 0.3
EU-15 (between countries)	14.3	11.8	– 2.5
EU-15 (within countries)	24.7	26.2	+ 1.5
EU-27 (between regions)	38.7	37.8	– 0.9
EU-27 (between countries)	29.1	25.7	– 3.4
EU-27 (within countries)	25.5	27.8	+ 2.3

Source: Ministero dello Sviluppo Economico (2009).

Although the 'gap' seems to be highly persistent in its sign as well as in terms of regional rankings, over time phases of increase and decrease are observed in the level of regional inequalities. Regional convergence within countries follows an 'accordion effect': alternate phases of regional convergence and divergence with limited mobility between the groups of rich and lagging-behind regions.

Looking at the regional convergence among European regions there is general agreement on the existence of an increase in regional inequalities at the beginning of the last century until World War II, followed by a decrease in regional inequalities (i.e. convergence) from the 1950s to the 1970s (Dunford, 1994). During the 1980s and the early 1990s regional disparities in the European Union showed no tendency to decrease. On the contrary, they increased (Fagerberg and Verspagen, 1996; Magrini, 1999). The last fifteen years have been characterised by a significant stability in the evolution of regional disparities across Europe (Puga, 2002; Ezcurra et al., 2005) or limited 'club convergence' (Canova, 2004).

Italy represents an emblematic case of the above described 'accordion effect', but the pattern is similar in most EU countries. Analysing the evolution of regional disparities in Italy over a very long period of time (1891-2004), alternate convergence and divergence are evident. In the period until 1913, with the early period of modernisation of the economy, the formation of regional disparities surfaces; between 1920 and 1939 disparities among regions widen, especially between the North and the South; between the 1951 and the early 1970s there is a decline in disparities; from the oil crises onward, a new deepening of North-South disparities is noted, with some decline in the last years (Daniele and Malanima, 2007).

In the case of Greece, regional disparities were reduced in the 1970s and the 1980s, while there is a clear process of divergence in the period 1991-2004 (Petrakos and Artelaris, 2008). At least part of the reduction in regional disparities, especially in the 1980s, is attributed to the prolonged recession of the economy that restrained the dynamism of the development centre of the country (Michelis et al., 2004).

The Iberic peninsula follows a similar pattern. In Spain the process of early industrialisation, which is highly concentrated in the Basque Countries, Catalonia and the Region of Madrid, is associated with an upswing of regional inequalities (Martinez-Galarraga et al., 2009). The post World War II period is characterised by a process of regional convergence that is interrupted by the first oil crisis. From the 1980s regional inequality in terms of per capita GDP is again increasing, although mildly.

In Portugal, the direction of regional inequalities goes mainly from the relative poor inland areas (with a declining share of GDP and population) to the coastal areas. Although in Portugal spatial differences have been highly persistent over time, in the last decades the regional ranking has observed an important change with the relative fall of the Norte – which gravitates around the industrial city of Porto – and the rise of the region of Algarve (Pires, 2005; INE, 2008; OECD, 2008).

Even in the case of East Germany, twenty years after the fall of the Berlin Wall, it seems that the catching-up process came to a halt. Eastern GDP per capita improved from 49% of the Western level in 1991 to 67% in 1996, since when convergence has stalled (Kosfeld and Lauridsen, 2004; Juessen, 2009).

The stylised facts on regional convergence within countries presented here, therefore, seem to corroborate the existence of an 'accordion effect', an (endogenous?) instability in convergence-divergence patterns.

3. BOUNCING BETWEEN THEORIES OF REGIONAL ECONOMIC CONVERGENCE

When considering the theoretical literature on convergence, a wide array of arguments arise predicting either the long-term reduction or the persistence and self-reinforcing nature of economic inequalities across countries and regions. Economic theory does not provide an unambiguous analysis but identifies some contradicting mechanisms and factors that generate economic convergence or divergence in per capita income levels.

Following Solow (1956), the neoclassical growth models predict that poor regions will grow faster than rich ones. Over time this translates into a reduction of regional disparities, although there is no presumption of complete convergence if regions differ in their structural characteristics. The prediction is based on the key hypothesis of production technologies that exhibit non-increasing returns to scale in productive factors. In a competitive environment, regional labour and capital mobility as well as regional trade will also work in favour of factor price convergence (à la Heckscher-Ohlin), reinforcing the negative relation between growth and regional disparities.

Endogenous growth models, which introduce increasing returns in the production function and postulate that human capital and innovation are central to growth, permit several possibilities with regard to convergence behaviour: some variants (including models that assume that technological advance is highly localised and its diffusion slow) predict persistent or even divergent differences in national (or regional) per capita income. Others allow for 'conditional' convergence to different long-run steady states that depend on initial national (regional) differences in institutional set-up, economic structure, tastes and so on. Still others allow for so-called 'club' convergence among countries (regions) with similar structural and related conditions.

Another set of theoretical models, belonging to the so-called new economic geography, has gained much attraction for its arguments on centralising and decentralising forces in geographic economic space, which could lead to convergence or divergence of regional incomes (Krugman, 1991a,b; Krugman and Venables, 1995; Fujita et al., 1999). Depending, among other things, on the relative importance of transport costs and localisation economies, some new economic geography models predict a persistent core-periphery pattern of regional per capita income or divergent regional income paths, while others predict initial divergence of regional per capita incomes, followed by convergence, as centrifugal forces come to outweigh the centripetal attraction of localisation economies.

Many of these theoretical predictions contrast with the stylised facts presented in the above section.

Ambiguity also rests on empirical investigations of the convergence/divergence debate. In fact, the ample body of empirical research on regional convergence has not yet reached a common answer as to whether, and under which conditions, a reduction in regional per capita income differentials actually takes place. Results differ profoundly according to the datasets and the approaches used, the period for which regressions are estimated, and the geographical scale of regions analysed. To date the existing empirical literature has failed to identify convincing empirical regularities regarding the dynamics of regional inequalities.

The discontinuity in regional convergence implies that those economic forces that were working toward a reduction (widening) of regional inequalities are reverted at some point in time. Why? In the next session we formulate our hypothesis to explain the pattern of regional convergence we observe.

4. SHOCKS AND REGIONAL CONVERGENCE

Consider two regions with a different level of development and assume that the less developed one is converging as illustrated by Figure 5.1. At some point in time (t_1) we can have a symmetric shock with asymmetric effects or an asymmetric shock (that is a shock which produces effects only in one region). These shocks can be positive or negative: they can accelerate the rate of convergence or they can change the previous pattern. They can produce a turning point and they can have long-lasting effects. Our hypothesis is, therefore, that exogenous shocks of various kinds (economic integration, financial crises, sectoral shocks, etc.) can explain variations in the convergence/divergence pattern.[2] What matters in terms of the impact on the regional convergence/divergence pattern is the length of the shock and the structural change provoked.[3]

Regions react to external shocks differently, depending on the underlying social, economic and geographic conditions. The vulnerability of the regions depends on their initial strengths and weaknesses: size of the internal market and access to external markets, firm concentration, endowments in natural resources and in physical, human and social capital, factor mobility, degree of sectoral specialisation, etc. It depends on broader national factors (in particular, the institutional setting) too.

Usually, less developed regions are hit by the negative shocks more severely than rich regions because of the fact that existing firms localised in central regions are on average more modern and technologically more advanced, and thus better able to adjust their production to the shocks and to retain workers.[4] Moreover, it is more likely in the lagging areas – where workforce turnover and sectoral mobility is structurally lower than in rich and dynamic areas – that spells of unemployment in the workforce induced by adverse shocks lead to a permanent loss of skills and that the stock of equipment and infrastructure decrease and become obsolete due to lower investment (hysteresis).

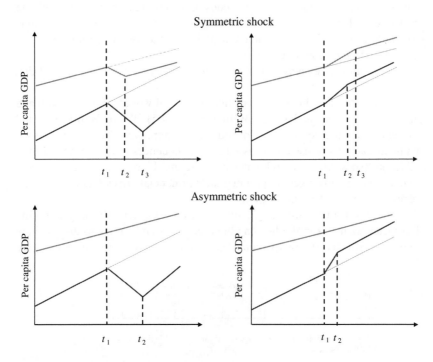

Figure 5.1   The impact of exogenous shocks on the regional convergence pattern

Innovation may be hampered as spending on research and development is one of the first outlays that businesses cut back on during a recession.[5] The current global economic crisis is having a profound impact on the firms' innovation behaviour across Europe, even if it is affecting countries to a different extent (Archibugi and Filippetti, 2010). As a result EU Member States are no longer converging in terms of innovative effort. It is reasonable to assume also that at the regional level the lagging areas are those decreasing their innovation expenditure more dramatically. This can lead to divergence in regional per capita income since, as far as the European case is concerned, differences in economic growth across European regions have already been explained by looking at the differences in generating innovation and adapting to technologies developed abroad (Fagerberg and Verspagen, 1996; Fagerberg et al., 1999; Cantwell and Iammarino, 2003).

Finally, after a negative shock, there are fewer economic resources to be devoted to regional policy goals, possibly also because of budget cuts at the national level. This may depress the odds of poorer areas catching up with the richer ones. Decreased use of regional policy instruments during recessions has long-lasting effects on regional disparities if the use of instruments is not increased during economic upturns.

Shocks and crises may, therefore, have a long-run effect on regional disparities.

Our hypothesis is in line with earlier theoretical work by Lucas (2000) and also the empirical analysis by Williamson (1965). While Williamson and Lucas analyse the consequence of industrialisation, we believe that their arguments can also be used to measure the consequences of other than industrialisation types of structural changes affecting both national growth and regional inequalities: economic integration, financial crises (banking or currency crises) and sectoral shocks.

To support our thesis we analyse several large exogenous shocks that hit the European countries in the last one hundred years and we try to discuss how they have affected the within-countries regional convergence pattern (Figure 5.2).

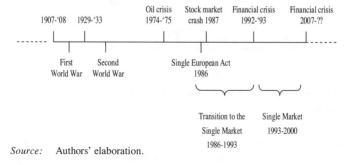

Source: Authors' elaboration.

Figure 5.2   The main exogenous shocks in Europe in the last one hundred years

4.1. Oil Crises and Regional Disparities

The first episode we study is the 1974-75 oil crisis. The 1970s were dominated by a slowdown in the rates of per capita growth all over Europe, provoked by the oil shocks. In several European countries this period is a turning point interrupting a rather long period of regional convergence. The oil shock had substantial effects on several industries and affected in turn the industrial composition, the locational advantages of regions and the pattern of trade. It is, in our opinion, at the root of three phenomena potentially affecting the convergence process.

First, while the vertical disintegration of industrial activities favoured the diffusion of mature activities (automobiles, consumer durables, petrochemicals) from the core to the periphery, the emergence of new high-value activities caused a renewal in the centripetal forces in order to benefit from agglomeration economies, R&D, human capital and physical infrastructure and amenities of the core regions.[6] This might have precluded the expected spatial diffusion, and thus the consequent convergence process.

Second, notwithstanding a certain change in the geographical location of clusters of high production regions, with the traditional core shifting southwards, due to the emergence of regions able to host new high-value activities to the detriment of those specialised in mature activities, we do not have a significant process of general diffusion in the location of these activities towards the poor peripheral regions.[7] The absence of convergence in GDP per capita was due basically to the inability of the poor regions to make significant moves up the ranking, as well as to the persistence of low value clusters in the traditional periphery.

We had therefore a concentric expansion of the economic activity, in which the inner periphery receives the positive effects of integration faster than the outer periphery. This phenomenon is well illustrated by the Italian case. The late 1970s was the period of the emergence of the 'Third Italy' (Bagnasco, 1977). At that time, it became apparent that while little economic progress was in sight in the relatively poor South, and the traditionally rich Northwest (Piedmont and Liguria) was facing a deep crisis, the Northeast and Centre of Italy showed fast growth demonstrating the dynamism of areas whose main industrial fabric was based on small and medium-sized enterprises clustered together in specific regions and able to grow rapidly, innovate their production, develop niches in export markets and offer new employment opportunities.

Third, the oil crisis led to a sudden decrease in the size of internal and cross-border migration that represented a powerful channel of convergence between the 1950s and the 1970s in countries like Italy and Spain. High unemployment rates in core regions, which played a role of 'sponge' for excess labour supply in peripheral regions, checked inter-regional mobility (Antolin and Bover, 1997; Bentolila, 1997; Faini et al., 1997). Internal migration changed not only in size but also in its nature: the migration from the peripheries to economic cores of low-skilled workers (often moving with the entire household), typical of the 1960s and 1970s, was replaced during the subsequent periods by migration of young and highly skilled individuals. The latter form of migration is likely to increase regional divergence – in particular in the longer term – since it makes more unequal the regional endowment of human capital, one of the most important sources of economic growth.

4.2. International Integration and Regional Disparities

The last few decades of European economic history are deeply characterised by a process that we might consider, from the point of view of single European regions, as an exogenous shock: the formation of the European Single Market and Economic and Monetary Union. Economic theory does not provide an unambiguous guide on the effects of increasing integration between countries on intra-country disparities. For proponents of neoclassical precepts, regional disparities are bound to disappear because of diminishing returns to capital. By promoting free movements of factors of production, further integration would lead to a more efficient resource allocation, and thus economic growth. To contrast with this approach, contributions to the new economic geography theory argue that, by promoting trade and factor mobility, deeper economic integration will create new opportunities of economies of scale, activity specialisation and economic agglomeration, which could generate regional disparities in growth and factor accumulation, and thus economic divergence.

We follow the latter reasoning and argue that there are several mechanisms at work which imply that deeper international economic integration – such as Economic and Monetary Union in Europe – generally leads to a widening gap between rich and poor regions within a country.

Firstly, the reduction in barriers to trade and factor mobility between countries is highly asymmetrical between core and peripheral regions. Economic transactions with foreign agents (firms and consumers) entail costs that are often very high: information costs in order to 'locate' transaction opportunities, communication costs with foreign actors, transport costs for sending/receiving goods and services, regulatory costs due to differences in legislation (fiscal system, product standards, safety regulation, etc.) or imposed by policymakers (i.e. trade policy). These costs, that we can for simplicity label 'transport costs', have both a variable component (i.e. increasing with the quantity of international transactions carried out; for instance freight and insurance costs) and a fixed component (for instance in case of regulatory costs). The complexity of international interactions implies that most of the firms, in particular small and medium enterprises, have to rely on specialised providers of services in order to access foreign markets (from logistics to legal services). The availability (cost) of these specialised inputs is larger (lower) in core regions where the density of economic activity is higher and where agents with international connections are mostly located.

The initial advantage of core regions implies that in a process of further international integration the change in 'transport costs' that follows are highly asymmetric. In particular, these costs will change more favourably where they are already low. In our opinion this asymmetric change in 'transport costs' has important consequences for the pattern of regional inequality.

In order to better understand this point, let us consider a stylised situation (illustrated in Figure 5.3) where, initially, a country composed of two regions with a different level of development (core and periphery) is weakly integrated with an emerging market (for instance Eastern Europe). Let us assume that the core (periphery) region is relatively capital (labour) abundant compared to the other region. In this initial framework of low international integration it is likely that, given the differential in economic development, labour will flow from where it is abundant to where it is scarce; i.e. from periphery to core. On the other hand, capital will flow from the core to the periphery in search of higher returns.

It is important to point out that, as predicted by trade models based on transport costs and increasing returns to scale in production, such as the new economic geography, some economic agents (hence part of the capital stock embedded in these activities) will find it convenient to move from the periphery to the core. These flows will likely characterise those sectors where economies of scale are strong. The rise of many industrial activities (for instance textile, footwear, furniture and other 'light' industries) in the periphery of Europe was the result of a process of intra-country production fragmentation. The convergence in the capital-labour ratio would then lead to a decline with respect to the initial regional disparities. In other words, this scenario will be characterised by regional convergence in per capita GDP.

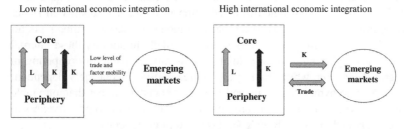

Low international economic integration   High international economic integration

Legend: L = labour; K = capital;
            = flows of production factors within the stylised country;
            = trade;
            = flows of production factors from the stylised country to the emerging market.
Source: Authors' elaboration.

Figure 5.3   *International integration: the effects of a reduction in 'transport costs'*

Let us now consider what would happen in this framework if barriers between this stylised country and a foreign emerging market are asymmetrically reduced (the reduction in 'transport costs' is higher for the core region, gaining an advantage in transaction technology with foreign agents). Due to the gap between core and periphery, labour will continue to flow from the latter to the former. The opening up of possibilities to interact with foreign agents will divert some of the capital from the periphery to the emerging market.

Capital owners will find it profitable to locate (or relocate) their capital abroad rather than to the periphery since, with lower 'transport costs', it is now convenient to locate in the emerging market and serve (through trade) the national market from there. This diversion of capital from the periphery to a foreign market is the result of a comparative advantage effect (in this simple example due to the labour abundance in the emerging market). What is more interesting is the flow of capital from where it is relatively scarce (the periphery) to where it is abundant (the core): this flow is the direct result of the asymmetric integration that generates a localisation advantage in the core region (a 'hub' effect). The asymmetric integration boosts the market potential of the core: some firms previously located in the periphery might find it an optimal strategy to relocate in the core and serve the consumer of the three markets (core, periphery and emerging market) from there.

The above-described hub effect should imply a larger increase in international trade flows in the core compared to the periphery: a story which shares some key aspects with the 'bazaar-economy' theory developed by Hans-Werner Sinn in a recent influential book (Sinn, 2005).[8]

We argue that an asymmetric integration has characterised the EU integration process, making the national cores more integrated among each other and increasing the relative distance of EU peripheries. As shown in Bouvet (2007), EMU has contributed to a reduction in regional inequality in richer EU countries, while it has exacerbated regional disparities among poorer countries. The opening of borders to trade is likely to amplify these internal trajectories, by making the wealthier regions more capable of competing in integrated markets, while leaving the poorer regions increasingly dependent on public employment and state and European transfers, rather than on viable entrepreneurial activities, as a consequence of their lack of competitiveness in more integrated markets (Rodríguez-Pose and Fratesi, 2004).

The Economic and Monetary Union is expected to bring more macroeconomic stability, which could promote a more equal income distribution, but on the other hand, labour market rigidities could make countries more vulnerable to asymmetric shocks. Moreover, increased competition induced by further integration and improved price transparency could put more pressure on the less developed Member States, which could ultimately lead to more inequalities (Padoa-Schioppa, 1987).

There are other channels through which international economic integration reinforces core regions (increasing regional divergence): (i) FDI inflows that are mainly directed to core regions, increasing the capital stock in rich regions (for example, Madrid attracted 65% of Spanish FDI inflows between 1993 and 2003); (ii) immigration inflows (in particular highly skilled individuals) are also directed to the most dynamic regions; (iii) new technologies/innovations are more likely to be 'absorbed' by the most productive and efficient firms that are typically more abundant in rich regions.

Interestingly, in Latin American countries' regional disparities tended to rise in the aftermath of trade liberalisation (Serra et al., 2006).[9] Although in these countries aggregate growth accelerated after trade liberalisation, wide discrepancies occurred across different regions within a country. The winners and losers from trade integration are geographically concentrated, and hence the initial benefits may have tended to favour more developed regions. For instance, in Mexico stronger divergence is found for the 1985-93 period covering the initial stages of reform and before the implementation of the NAFTA agreement. This confirms that these reforms had highly differentiated effects on different regions (Juan-Ramón and Rivera-Batiz, 1996). Following trade liberalisation reforms investment flowed into the border states and Mexico City because of their high levels of human capital and better communications and transportation infrastructure (Chiquiar, 2005).

4.3. Financial Crises and Regional Disparities

The financial crises have a pervasive impact on the real economy.[10] Cerra and Saxena (2005, 2008) indicate that permanent output loss is a consequence of most financial crises. The occurrence of a financial crisis negatively and permanently affects potential output (Furceri and Mourougane, 2009).[11] As it is known, often financial crises are associated with recessions (Kaminsky and Reinhart, 1999) and, as shown by Claessens et al. (2009), recessions associated with credit crunches and house price busts tend to be deeper and longer than other recessions.

A financial crisis represents a symmetric shock that can have asymmetric implications: usually, it hits first the 'core' regions, but it is fast propagating to the 'peripheries'. If lagging areas are hit more severely by this negative shock, this could cause divergence. There are indeed several reasons why disparities should grow during recessions under these circumstances.

First, since recessions may have permanent effects on the level of productivity, it follows that if productivity improvements differ across regions, then recessions may have permanent effects on regional economic disparities as well. The literature suggests several mechanisms that explain why recessions increase productivity (Aghion and Saint-Paul, 1998): (i) recessions tend to cut away the least productive activity and preserve only the most efficient firms (Caballero and Hammour, 1994); (ii) the opportunity costs of productivity-improving activities, such as reorganisation and training, are lower during recessions, consequently recessions speed up productivity improvement; (iii) during recessions the likelihood of bankruptcy is lower for firms that undertake reorganisation investments (the 'disciplinary effect'); (iv) if during economic downturns the difference between efficient and inefficient workers can be observed more readily, then a recession can help to improve worker selection, decreasing the probability of a mistaken occupational choice. The reason why productivity improvements differ across regions during recessions is that, generally speaking, firms in the initially richer regions are more likely to experience larger increases of productivity as they are often more advanced and well-equipped to handle corporate restructuring following an economic and/or financial crisis. In turn this leads to growing regional disparities.

Second, reasons why poorer regions are finding it increasingly difficult to cope during economic contractions have been sought in the timing and duration of regional cycles (Saint-Paul, 1997). Lagging areas have a less diversified economy and if they are specialised in sectors that tend to suffer more from longer and deeper downswings, this widens regional disparities.

Diminished migration flows from poor to rich regions are the fourth reason for regional divergence during contractions. A well established fact is the lower tendency of labour to migrate during periods of recession (Pissarides and McMaster, 1984; Attanasio and Padoa-Schioppa, 1991; Decressin, 1994; Dewhurst, 1998). Particularly important, moreover, is the mobility of highly educated individuals, who are the most prone to move away from the worst-hit regions (Mauro and Spilimbergo, 1999). This has serious consequences for the worst-off regions as they lose some of their most productive labour force, and this will have a long-lasting impact on their future economic growth.

The last reason concerns the fact that (in most observed cases) crisis policy responses focus more resources in core regions.

The 1990s crises in Finland, Norway and Sweden are among the most deep financial crises since World War II, and they were associated with recessions. In the case of Sweden, for example, the output loss was not fully reversed (Cerra and Saxena, 2008). There was a permanent output decline associated with Sweden's banking crisis. The decline led to a drop in Sweden's per capita GDP relative to other OECD countries.

The economic crisis of the early 1990s in Finland marked the end of a long period or regional economic convergence, which started in the 1930s and become particularly rapid in the 1960s and 1970s (Kangasharju, 1999; Pekkala, 1999) and had a strong repercussion on the regional structure, with subregions changing their relative positions in the GDP ranking. As shown by Pekkala (2000), the regional convergence occurred before the slump, while divergence occurred in the downturn and early recovery. Moreover, according to Kangasharju and Pekkala (2000) the regional effects of the recession have been more permanent in nature.

Although Finland as a whole flourished in the late 1990s, this was not true across all its regions. The positive aggregate development experienced by Finland was based on uneven regional growth, especially after the severe recession of the early 1990s. Regional competitiveness varied greatly. The new growth based on the export and information technology industries took place in a highly uneven way across the country. Especially in the early phase of growth, new jobs were created only in a few big centres, which affected the direction of the rapidly increasing migration flows, and concentration substantially accelerated after the severe recession of the early 1990s. The main reason for this divergence was the faster growth of productivity in the initially rich subregions. Slower decline in employment in the rich subregions also contributed to divergence. Inter-regional migration flows exerted a convergent effect on the GDP per capita, but not sufficiently to offset the disparity in productivity and employment. The developments of the 1990s also seem to have brought regional convergence to a halt (Tervo, 2005).[12]

4.4. Sectoral Shocks and Regional Disparities

Sectoral shocks too are important in explaining the regional convergence pattern. Here we briefly present the case of a positive sectoral shock: the large-scale development of international tourism that started in the 1960s. Structural changes in the supply of tourist services (for instance the emergence of large tour operators in Northern European countries) and a substantial decrease in mobility costs led to a boost in tourism along the Mediterranean coast (with the partial exception of the Italian Mezzogiorno). The Greek Islands, the Balearic and Canary Islands in Spain and the Algarve region in Portugal are among the obvious 'success stories' of regions that caught up with the national average in the last decades. International tourism played a crucial role in the development of these lagging regions and is by far the largest contributor to the formation of their GDP per capita. This result is of great importance for the development of regions which, for geographical or historical reasons, have failed to attract significant industrial activity.

5.   CONCLUSIONS AND POLICY IMPLICATIONS

Will the current crisis have long-term effects on regional convergence in Europe? Which could be the implications of the crisis on the European regional policy?

As we have shown in this chapter, the within-countries convergence/divergence pattern can be strongly affected by external shocks. Past shocks in Europe have had asymmetric effects on regional performances and represented a structural break in the dynamics of regional inequalities.

Although the European Union as a whole is considered to have moved out of recession at the end of 2009, there is still uncertainty over the path of recovery, over the impact of the ongoing increase in unemployment and the subsequent slowdown of aggregate demand (in most, though not all EU countries), over the fundamental health of the financial sector, and over the effect of more severe credit constraints for businesses and households.

All European regions have been affected to some extent by the crisis (depending on their initial situation, their sectoral specialisation, and the response of national and regional authorities), but the duration of the negative effects are likely to vary. The 'core' regions should be capable of taking advantage from the recovery, as happened after the previous crises (for example, capital cities and large urban regions led the rest of Europe to economic recovery after the oil shocks in the early 1970s (Rodríguez-Pose, 1998), while in the case of 'peripheral' regions there is the risk that the loss of jobs and firms in the recession could lead to structurally lasting lower levels of employment and economic activity.

Shocks influence convergence/divergence patterns also indirectly by changing policy variables. Although numerous measures that governments introduced to respond to the crisis mostly did not have a regional dimension, nevertheless some measures may implicitly be biased towards certain regions because they focus on sectors or activities (such as R&D or investment in infrastructure) that are more concentrated in some regions than in others.[13] In addition, there were changes in regional policy both at national and European level (cohesion policy). In some countries one witnessed a re-orientation of regional policy, but the changes made have not benefitted lagging areas, but rather relatively more developed regions, or all regions (Davies et al., 2010). In Germany, an example of a measure that benefits stronger regions is the temporary extension from the new Länder to all Länder of area eligibility under the Central Innovation Programme for SMEs (ZIM), which is the single most important federal programme to fund R&D and innovation activities of SMEs. In England and Scotland changes to regional aid schemes have extended the designation category to the whole territory providing grants to SMEs outside Article 87(3).

In other countries economic resources previously devoted to regional policy goals have been cut in order to raise resources to tackle the overall negative effects of the crisis. In Italy the fiscal stimulus package includes a reduction in domestic regional funding. The resources taken from the Fund for Under-utilised Areas have been reallocated to other types of expenditure.[14]

At the European level, as part of the EU's anti-crisis measures, the European Commission has introduced a series of measures in order to simplify the implementation of its cohesion policy and to provide additional flexibility to Member States in using the corresponding resources (by closing 2000-06 programmes and by allowing domestic authorities to reallocate funds in the 2007-13 programmes, with the aim of accelerating spending).[15] It is fair to say that these changes are questionable since cohesion policy is an instance of long-term structural policy and should not be viewed as an anti-crisis weapon.

The regional policy changes induced by the crisis could thus exacerbate the negative impact of the shock on the regional convergence.

Moreover, the necessary public spending cuts to reduce public sector indebtedness generated by the financial crisis and economic recession could have a greater impact on weaker regions whose local authorities may not be able to provide adequate public services.

Like past shocks the current one might lead to a discontinuity in regional inequalities within EU countries. What should policymakers, in the light of this, do with respect to EU regional policy?

First, since the shock is likely to have strongly heterogeneous regional effects, place-based development policies should be considered as a necessary policy tool. The risk of diversion of public funds from regional policy, which by nature is, or should be, a set of medium/long-term policies aimed at addressing structural deficits of peripheral regions, to shock-induced policies that have short-term objectives and are often targeted mainly to central regions, could produce a long-lasting adverse impact on convergence processes.

Second, equity (and not only efficiency) should be an objective of regional policy (Barca, 2009). As a consequence, regional policy should address the effects of 'circumstances' (including those that are place-related), since the economic performance of a region does not depend simply on 'effort'. An interesting example of the importance of the 'circumstances' is given by the 'maquiladora' industry in Mexico, concentrated in Mexican states along the Mexico-US border.[16] As shown by Hanson (2002), one of the main factors accounting for their success is the proximity to the large, high-wage economy of the United States. It is evident that this factor is not specifically related to 'effort' or to specific comparative advantages of the Mexican border region.[17]

On efficiency grounds, what the EU needs is a long-term development strategy aiming at (i) reducing underutilisation of resources and social exclusion through the production of integrated bundles of public goods and services; (ii) reducing 'remoteness' by building 'market potential' (investment in material, but above all in immaterial infrastructures that integrate lagging areas with emerging markets); (iii) increasing human capital endowment and innovation potential of the lagging areas in order to make these regions able to adapt their economic and social structure to structural change induced by external shocks. For this reason it is important to have a differentiated approach: growth strategies that worked for some regions are not necessarily suitable for other regions.

To conclude, it is important to underline that, differently from past episodes, the current shock comes at a time when economic distances in the global market have been substantially reduced. Many emerging markets (some of them only mildly affected by the global economic downturn) are 'closer' than ever before to EU markets. This could imply that – if the effort toward regional policy is reduced or put in 'stand-by' – the post-crises landscape of the European periphery might be one of increased economic desertification with substantial job losses in traditional sectors directly competing with emerging markets.

NOTES

1. In the United Kingdom regional policies were initiated already in the 1930s.
2. Easterly et al. (1993) provide some evidence on the significance of shocks, especially shocks to terms of trade, in explaining the variation in growth during the 1970s and the 1980s at country level. Rodrik (1999) suggests that external shocks alone cannot explain this variation in the country growth paths after the mid-1970s. His idea is that what is relevant is the interaction of these shocks with both latent social conflicts and the institutions of conflict management.
3. It is important to point out that we do not consider the association between business cycles and the evolution of regional disparities (as Rodríguez-Pose and Fratesi, 2006), but we study the effect of specific events which provoke structural and long-lasting change in the regional economies.
4. In some cases, economic downturns can lead to narrower interregional disparities. This happens when the economies of lagging areas depend on protected sectors such as, for example, public services.
5. A large body of literature has demonstrated the fundamental role played by innovation and technological capabilities for fostering long-term growth performance (Fagerberg, 1994; Castellacci, 2004; Fagerberg and Godinho, 2005).
6. In particular, large metropolitan areas have benefited from the coexistence of developed financial markets and political power (Rodríguez-Pose, 1998).
7. The 1980s confirmed the declining growth trend of traditional industrial regions, which have been unable to respond rapidly to structural change and cope with new scenarios.
8. Sinn (2005) argues that the strong export performance of Germany in the last decade is due to the rise in value-added of German exports accounted for by imported intermediate inputs (mainly from China), rather than being explained by a boost in competitive advantage of

German firms. Sinn shows that the rise in export is not accompanied by a rise in industrial employment. In other words, according to the author, the German economy acts more and more like a European (or even world) bazaar where goods are imported from low-cost producers and exported to foreign markets with a tiny profit margin. Our story of asymmetric trade integration explains why this 'bazaar economy' is located in Germany, rather than in other EU countries.

9. The results of Serra et al. (2006) suggest that within six large middle-income Latin American countries (Argentina, Brazil, Chile, Colombia, Mexico and Peru) there is limited evidence of regional convergence between 1970 and the early years of the present decade.

10. Financial and macroeconomic variables interact closely through wealth and substitution effects, and through their impacts on firms' and households' balance sheets (e.g. Blanchard and Fischer, 1989; Obstfeld and Rogoff, 1999).

11. In Europe not only has actual economic activity been affected by the crisis, but also potential output is likely to have been affected, and this has major implications for the longer-term growth outlook and the fiscal situation (European Commission, 2009).

12. It is interesting to note that both the period of convergence in the late 1960s and early 1970s and the period of absence of convergence after the recession of the early 1990s were characterised in Finland by strong internal migration. In the first wave, people moved from rural areas to the cities and from the north to the south (in addition, a considerable part of this migration was directed at Sweden), while, in the second wave, the greatest flows were from rural and smaller urban areas to a few big centres (Tervo, 2005).

13. In many countries (e.g. Germany, France, Norway, the United Kingdom) additional funding has been allocated to R&D and innovation. These activities are usually geographically concentrated in the central areas and in the big cities. This is, for example, the case of the United Kingdom, where the highest concentration of research-intensive universities and firms is in London and South East England (Davies et al., 2010).

14. The Fund for Under-utilised Areas finances economic development instruments mainly in the southern regions for which 85% of the total resources is reserved.

15. For a more comprehensive view of the role of cohesion policy in responding to the crisis, see European Commission (2008).

16. Maquiladoras import parts and components from abroad, assemble the inputs into final goods, and then export their output. They are most active in the electronics, auto parts, and apparel industries.

17. On the contrary, wages in border states are much higher than in the rest of the country while the former are not more productive than workers elsewhere in the country (Hanson, 2002).

REFERENCES

Aghion, P. and G. Saint-Paul (1998), 'Uncovering some Causal Relationship between Productivity Growth and the Structure of Economic Fluctuations: a Tentative Survey', *Labour*, **12**, 279-305.

Antolin, P. and O. Bover (1997), 'Regional Migration in Spain: the Effect of Personal Characteristics and of Unemployment, Wage and House Price Differentials using Pooled Cross-sections', *Oxford Bulletin of Economics and Statistics*, **59**, 215-235.

Archibugi, D. and A. Filippetti (2010), 'Is the Economic Crisis Impairing Convergence in Innovation Performance across Europe?', ssrn.com/abstract=1551382.

Attanasio, O. and F. Padoa-Schioppa (1991), 'Regional Inequalities, Migration and Mismatch in Italy', in: F. Padoa-Schioppa (ed.), *Mismatch and Labour Mobility*, Cambridge: Cambridge University Press, pp. 237–320.

Bagnasco, A. (1977), *Tre Italie: la Problematica Territoriale dello Sviluppo Italiano*, Bologna: Il Mulino.

Barca, F. (2009), 'Agenda for a Reformed Cohesion Policy', http://ec.europa.eu/ regional_policy/policy/future/barca_en.htm.

Barro, R.J. and X. Sala-i-Martín (1991), 'Convergence across States and Regions', *Brookings Papers on Economic Activity*, **1991**(1), 107-182.

Bentolila, S. (1997), 'Sticky Labour in Spanish Regions', *European Economic Review* **41**, 591-598.

Blanchard, O.J. and S. Fischer (1989), *Lectures on Macroeconomics*, Cambridge, MA: MIT Press.

Bouvet, F. (2007), 'Dynamics of Regional Income Inequality in Europe and Impact of EU Regional Policy and EMU', http://ec.europa.eu/economy_finance/events /2007/researchconf1110/bouvet_en.pdf.pdf.

Caballero, R. and M. Hammour (1994), 'The Cleansing Effect of Recessions', *American Economic Review*, **84**, 1350-1368.

Canova, F. (2004), 'Testing for Convergence Clubs: a Predictive Density Approach', *International Economic Review*, **45**, 49-78.

Cantwell, J. and S. Iammarino (2003), *Multinational Enterprises and European Regional Systems of Innovation*, London: Routledge.

Castellacci, F. (2004), *Innovation and Economic Growth in Europe: Evolutionary Perspectives*, Oslo: Centre for Technology, Innovation and Culture.

Cerra, V. and S.C. Saxena (2005), 'Eurosclerosis or Financial Collapse: why did Swedish Incomes Fall Behind?', *IMF Working Paper*, 05/29.

Cerra, V. and S.C. Saxena (2008), 'Growth Dynamics: the Myth of Economic Recovery', *American Economic Review*, **98**, 439-457.

Chiquiar, D. (2005), 'Why Mexico's Regional Income Convergence Broke Down', *Journal of Development Economics*, **77**, 257-275.

Claessens, S., M.A. Kose and M.E. Terrones (2009), 'What Happens During Recessions, Crunches and Busts?', *Economic Policy*, **24**(60), 653-700.

Cuadrado-Roura, J.R. (2001), 'Regional Convergence in the European Union: from Hypothesis to the Actual Trends', *Annals in Regional Science*, **35**, 333-356.

Daniele, V. and P. Malanima (2007), 'Il Prodotto delle Regioni e il Divario Nord-Sud in Italia (1861-2004)', *Rivista di Politica Economica*, Marzo-Aprile.

Davies, S., S. Kah and C. Woods (2010), 'Regional Dimension of the Financial and Economic Crisis', *European Policy Research Paper*, no. 70.

Decressin, J. (1994), 'Internal Migration in West Germany and Implication for East-West Salary Convergence', *Weltwirtschaftliches Archiv*, **130**, 231-257.

Dewhurst, J. (1998), 'Convergence and Divergence in Household Incomes per Head in the United Kingdom, 1984-93', *Applied Economics*, **30**, 31-35.

Dunford, M. (1994), 'Winners and Losers: the New Map of Economic Inequality in the European Union', *European Urban and Regional Studies*, **1**, 95-114.

Easterly, W., M. Kremer, L. Pritchett and L.H. Summers (1993), 'Good Policy or Good Luck: Country Growth Performance and Temporary Shocks', *Journal of Monetary Economics*, **32**, 459-483.

European Commission (2008), *Cohesion Policy: Investing in the Real Economy*, COM(2008) 876 final, Brussels.

European Commission (2009), 'Economic Crisis in Europe: Causes, Consequences and Responses', *European Economy*, **7**, Luxembourg: European Communities.

Ezcurra, R., C. Gil, P. Pascual and M. Rapún (2005), 'Inequality, Polarisation and Regional Mobility in the European Union', *Urban Studies*, **42**, 1057-1076.

Fagerberg, J. (1994), 'Technology and International Differences in Growth Rates', *Journal of Economic Literature*, **32**, 1147-1175.

Fagerberg, J. and M.M. Godinho (2005), 'Innovation and Catching-up', in: J. Fagerberg, D.C. Mowery and R.R. Nelson (eds), *The Oxford Handbook of Innovation*, Oxford: Oxford University Press, pp. 514-542.

Fagerberg, J., P. Guerrieri and B. Verspagen (1999), *The Economic Challenge for Europe*, Cheltenham, UK and Northampton, MA, USA: Edward Elgar.

Fagerberg, J. and B. Verspagen (1996), 'Heading for Divergence? Regional Growth in Europe Reconsidered', *Journal of Common Market Studies*, **34**, 431-448.

Faini, R., G. Galli, P. Gennari and F. Rossi (1997), 'An Empirical Puzzle: Falling Migration and Growing Unemployment Differentials among Italian Regions', *European Economic Review*, **41**, 571-579.

Fujita, M., P. Krugman and A.J. Venables (1999), *The Spatial Economy: Cities, Regions and International Trade*, Cambridge, MA: MIT Press.

Furceri, D. and A. Mourougane (2009), 'The Effect of Financial Crises on Potential Output: New Empirical Evidence from OECD Countries', *OECD Economics Department Working Papers*, no. 699.

Hanson, G.H. (2002), 'The Role of Maquiladoras in Mexico's Export Boom', http://migration.ucdavis.edu/rs/more.php?id=8_0_2_0.

INE (2008), *Contas Regionais: 1995-2005*, Istituto Nacional de Estatistica, Portugal.

Juan-Ramón, V.H. and L.A. Rivera-Batiz (1996), 'Regional Growth in Mexico: 1970-'93', *IMF Working Paper*, 96/92.

Juessen, F. (2009), 'A Distribution Dynamics Approach to Regional GDP Convergence in Unified Germany', *IZA Discussion Paper*, no. 4177.

Kaminsky, G. and C. Reinhart (1999), 'The Twin Crises: the Causes of Banking and Balance of Payments Problems', *American Economic Review*, **89**, 473-500.

Kangasharju, A. (1999), 'Relative Economic Performance in Finland: Regional Convergence, 1934-1993', *Regional Studies*, **33**, 207-217.

Kangasharju, A. and S. Pekkala (2000), 'The Effects of Aggregate Fluctuations on Regional Economic Disparities', *Pellervo Economic Research Institute Working Paper*, no. 29.

Kosfeld, R. and J. Lauridsen (2004), 'Dynamic Spatial Modelling of Regional Convergence Processes', *Empirical Economics*, **29**, 705-722.

Krugman, P. (1991a), 'Increasing Returns and Economic Geography', *Journal of Political Economy*, **99**, 483-499.

Krugman, P. (1991b), *Geography and Trade*, Cambridge, MA: MIT Press.

Krugman, P. and A. Venables (1995), 'Globalization and the Inequality of Nations', *Quarterly Journal of Economics*, **110**, 857-880.

Lucas, R.E. (2000), 'Some Macroeconomics for the 21st Century', *Journal of Economic Perspectives*, **14**, 159-168.

Magrini, S. (1999), 'The Evolution of Income Dispersion among the Regions of the European Union', *Regional Science and Urban Economics*, **29**, 257-281.

Martinez-Galarraga, J., J.R. Rosés and D.A. Tirado (2009), 'The Upswing of Regional Income Inequality in Spain 1860-1930', *Universidad Carlos III de Madrid Working Papers in Economic History*, no. 5.

Mauro, P. and A. Spilimbergo (1999), 'How do the Skilled and the Unskilled Respond to Regional Shocks? The Case of Spain', *IMF Staff Papers*, **46**, 1-17.

Michelis, L., A.P. Papadopoulos and G.T. Papanikos (2004), 'Regional Convergence in Greece in the 1980s: an Econometric Investigation', *Applied Economics*, **36**, 881-888.

Ministero dello Sviluppo Economico (2009), *Rapporto Annuale del DPS 2008*, Rome.

Obstfeld, M. and K. Rogoff (1999), *Foundations of International Macroeconomics*, Cambridge, MA: MIT Press.

OECD (2008), *Territorial Reviews: Portugal*, Paris: Organisation for Economic Co-operation and Development.

OECD (2009), *How Regions Grow. Trends and Analysis*, Paris: Organisation for Economic Co-operation and Development.

Padoa-Schioppa, T. (1987), *Efficiency, Stability and Equity: a Strategy for the Evolution of the Economic System of the European Community*, Oxford: Oxford University Press.

Pekkala, S. (1999), 'Regional Convergence across Finnish Provinces and Subregions, 1960-1994', *Finnish Economic Papers*, **12**, 28-40.

Pekkala, S. (2000), 'Aggregate Economic Fluctuations and Regional Convergence: the Finnish Case, 1988-95', *Applied Economics*, **32**, 211-220.

Petrakos, G. and P. Artelaris (2008), 'Regional Inequalities in Greece'. in: H. Coccossis and Y. Psycharis (eds), *Regional Analysis and Policy: The Greek Experience*, Heidelberg: Physica-Verlag, pp. 121-139.

Pires Armando, J.G. (2005), 'Market Potential and Welfare: Evidence from the Iberian Peninsula', *Portugal Economic Journal*, **4**, 107-127.

Pissarides, C. and I. McMaster (1984), 'Regional Migration, Wages and Unemployment: Empirical Evidence and Implication for Policy', *LSE Centre for Labour Economics Discussion Paper*, 204.

Puga, D. (2002), 'European Regional Policy in Light of Recent Location Theories', *Journal of Economic Geography*, **2**, 373-406.

Rodríguez-Pose, A. (1998), *Dynamics of Regional Growth in Europe: Social and Political Factors*, Oxford: Clarendon Press.

Rodríguez-Pose, A. and U. Fratesi (2004), 'Between Development and Social Policies: the Impact of Structural Funds in Objective 1 Regions', *Regional Studies*, **38**, 97-114.

Rodríguez-Pose, A. and U. Fratesi (2006), 'Regional Business Cycles and the Emergence of Sheltered Economies in the Southern Periphery of Europe', BEER paper no. 7.

Rodrik, D. (1999), 'Where did all the Growth Go? External Shocks, Social Conflict, and Growth Collapse', *Journal of Economic Growth*, **4**, 385-412.

Saint-Paul, G. (1997), 'Business Cycle and Long-run Growth', *Oxford Review of Economic Policy*, **13**, 145-153.

Serra, M.I., M.F. Pazmino, G. Lindow, B. Sutton and G. Ramirez (2006), 'Regional Convergence in Latin America', *IMF Working Paper*, 06/125.

Sinn, H.W. (2005), 'Basar-Ökonomie Deutschland. Exportweltmeister oder Schlusslicht', *ifo Schnelldienst* 58, Munich.

Solow, R.M. (1956), 'A Contribution to the Theory of Economic Growth', *Quarterly Journal of Economics*, **70**, 101-108.

Tervo, H. (2005), 'Regional Policy Lessons from Finland', in: D. Felsenstein and B.A. Portnov (eds), *Regional Disparities in Small Countries*, Berlin: Springer Verlag, pp. 267-282.

Tondl, G. (2001), *Convergence After Divergence? Regional Growth in Europe*, Berlin: Springer Verlag.

United Nations (1955), *Economic Survey of Europe in 1954*, Geneva: UN Department of Economic and Social Affairs.

Williamson, J.G. (1965), 'Regional Inequality and the Process of National Development: a Description of the Patterns', *Economic Development and Cultural Change*, **13**, 1-84.

6. Do the European Union's Bilateral Investment Treaties Matter? The Way Forward after Lisbon

Selen Sarisoy Guerin

1. INTRODUCTION

The Lisbon Treaty entered into force on 1 December 2009 and has brought at least one significant change in the area of the EU's common commercial policy. The 'Treaty on the Functioning of the European Union' now identifies foreign direct investment as an area of exclusive EU competence. This means that the EU is now the sole negotiator of international investment treaties and that member states in principle can no longer negotiate bilateral agreements on foreign direct investment with third countries.[1] Although the issue of how the transfer of competences in this area from member states to the EU should be handled has in the first place to be left to EC lawyers, there are several important questions that economists should address so as to contribute to EU's future investment policy.

The aim of this chapter is to deal with several important questions that are relevant to the EU's future investment policy. The EU Commission has drafted a proposal on the Regulation on International Investment (July 2010) on establishing transitional arrangements for the existing bilateral investment treaties of the 27 member states. Hence, the first question we address in this chapter is to empirically test whether the existing member state Bilateral Investment Treaties (BITs) have the desired positive impact on FDI outflows to the host developing countries. By default BITs are intended to promote and protect investment in the contracting country by the counterparty investor. Typically, the BITs define the type of investment and investor that is covered. In addition to this, BITs are intended to protect the investor against arbitrary expropriation by the host country government without compensation, and offer an investor-to-state dispute settlement mechanism. BITs are therefore essentially intended to reduce risk to investment.

We also address two more policy relevant questions: 1) in its *Roadmap* (2010), the European Commission raises the question about what a EU BIT should look like; to deal with this issue, we first ask whether some member states' BITs could be identified as having a significantly more positive effect on FDI than others[2] (the impact of the BIT can work through two channels: by effectively reducing risk to investment and by increasing market access through FDI liberalisation);[3] 2) we address the question with which countries the EU should negotiate its new investment treaties. As the *Roadmap* indicates, when the transition period of grandfathering of existing BITs comes to an end, the EU is going to choose a number of third countries to negotiate with.

The empirical literature on the impact of bilateral investment treaties on FDI flows is ambiguous. While several studies indicate that the relationship between BITs and FDI is positive and statistically significant (e.g. Busse et al., 2008; Egger and Pfaffermayr, 2004; Neumayer and Spess, 2005; Salacuse and Sullivan, 2004), several others either find a negative or not statistically significant relationship (e.g. Hallward-Driemeier, 2003 and Rose-Ackerman and Tobin, 2004). Recent literature has recognised that several of these studies fail to find a significant relationship between BITs and FDI as they do not account for endogeneity. Indeed it is difficult to assess the impact of BITs on FDI while the selection of the BIT partner is endogenously determined. In addition to reverse causality, the potential endogeneity in the BIT/FDI literature is further exacerbated by an omitted variables bias.

We use large panel data of bilateral FDI inflows to 25 middle-income developing countries from 14 OECD member countries over the period 1992-2006 to examine the impact of member state BITs on FDI. This period captures both the surge in global FDI flows and the number of BITs signed and implemented. As ICSID statistics indicate, the number of BITs in the world increased from 636 in 1992 to 2270 in 2006. Analogous to literature on the impact of free trade agreements on trade, we use a BIT treatment effect à la Baier and Bergstrand (2007).

In order to address concerns over potential endogeneity in our model, we use a modified gravity-type model and estimate the relationship between BITs and FDI by a fixed-effects model controlling for both country-pair fixed effects and time effects. Models estimated with country-pair fixed effects are shown to effectively eliminate the selection bias (e.g. Razin et al., 2003).

We find a positive and statistically significant impact of the existing BITs on member states' FDI in the sample developing countries. We test the robustness of our results against the omitted variable bias, strict exogeneity and also sensitivity against different estimation techniques. The positive impact of BITs on EU FDI in the developing countries is robust when the level of economic and political reform in the host country is controlled for by introducing the level of privatisation proceeds in the host country, an index of risk of expropriation, the level of democratic development and the level of trade linkages. The economic impact of BITs on member states' FDI outflows is stronger in estimations using both random effects and pooled OLS models. Following Baier and Bergstrand (2007), we control for strict exogeneity and we find no feedback effect from FDI outflows to BITs.

Our results indicate that 1) in our sample there is evidence that both OECD and specifically EU BITs have a positive and robust impact on FDI outflows; in the case of EU BITs, FDI outflows have increased by 22 percent following the entry into force of the treaties; 2) among the member state BITs, only the BITs of Austria and France had a statistically significant positive effect on their FDI outflows; there is also evidence that BITs of Austria exert a positive influence on FDI outflows through protection of investment and reducing risk, whereas in France's BITs have provided significant market access; 3) among the EU15's BIT partners Romania, Slovenia, the Philippines and South Africa have positively benefited from signing BITs with the EU.

The next section discusses both patterns of FDI outflows of the EU and its selection of BIT partners. Section 3 is about the description of data and methodology and section 4 follows with results. Section 5 concludes.

2. FOREIGN DIRECT INVESTMENT AND BILATERAL INVESTMENT TREATIES OF THE EU

In this section we examine the outward FDI performance of the EU and present some qualitative analysis of its bilateral investment treaties. The EU27 is the number one source of FDI flows globally. Total FDI outflows of the EU27 has peaked at €1.2 trillion in 2007 (more than four times FDI outflows invested by the US) with FDI outward stocks reaching €8.2 trillion in the same year. As FDI is also home biased like trade, the majority of EU27 FDI outflows are destined to other member states. Intra-EU27 FDI outflows reached €707 billion, leaving €530 billion for extra-EU27 outflows in 2007.[4] In terms of most favoured extra-EU destinations, North America is by far the largest recipient of EU FDI outflows with a peak in 2007 at €199 billion. In other regions of the world, the EU27 invested €25.2 billion in Latin America, €17.9 billion in Africa and €53.9 billion in Asia.

The first question one would ask is whether countries that have signed bilateral investment treaties with the EU are receiving significantly larger amounts of FDI compared to non-BIT partners. As a start, we can see in

Table 6.1 that the EU27 has signed 1557 BITs to date compared to Japan and the US that have signed 11 and 48 BITs only, respectively (ICSID, 2010).

Table 6.1　　EU27 FDI and BITs up to 2007

	Number of BITs	Extra-EU27 outward FDI stock (millions of euro)
Austria	65	35,644
Belgium-Luxembourg	77	NA
Bulgaria	54	376
Czech Rep.	79	446
Denmark	43	48,910
Cyprus	16	4,781
Finland	62	17,864
France	103	354,660
Estonia	23	621
Greece	38	9,849
Hungary	58	5,097
Germany	147	334,900
Ireland	1	36,424
Italy	83	80,521
Netherlands	105	203,612
Malta	22	209
Latvia	43	431
Lithuania	42	487
Poland	62	6,354
Portugal	45	16,215
Romania	84	571
Slovakia	40	205
Slovenia	36	4,621
Spain	61	187,820
Sweden	66	78,481
UK	102	603,075
Total EU	1,557	
US	48	2,272,056
Japan	11	489,456

Source:　ICSID, Eurostat.

Among the member states, with 147 BITs signed, Germany is by far the most active proponent of BITs. Germany is also the member state with the oldest BIT in the world: Germany has negotiated and signed its first BITs with Pakistan and the Dominican Republic in 1959. Germany has negotiated several BITs with many countries in Africa and Asia in the 1960s as well.

Nevertheless, among the member states, the UK has the largest extra-EU FDI outward stocks accumulated, followed by France and then Germany (Table 6.1).[5] One can observe that the EU member states that have the highest number of BITs also have the largest stocks of FDI invested abroad. This may suggest that indeed the promotion and protection offered by BITs may be encouraging FDI outflows.

There are several other factors that play a role in the selection of a host location for FDI. The empirical literature indicates that country size and income play a positive role whereas distance deters investment much the same as for trade. Factors that facilitate flow of information such as sharing a common language, common law origins, having signed a regional trade agreement, and indeed trade flows themselves all encourage FDI. Hence the selection of the BIT partner may not be exogenous. For example, among all the developing countries of the world only a subset of them receive the majority of FDI. Indeed the so-called emerging market economies have been highly successful in attracting FDI.

As can be seen in Table 6.2 there are diverse patterns in terms of the region that each member states prefer for their BIT partners. For example, Germany has signed BITs with 47 countries out of 53 in Africa, 26 out of 41 in Asia and 22 out of 32 in Latin America. On the other hand, France has signed BITs with most countries in Latin America (20 out of 32) and least with countries in Africa (21 out of Africa). Overall the coverage ratio of BITs is higher for Asia than for Latin America and lowest for Africa. Detailed examination of data does not always suggest that the date of signature of a BIT has an immediate impact on FDI flows. For example, for several African countries the flows have always been small both before and after the BIT. In contrast for emerging market economies like Brazil, FDI flows have always been large.

Table 6.3 below shows in the first column the number of member states that have signed a BIT with an emerging market economy. These countries have been the few in each region to receive the majority of FDI. Indeed with the exception of Brazil and Colombia, the majority of EU15 member states and some of the new member states have signed BITs with all the emerging market economies.[6]

Table 6.2   *Regional allocation of EU27 BITs (in force as of 2007)*

	Africa	Asia	Latin America
Austria	8	16	7
Belgium-Luxembourg	17	19	11
Bulgaria	4	7	1
Cyprus	2	3	–
Czech Rep.	4	11	12
Denmark	8	13	8
Estonia		2	
Finland	6	16	12
France	21	24	20
Germany	47	26	22
Greece	6	8	3
Hungary	4	12	5
Italy	18	15	12
Latvia	1	9	
Lithuania		8	2
Malta	3		–
Netherlands	27	19	18
Poland	3	14	3
Portugal	12	6	8
Romania	10	15	8
Slovak Rep.	1	8	1
Slovenia	1	3	–
Spain	8	11	19
Sweden	11	16	10
UK	21	23	19
Total	243	304	201

Source: ICSID, World Bank.

Even though Brazil has not ratified any of its bilateral investment treaties, the EU has FDI outward stocks of €112 billion in Brazil. Contrary to what one might expect, FDI stocks in China are limited and less than FDI stocks in Turkey. Even though 24 member states have signed BITs with China, with the exception of Austria-China and Belgium-Luxembourg-China BIT, the majority have been signed in the last decade.

Table 6.3   *EU27 BIT partners, FDI stocks, income (million €) and return (end 2008)*

	Number of BITs with the EU	EU27 FDI stock	FDI income	Rate of return (in %)
Argentina	18	44,103	4,139	9
Brazil	9	112,520	9,288	8
Chile	17	12,324	1,762	14
China	24	47,285	3,431	7
Colombia	2	7,178	745	10
Egypt	23	20,933	1,821	9
India	19	19,362	1,825	9
Indonesia	15	13,106	1,457	11
Malaysia	15	12,979	1,590	12
Mexico	14	49,048	3,765	8
Morocco	17	14,133	637	5
Russia	21	91,955	6,324	7
South Africa	13	46,345	4,362	9
Philippines	13	6,260	509	8
Thailand	12	10,625	395	4
Turkey	23	51,660	2,731	5
Czech Rep.	25	67,735	7,005	10
Bulgaria	22	11,443	849	7
Poland	23	86,899	6,525	8
Romania	22	31,163	2,492	8
Slovenia	21	5,513	355	6
Slovak Rep.	21	24,401	1,578	6
Korea	19	28,888	3,362	12

Source: ICSID, World Bank and Eurostat and author's own calculations.

In Table 6.3, column 3, we present FDI investment income flows from each emerging market economy to EU27. One important criterion for the choice of investment location is the return to investment given risk. Anecdotal evidence indicates that investors first choose a region and then a country in that region to invest. This may explain why a few countries in each region receive the majority of FDI inflows. If the decision to negotiate a BIT is endogenous, then we would expect to see large flows prior to signature of the BIT. High returns may also encourage investment that in return may increase the probability of selection into a BIT. Among the emerging market economies, Chile presents the highest return to EU FDI, with 14 percent, followed by Malaysia, Indonesia and South Korea. All of these countries have signed BITs with the EU15 and some of the new member states. Turkey, that has signed 21 BITs with the EU27, so far has a low rate of return, 5 percent, like Morocco. Return to FDI has also been modest in China, with 7 percent return to EU investment, where there are 24 BITs signed.

In this section we have presented some patterns in FDI outflows and selection of BIT partners of the EU. The EU is the world's largest FDI investor and is the first ever BIT negotiator. Member states apparently rely on BITs to a larger extent than the US and Japan. The qualitative analysis in this section shows that each member state has negotiated several BITs with a different set of countries in each region. However, there is a tendency to negotiate BITs more with Asian and Latin American countries than with African countries. Finally, EU member states have negotiated BITs with all emerging market economies that have been successful in attracting FDI. There seems to be also a positive correlation between the total number of BITs signed and FDI outflows.

3.   DATA AND METHODOLOGY

In this section we describe the data and methodology used in order to test the differential impact of EU's BITs on FDI outflows. To this end we have constructed a large dataset of bilateral FDI flows using OECD's *International Investment Statistics* database. The panel dataset includes 14 OECD countries as reporters and 25 middle-income emerging market economies as partners over the period 1992-2006. The dataset covers over 90 percent of EU's FDI outflows.

We model the EU's FDI outflows using a modified gravity model. Gravity models have been extensively used in modelling bilateral trade flows and recently also FDI flows. They have been empirically highly successful and are well grounded in economic theory. We argue that among several panel estimation techniques, using the fixed-effects model is theoretically the most suitable. As Baier and Bergstrand (2007) show, fixed effects models on panel data including bilateral (country-pair) fixed-effects and country-and-time dummies are superior to other estimation methodologies such as pooled OLS, or random-effects models. One of the most important advantages of using a fixed-effects model on our panel data is that we will be able to control for the unobserved endogeneity that is raised as a concern in literature. After all, it is widely accepted that investment policy cannot be exogenous to investment volumes. Solving the problem of endogeneity is cumbersome using alternative methods such as instrumental variable techniques because it is difficult to find good proxies for investment policy variables like a BIT.

Unlike other estimation techniques (e.g. OLS on cross-section data that produces biased estimates, or a random-effects models that assumes no correlation between unobservables and the BIT variable), a fixed-effects estimator is unbiased and a consistent estimator of the treatment effect of a BIT. The downside of the fixed-effects estimator is that one cannot include time-invariant variables in the model as fixed-effects take into account the 'within' variation in the data and hence wipe out any time-invariant variables in the model. In other words, all time-invariant variables that are part of the standard gravity models such as bilateral distance, common language, adjacency, etc. will be subsumed by the country-pair fixed effect a_{ij}.

One final concern regarding the choice of fixed-effects estimator is that due to the particular shape of our dataset, where n (number of country pairs = 350) is large and the time-series dimension of our dataset is relatively short ($T = 14$), the fixed-effect estimator suffers from the so-called 'incidental parameter' problem (Baltagi, 2001), and hence produces inconsistent estimates of dummy variable coefficients. In order to adjust for that, we will also present results for the 'within effect' estimator.

In order to estimate the treatment effect of the EU's BITs on EU's FDI outflows with its investment partners we estimate the following equation:

$$
\ln FDI_{ijt} = \alpha_{ij} + \beta_1 \ln GDP_{it} + \beta_2 \ln GDP_{jt} + \beta_3 \ln income_{it} \\
+ \beta_4 \ln income_{jt} + \mu BIT_{ijt} + \sum_k \gamma_k X_{ikt} + u_{ijt} \quad .
$$

$$(6.1)$$

The dependent variable, $\ln(FDI)$ is the natural log of 14 OECD member country FDI outflows in constant US dollars to their 25 investment partners. In order to control for the impact of the size of the OECD country and the emerging market economies, we introduce the log of real GDP of both the reporter (i) and the partner (j) at time t. We also introduce real GDP per capita of both the investor and host as proxies of income.

We would expect a positive relationship between the GDP per capita and FDI volumes as the two countries become more similar in level of income. In an analogy to the Linder hypothesis, we expect that the more similar the demand structure of two countries are, as proxied by GDP per capita, the more intense the potential flows between them will be.[7] All GDP and GDP per capita variables are from IMF's *World Economic Outlook* April 2010 database. We use a BIT dummy variable that takes on the value 1 when the reporting OECD country signed a BIT with the partner country and zero otherwise. The data on the dates of BITs are from the database of the *International Center for Settlement of Investment Disputes*.[8] Finally, as a set of control variables and to test the robustness of the BIT dummy we introduce several additional country-specific variables X, such as bilateral trade flows, privatisation proceeds in the host country (in US$), a dummy for ex-colony, degree of democratisation (*POLITY*) and a measure of risk for expropriation (*RISK*).

4. RESULTS

In this section we present results on the differential impact of bilateral investment treaties on FDI outflows. In Table 6.4, we test first the impact of OECD BITs in general in our sample. As the ICSID statistics indicate, our sample period, 1992-2006, covers a period of greater activity where the number of BITs in the world increased from 636 in 1992 to 2,270 in 2006. In Table 6.4 we regress FDI outflows from OECD countries to emerging market economies on standard gravity variables, GDP, income per capita, distance, a set of control variables such as bilateral trade flows, privatisation proceeds in US$, and a dummy for ex-colony. We control for trade flows as countries that trade more also tend to invest more. In other words, trade can act as a channel for information, increasing familiarity and hence reducing transaction costs in a host country. We use privatisation proceeds in US$ millions from the World Bank's *Privatization Database* to control for the level of economic reform the emerging economies went through.

Both for theoretical and econometric reasons, we focus on the results of the fixed-effects estimator in column 1, but we present random-effects and pooled OLS results in column 2 and 3 as well. The results in column 1 indicates that BITs have a statistically significant and a positive impact on the FDI outflows from 14 OECD source countries to their BIT partner. The coefficient of BIT indicates that when the BIT is implemented the source country FDI increases by 32 percent.[9] Other variables that are statistically significant have the expected positive sign, with the exception of GDP per capita of the host country. In columns 2 and 3 we can control for time-invariant variables such as distance and colony. Controlling for distance and colonial history, BITs have a robust positive impact on FDI in both random-effects and pooled OLS models.

In Table 6.5 we test the robustness of EU's BITs using the same specification as in Table 6.4. Both in fixed-effect and random effect models EU BITs have a statistically significant and positive impact on FDI, indicating an estimated 22 and 20 percent increase in FDI respectively.

Table 6.4   OECD bilateral investment treaties

| | Dependent variable: ln FDI_{ijt} | | |
	Fixed-effects	Random-effects	OLS
Ln GDP_{it}	2.74 (0.84)***	0.05 (0.09)	0.06 (0.05)
Ln GDP_{jt}	2.22 (2.52)	-0.07 (0.08)	0.02 (0.05)
Ln $income_{it}$	-2.11 (0.84)***	0.52 (0.08)***	0.57 (0.04)***
Ln $income_{jt}$	-2.51 (2.56)	0.52 (0.19)***	1.23 (0.14)***
BIT dummy	0.28 (0.10)***	0.42 (0.09)***	0.14 (0.08)*
Ln $privatisation$	0.05 (0.01)***	0.04 (0.02)**	0.08 (0.02)***
Ln $trade$	1.09 (0.11)***	1.05 (0.07)***	0.89 (0.04)***
Ln $distance$		0.10 (0.10)	0.09 (0.02)***
$colony$ dummy		0.66 (0.63)	0.96 (0.19)***
Overall adj-R^2	0.20	0.48	0.51
'Within' R^2	0.17	0.16	
N	2,079	2,079	2,079
F value	7.19		
Time dummies	YES	YES	YES

Note: Regression with robust standard errors for correction of heteroskedasticity in parentheses; *** denotes significance at 1%; ** significant at 5%;* significant at 10%.

Table 6.5   EU bilateral investment treaties

| | Dependent variable: ln FDI_{ijt} | | |
	Fixed-effects	Random-effects	OLS
Ln GDP_{it}	-1.72 (1.02)*	0.11 (0.06)	0.02 (0.05)
Ln GDP_{jt}	-5.85 (3.10)*	0.12 (0.08)	0.06 (0.05)
Ln $income_{it}$	2.11 (1.00)**	0.41 (0.08)***	0.57 (0.04)***
Ln $income_{jt}$	6.55 (3.24)**	0.99 (0.21)***	1.27 (0.15)***
EU-BIT dummy	0.20 (0.12)*	0.18 (0.10)*	0.09 (0.08)
Ln $privatisation$	0.05 (0.02)***	0.05 (0.02)***	0.08 (0.02)***
Ln $trade$	0.50 (0.14)***	0.82 (0.06)***	0.89 (0.04)***
Ln $distance$			0.06 (0.05)
$colony$ dummy			0.96 (0.19)***
Overall adj-R^2	0.11	0.50	0.51
'Within' R^2	0.20	0.20	
N	2,107	2,107	2,079
F value	7.33		
Time dummies	YES	YES	YES

Note: Regression with robust standard errors for correction of heteroskedasticity in parentheses; *** denotes significance at 1%; ** significant at 5%;* significant at 10%.

In Table 6.6 we test the robustness of EU BIT by introducing several potential explanatory variables to reduce the probability of endogeneity due to

omitted variable bias. In this table and the ones that follow we present results only from the fixed-effects estimator. We add the *POLITY2* variable from the POLITY IV project of University of Maryland to measure the level of democracy in the host country. This index ranges from −10 to 10, increasing as the host countries political freedom improves. We expect that as a country becomes more democratic it should receive more FDI: political reform and economic reform are shown to be positively correlated (see e.g. Persson, 2005).

Table 6.6   *EU bilateral investment treaties – the effect of POLITY2 and RISK*

	Dependent variable: ln $(FDI)_{ijt}$	
	Fixed-effects	Fixed-effects
ln GDP_{it}	-1.74 (1.03)*	-1.55 (1.42)
ln GDP_{jt}	-5.85 (3.11)*	-9.08 (4.39)**
ln *income*$_{it}$	2.11 (1.01)**	1.84 (1.41)
ln *income*$_{jt}$	6.55 (3.25)**	9.32 (4.56)**
EU BIT dummy	0.21 (0.10)*	0.24 (0.14)*
ln *privatisation*	0.05 (0.02)***	0.07 (0.02)***
ln *trade*	0.49 (0.13)***	0.36 (0.17)**
POLITY2	-0.01 (0.01)	
RISK		0.04 (0.02)**
Overall adj-R^2	0.11	0.13
'Within' R^2	0.20	0.21
N	2,107	1,538
F value	7.24	6.22
Time dummies	YES	YES

Note: Regression with robust standard errors for correction of heteroskedasticity in parentheses; *** denotes significance at 1%; ** significant at 5%;* significant at 10%.

We argue that the effect of a BIT may work through two channels. First, the BIT may encourage FDI by reducing risk of expropriation. Second it may provide better market access. In general EU BITs provide post-establishment rights granting the investor equal rights as the domestic investor. However, there are some BITs that also provide FDI liberalisation through granting MFN rights by including pre-establishment clauses. In an attempt to discriminate between the two channels mentioned above, we introduce a political risk index (*RISK*) referred to the host economy and ranging from 0 (highest risk) to 25 (lowest risk). This index is computed by Eschenbach et al. (2004) and is based on the *Euromoney* political risk index. It provides a (subjective) assessment of the risk of non-payment or non-servicing of payment for goods or services, loans, trade-related finance and dividends, as well as of the risk of non-repatriation of capital. This index is a proxy for the risk of expropriation, and helps us control for the effect of political risk on FDI inflows. In column 1 of Table 6.6, the effect of the EU BIT dummy is robust to the inclusion of the *POLITY2* dummy. In column 2 we control for *RISK* in the host country as well and as a result the economic impact of the EU BIT increases slightly and *RISK* has a positive impact as expected. This may suggest that BITs do not only provide investor protection to EU investors but also increase market access.

Table 6.7   EU bilateral investment treaties – country effects

	Dependent variable: ln FDI_{ijt}	
	Fixed-effects	Fixed-effects
Austria BIT	0.82 (0.35)**	0.64 (0.48)
Denmark BIT	0.04 (0.64)	0.33 (0.68)
Finland BIT	0.11 (0.36)	0.26 (0.44)
France BIT	1.16 (0.31)***	1.09 (0.38)***
Germany BIT	-0.44 (0.36)	-0.60 (0.46)
Italy BIT	-0.05 (0.25)	0.20 (0.30)
Netherlands BIT	0.35 (0.34)	0.41 (0.38)
Portugal BIT	-0.87 (0.49)*	-0.96 (0.74)
Spain BIT	0.43 (0.32)	0.33 (0.34)
Sweden BIT	0.45 (0.64)	
UK BIT	-0.33 (0.34)	-0.28 (0.38)
ln GDP_{it}	-7.38 (3.20)**	-10.36 (4.46)*
ln GDP_{jt}	-1.70 (1.02)*	-1.48 (1.42)
ln $income_{it}$	8.32 (3.34)***	10.78 (4.64)**
ln $income_{jt}$	2.11 (1.00)**	1.79 (1.41)
ln *privatisation*	0.04 (0.02)**	0.07 (0.02)***
ln *trade*	0.48 (0.14)***	0.36 (0.17)**
RISK		0.05 (0.02)*
Overall adj-R^2	0.11	0.13
'Within' R^2	0.22	0.22
N	2,107	1,538
F value	6.24	5.35
Time dummies	YES	YES

Note: Regression with robust standard errors for correction of heteroskedasticity in parentheses. *** denotes significance at 1%; ** significant at 5%;* significant at 10%.

Table 6.7 presents results from BITs of different member states. The motivation here is to see whether there is a pattern in which certain member states' BITs deliver better results. Indeed, we can see that the coefficient of BITs is positive for several member states but only statistically significant for Austria and France. There is evidence in our sample that Portugal has been

Global European Governance

negatively affected by its BITs. However, when we control for the risk of expropriation, only France remains to have benefitted from its BITs. This may indicate that Austria might be choosing its BITs partners among the riskier emerging economies to protect from expropriation. France, on the other hand, might be achieving market access as well.

Table 6.8   EU bilateral investment treaties and host country effects

	Dependent variable: ln FDI_{ijt}	
	Fixed-effects	Fixed-effects
Argentina	0.39 (0.41)	0.34 (0.41)
Chile	-0.41 (0.38)	-0.32 (0.48)
China	-0.58 (0.71)	
Bulgaria	-0.32 (0.40)	-0.90 (0.53)*
Czech Rep.	-0.42 (0.71)	-0.94 (0.88)
Egypt	0.37 (0.72)	0.51 (0.75)
Hungary	-2.71 (1.35)**	-2.65 (1.33)**
Indonesia	-0.55 (0.27)	-0.00 (0.56)
India	0.18 (0.27)	0.02 (0.35)
Mexico	0.55 (0.56)	0.82 (0.57)
Morocco	-0.41 (0.57)	-0.33 (0.83)
Philippines	0.90 (0.47)**	1.00 (0.54)*
Poland	-0.20 (0.53)	-0.21 (0.57)
Romania	1.09 (0.33)***	1.01 (0.38)***
Russia	-0.66 (0.89)	
South Africa	0.62 (0.36)*	0.56 (0.41)
Slovenia	1.16 (0.64)*	
Slovak Rep.	-0.05 (0.84)	0.85 (0.99)
Thailand	0.40 (0.75)	0.82 (0.99)
Turkey	0.02 (0.53)	0.18 (0.53)
ln GDP_{it}	-6.22 (3.13)**	-9.80 (4.41)**
ln GDP_{jt}	-1.49 (1.12)	-1.75 (1.51)
ln $income_{it}$	7.08 (3.28)**	10.19 (4.59)**
ln $income_{jt}$	1.92 (1.09)*	2.09 (1.50)
ln *privatisation*	0.05 (0.02)***	0.07 (0.02)***
ln *trade*	0.45 (0.14)***	0.32 (0.18)*
RISK		0.04 (0.02)*
Overall adj-R^2	0.12	0.13
'Within' R^2	0.22	0.23
N	2,107	1,538
F value	6.71	5.80
Time dummies	YES	YES

Note: Regression with robust standard errors for correction of heteroskedasticity in parentheses. *** denotes significance at 1%; ** significant at 5%;* significant at 10%.

In Table 6.8 we explore the differential impact of BITs due to the selection of the BIT partner. In other words, we ask the question which host countries have benefited from the EU's BITs. Our results indicate that only the Philippines, Romania and Slovenia have increased FDI inflows after the implementation of the EU BITs, whereas Hungary has received less FDI.[10] Finally we check the robustness of our results and test for endogeneity by introducing a dummy on BITs for $t+1$, following Baier and Bergstrand (2007). We find no feedback effect in our sample.[11]

5.   CONCLUSION

In this chapter we addressed several policy-relevant issues regarding the bilateral investment treaties of the EU. Since the Lisbon Treaty, the right to negotiate investment treaties has been transferred from the member states to the European Commission. As the world's largest source of FDI outflows the EU27 has 1557 BITs signed, compared to the US that has only 48 and Japan 11. As the existing BITs will be grandfathered, several questions await. First and foremost we explored the question whether the EU's BITs have a significantly positive impact on outflows or not. Second, we asked the question which member states and which BIT partners have had a significant experience after the implementation of the BIT.

In our sample we find that both OECD BITs and EU BITs have a statistically significant and positive impact on FDI outflows. This result is robust to standard controls, but particularly also to the inclusion of variables such as privatisation proceeds that control for the level of economic reform, the level of trade linkages, the level of democratic freedom and a measure of risk of expropriation. Our results are also robust to the selection estimators. We control for endogeneity in our estimations by using the fixed-effects estimator as our preferred estimator on a large panel dataset. As most of the time the endogeneity is due to uncontrolled unobserved heterogeneity, using fixed-effects on panel data is an efficient method to deal with this issue. We also test strict exogeneity of our results by using a method suggested by Baier and Bergstrand (2007) and we find no feedback effect in our sample.

Our results have several important policy implications. First, it is important to ensure investor security throughout the transition period. As our results indicate, BITs have been an effective tool so far. Next, it is important to make proper decisions on the shape and contents of an EU BIT. This could be based on best practice. Here, our results are only suggestive as we do not consider the details of the BITs. Even though there is a basic format to all BITs with standard sections there may indeed be several significant differences in the language used. For example, one important difference between

US BITs and EU BITs is that the US BITs do provide FDI liberalisation. In further research we will also address these differences.

In terms of the future EU investment partners, the third countries that have benefitted positively from signing BITs with EU member states should be given a longer transition period while member states adjust individual BITs to harmonise to a common EU BIT format.

NOTES

1. The member states may still be empowered to negotiate their individual BITs.
2. We accept that this is a somewhat crude attempt to identify differences between each member state's BIT. However, it is a reasonable assumption that while BITs, in essence, may change from member state to member state, it is likely that the underlying texts are almost exactly the same for each third party (e.g. the text of the BIT for Austria-Argentina is the same as for Austria-Philippines).
3. Contrary to the BITs signed by the US and recently by Canada, EU BITs rarely provide FDI liberalisation through offering MFN treatment during the pre-establishment period of the investment.
4. In detail, extra-EU15 outflows were €580 billion in 2007 indicating that the 12 new member states have actually disinvested during 2007.
5. The same holds true even when one examines global (including other EU member states) FDI outward stocks of Germany and UK.
6. The case of Brazil stands out from the others as 9 member states have signed BITs with Brazil but they were not implemented. This was due to political and constitutional concerns by Brazil.
7. We have also used the log difference in incomes per capita in our specifications. However, this variable was not robustly significant and did not add any explanatory power to the model. The results can be obtained from the author.
8. For the date of BIT, we use the date for implementation and not the date for signature. Later we will also use the date of signature to measure the signalling effect of BITs.
9. $\text{Exp}(0.28) = 1.32$.
10. With the exception of Ireland, all EU15 member states have signed BITs with the 10 new member states in the early 1990s that are still in place. Among the new member states, Hungary has signed BITs earlier in the 1980s, hence our results may not be capturing the full effect of Hungary's BITs.
11. The results are available upon request.

REFERENCES

Baier, S.L. and J. Bergstrand (2007), 'Do Free Trade Agreements Actually Increase Members' International Trade?', *Journal of International Economics*, **71**, 72-95.

Baltagi, B.H. (2001), *Econometric Analysis of Panel Data*, Chichester: Wiley and Sons.

Busse, M., J. Königer and P. Nunnenkamp (2008), 'FDI Promotion through Bilateral Investment Treaties: More than a Bit?', *Review of World Economics*, **146**, 147-177.

Egger, P. and M. Pfaffermayr (2003), 'The Impact of Bilateral Investment Treaties on Foreign Direct Investment', *Journal of Comparative Economics*, **32**, 788-804.

Eschenbach, F., J.F. Francois and S. Nitzsche (2004), 'Economic Growth in 130 Countries: a New Dataset on Development and Finance', http://www.i4ide.org/francois/data.htm.

European Commission (2010), 'Roadmap: Commission Communication on EU Investment Policy', http://ec.europa.eu/governance/impact/planned_ia/docs/87_trade_eu_investment_policy_en.pdf.

Hallward-Driemeier, M. (2003), 'Do Bilateral Investment Treaties Attract FDI? Only a Bit and They Could Bite', *World Bank Policy Research Paper*, WPS 3121.

ICSID (2010), *The ICSID Case-Load Statistics: Issue 2010-2*, Washington D.C.: International Centre for Settlement of Investment Disputes.

Neumayer, E. and L. Spess (2005), 'Do Bilateral Investment Treaties Increase Foreign Direct Investment to Developing Countries?', *World Development*, **33**, 1567-1585.

Persson, T. (2005), 'Forms of Democracy, Policy and Economic Development', Institute for International Economic Studies, Stockholm University, mimeo.

Razin, A., Y. Rubinstein and E. Sadka (2003), 'Which Countries Export FDI, and How Much?', *NBER Working Paper*, no. 10145.

Rose-Ackerman, S. and J. Tobin (2004), 'Foreign Direct Investment and the Business Environment in Developing Countries: the Impact of Bilateral Investment Treaties', *Yale Law School & Economics Research Paper*, no. 293.

Salacuse, J. and N. Sullivan (2004), 'Do BITs Really Work? an Evaluation of Bilateral Investment Treaties and their Grand Bargain', *Harvard International Law Journal*, **46**, 67-130.

PART II

The Economic Crisis and Global Economic Imbalances

7. The Effects of the US Economic and Financial Crises on Euro Area Convergence

Fabio C. Bagliano and Claudio Morana

1. INTRODUCTION

Since the 1980s the European economy has undergone a progressive process of economic integration, involving both real and financial markets. This process has not been monotonous, with the main stages marked by the introduction of the European Exchange Rate Mechanism (ERM) in March 1979, the ratification of the Maastricht Treaty in November 1993, and the start of the Economic and Monetary Union (EMU) in January 1999. Many studies have approached the integration process from different perspectives, focusing on business cycle synchronisation, inflation convergence and persistence, and financial markets integration. Though the available empirical evidence is not fully clear-cut, the finding of a stronger co-movement in real and financial variables across euro area countries over the 1990s is fairly robust. Yet, so far EMU does not seem to have contributed decisively to further increasing euro area economic and financial integration, relatively to pre-EMU levels. For instance, as regards real convergence and the existence of a euro area business cycle, the evidence suggests that business cycle synchronisation across euro area countries is still weak (Camacho et al., 2005; de Haan et al., 2008), concerns subsets of countries rather than the whole area (Mink et al., 2007; Aguiar-Contraria and Soares, 2009; Giannone et al., 2009)[1], and with stronger regional than international coordination (Montoya and de Haan, 2007). International trade emerges as one of the key sources of euro area business cycle synchronisation (Bower and Guillemineau, 2006), with a positive effect also on nominal convergence (Honohan and Lane, 2003). Convergence in inflation trends seems to have occurred within the euro area, though persistent inflation differentials remain, due to cyclical dynamics (Angeloni and Ehrmann, 2004; Cavallero, 2010). Evidence of recent divergence in inflation rates has been provided by Busetti et al. (2007).

Moreover, financial market integration, while benefiting at least from the start of the EMU from the elimination of currency risk (Fratzscher, 2002), leading to a decrease in stock market volatility for the most volatile markets of the euro zone, i.e. Italy and Spain, relative to the least volatile ones, i.e. France and Germany (Morana and Beltratti, 2002), as well as to a reduction in the equity home bias for portfolios owned by European institutional investors (Adam et al., 2002), would be still in progress. For instance, market participation of households across euro zone countries is indeed still heterogeneous (Guiso et al., 2003). Actually, the degree of stock market integration could even have decreased in the last few years relative to the 1990s, as stock markets co-movements appear to be stronger for subsets of countries rather than for the whole area (Morana, 2010).

Since economic and financial integration between the euro area and the US is strong (Giannone et al., 2009; Morana, 2010), it is likely that the ongoing crisis, which heavily hit also the US economy, may have had an impact on the process of convergence in the euro area. This is consistent with the fact that apparently symmetric shocks may have had different effects across countries, according to the country-specific degree of shock persistence. The convergence process should however imply both a progressive reduction in the cross-country dispersion about the mean/median euro-area value of various macroeconomic indicators, as well as a more symmetric cross-sectional distribution. To provide a first look at the evidence, Figure 7.1 depicts the recent behaviour (2007-09) of the distribution of several macroeconomic variables across 14 euro-area countries, showing that the crisis has so far had quite a deep impact on euro-area economic activity and some effects on its cross-sectional dispersion as well. In 2009 median GDP growth became negative (−3.6%), with a cross-sectional distribution featuring negative skewness and increased dispersion with respect to the previous two years. Some changes in the cross-sectional distributions of the output gap, the inflation rate and the unemployment rate can also be detected. All variables show pronounced skewness, and changes also in the dispersion around median values (−5.2%, 0.2% and 8.2% in 2009 for the output gap, the inflation rate and the unemployment rate, respectively).

In the light of the above evidence, the chapter investigates the linkages between the US and the euro-area economies over the 1980-2009 period, aiming at assessing whether spillovers of macroeconomic and financial shocks from the US may have affected the convergence process of nominal and real variables in the euro area.

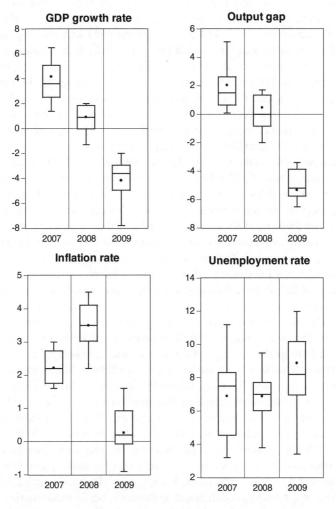

Note: The box plots in this and the following figures show, for each distribution, the mean
value (represented by a dot), the median value (a straight line), the interquartile range
(IQR, containing 50% of the observations, represented by a box), and the values that
are outside the first and third quartiles but within the first (third) quartile minus (plus)
1.5 times the IQR (represented by vertical lines ending with a staple).

Figure 7.1   *Box plots of the distribution of GDP growth, output gap,*
inflation rate and unemployment rate in 2007-09 for 14
euro-area countries (in percentage)

While there is a vast literature on the economic and financial convergence in the euro area, we are unaware of other papers which have so far dealt with the likely consequences of the US crisis on the euro area convergence process. The chapter tries to innovate in terms of the depth and wideness of the analysis and econometric methodology, providing an accurate investigation of the euro area-US macro/finance interface. In addition to 14 euro-area member countries and the US, 35 additional economies, covering advanced and major emerging countries, have been considered, in order to set the analysis in a proper open economy framework. The econometric model counts about 300 equations, considering key macroeconomic and financial variables, and is set in the factor vector autoregressive (F-VAR) framework.

The contribution of US crises to the euro-area convergence process has then been assessed by measuring the dynamic responses of key euro-area country macroeconomic variables to real and financial shocks originating in the US. The features of the cross-sectional distribution of such dynamic responses over different horizons is subsequently assessed in order to gauge the likely short- and medium-term consequences of the ongoing crisis.

The findings of the chapter indeed point to a likely contribution of US real and financial factors to real divergence in the euro area. In fact, a slowdown in US economic activity may not only lead to a contraction in the first moment of the cross-sectional distribution of GDP growth in the euro area, but also to an increase in second and third moments. US financial factors may also contribute to the increase in dispersion and skewness of the euro area GDP growth distribution, but are less likely to affect its first moment. Differently, neither real nor financial US factors are likely to have affected the process of nominal convergence in the euro area during the current crisis, given the near independence of the euro area inflation rate distribution from the US real and financial cyclical dynamics. Not surprisingly, both real and financial US factors are found to be important for euro area financial convergence, consistent with the strong economic and financial integration of the two areas and the leading role of the US economy. Destabilising US financial conditions may then have contributed to destabilising financial markets in the euro area. In particular, US excess liquidity and real estate and stock prices, seem to have contributed to euro area stock market fluctuations. Moreover, the downturn in US GDP growth would have contributed to the contraction in euro area stock prices, as well as to the increase in volatility and downside risk for both house and stock prices.

The rest of the chapter is organised as follows. The next section introduces the econometric methodology, while in section 3 the data and their properties are presented. Then, section 4 discusses the specification and estimation of the F-VAR model and shows the main results. Finally, conclusions are drawn in section 5.

2.   ECONOMETRIC METHODOLOGY

The econometric model is composed of two sets of equations. The first one refers to the US economy (with variables collected in vector X_t), while the second to the other $m-1$ non-US countries (collected in vector Y_t). The joint dynamics of q macroeconomic variables for each of the m countries of interest (in vector $Z_t = [X_t \ \ Y_t]$) are modelled by means of the following F-VAR model:

$$F_t = \mathbf{\Phi}(\mathrm{L})F_{t-1} + \eta_t \tag{7.1}$$

$$G_t = \mathbf{\Psi}(\mathrm{L})G_{t-1} + \zeta_t \tag{7.2}$$

$$Z_t - \mu_t = \mathbf{\Lambda} F_t + \mathbf{\Xi} G_t + \mathbf{D}(\mathrm{L})(Z_{t-1} - \mu_{t-1}) + v_t \tag{7.3}$$

In (7.3) $Z_t \sim \mathrm{I}(0)$ is the $n \times 1$ stationary vector of variables of interest, with $n = m \times q$, and $\mu_t = [\mu_t^X \ \ \mu_t^Y]$ is an $n \times 1$ vector of deterministic components, including an intercept term, and linear or non-linear trend components. F_t is an $r \times 1$ vector of observed or unobserved common factors, generated by the autoregressive process in (7.1), where $\mathbf{\Phi}(\mathrm{L})$ is an $r \times r$ finite order matrix lag polynomial, and η_t is a vector of i.i.d shocks driving the F_t factors. G_t is an $s \times 1$ vector of non-US factors, generated by the autoregressive process in (7.2), where $\mathbf{\Psi}(\mathrm{L})$ is an $s \times s$ finite order matrix lag polynomial, and ζ_t is a vector of i.i.d. shocks driving the G_t factors. The effects of both sets of factors on the US and non-US variables in Z_t is captured by the loading coefficients collected in the matrices $\mathbf{\Lambda} = [\mathbf{\Lambda}^X \ \ \mathbf{\Lambda}^Y]'$ and $\mathbf{\Xi} = [\mathbf{\Xi}^X \ \ \mathbf{\Xi}^Y]'$ (of dimension $n \times r$ and $n \times s$, respectively). Finally, $\mathbf{D}(\mathrm{L})$ is an $n \times n$ finite order matrix lag polynomial, partitioned as

$$\mathbf{D}(\mathrm{L}) = \begin{bmatrix} \underset{q\times q}{\mathbf{D}_{XX}(\mathrm{L})} & \underset{q\times(m-1)q}{\mathbf{0}} \\ \underset{(m-1)q\times q}{\mathbf{D}_{YX}(\mathrm{L})} & \underset{(m-1)q\times(m-1)q}{\mathbf{D}_{YY}(\mathrm{L})} \end{bmatrix}$$

with

$$\mathbf{D}_{YY}(\mathrm{L}) = \begin{bmatrix} \underset{q\times q}{\mathbf{d}_{11}(\mathrm{L})} & \mathbf{0} & \dots & \mathbf{0} \\ \mathbf{0} & \underset{q\times q}{\mathbf{d}_{22}(\mathrm{L})} & \dots & \mathbf{0} \\ \vdots & \vdots & \ddots & \vdots \\ \mathbf{0} & \mathbf{0} & \dots & \underset{q\times q}{\mathbf{d}_{m-1,m-1}(\mathrm{L})} \end{bmatrix}$$

and $v_t = [v_t^X \; v_t^Y]'$ is the $n \times 1$ vector of reduced-form idiosyncratic (i.e. country-specific) i.i.d. disturbances. It is assumed that all polynomial matrices $\Phi(L)$, $\Psi(L)$, and $D(L)$ have all roots outside the unit circle. Moreover, $E(\eta_{jt} v_{is}) = E(\eta_{jt} \zeta_{is}) = E(\zeta_{jt} v_{is}) = 0$ for all i, j, t and s.

The specification of the model has important implications for cross-country linkages: firstly, US idiosyncratic shocks (v_t^X) do not only affect the US (through $D_{XX}(L)$), but also the other countries (through $D_{YX}(L)$). Differently, non-US idiosyncratic disturbances (v_t^Y) do not affect US variables, while only own-country linkages are relevant for the other countries ($D_{YY}(L)$ is block diagonal). The specification selected is then consistent with the view that the US play a leading role in the transmission of macro-economic shocks, interpreting US macroeconomic dynamics in terms of global dynamics (see for instance Bagliano and Morana, 2009 and Beltratti and Morana, 2010). This, however, does not prevent interlinkages between the US and the other countries, which are parsimoniously described by means of the non-US factors G_t.

By substituting (7.1) and (7.2) into (7.3), the dynamic factor model can be written in standard vector autoregressive form as

$$
\begin{pmatrix} F_t \\ G_t \\ Z_t - \mu_t \end{pmatrix} = \begin{pmatrix} \Phi(L) & 0 & 0 \\ 0 & \psi(L) & 0 \\ \Lambda\Phi(L) & \Xi\Psi(L) & D(L) \end{pmatrix} \begin{pmatrix} F_{t-1} \\ G_{t-1} \\ Z_{t-1} - \mu_{t-1} \end{pmatrix} + \begin{pmatrix} \varepsilon_t^F \\ \varepsilon_t^G \\ \varepsilon_t^Z \end{pmatrix} \qquad (7.4)
$$

where

$$
\begin{pmatrix} \varepsilon_t^F \\ \varepsilon_t^G \\ \varepsilon_t^Z \end{pmatrix} = \begin{pmatrix} I_r \\ 0 \\ \Lambda \end{pmatrix} \eta_t + \begin{pmatrix} 0 \\ I_s \\ \Xi \end{pmatrix} \zeta_t + \begin{pmatrix} 0 \\ 0 \\ v_t \end{pmatrix} \quad ,
$$

or $\qquad Z_t^* = H^*(L) Z_{t-1}^* + \varepsilon_t \quad ,$ $\qquad\qquad\qquad\qquad (7.5)$

with $\qquad Z_t^* = \begin{bmatrix} F_t & G_t & Z_t - \mu_t \end{bmatrix}'$, and variance-covariance matrices

$$
E(\varepsilon_t \varepsilon_t') = \Sigma_\varepsilon = \begin{pmatrix} \Sigma_\eta & 0 & \Sigma_\eta\Lambda' \\ 0 & \Sigma_\zeta & \Sigma_\zeta\Xi' \\ \Lambda\Sigma_\eta & \Xi\Sigma_\zeta & \Lambda\Sigma_\eta\Lambda' + \Xi\Sigma_\zeta\Xi' + \Sigma_v \end{pmatrix}
$$

and $\Sigma_\eta = E(\eta_t \eta_t')$, $\Sigma_\nu = E(\nu_t \nu_t')$, and $\Sigma_\zeta = E(\zeta_t \zeta_t')$. The inversion of the F-VAR form to obtain the reduced vector moving average (VMA) form for the Z_t^* process, as well as the identification of the structural shocks, is discussed in Bagliano and Morana (2010).

In our analysis, the impact of a change in the variables of interest (X_t, F_t, G_t) on the Y_t block is investigated by exploiting the reduced form VAR structure of the model:

$$(\mathbf{I} - \mathbf{D}_{YY}(L))(Y_t - \mu_t^Y)$$

$$= \left(\mathbf{\Lambda}^Y \mathbf{\Phi}(L) \quad \mathbf{\Xi}^Y \mathbf{\Psi}(L) \quad \mathbf{D}_{YX}(L)\right) \begin{pmatrix} F_{t-1} \\ G_{t-1} \\ X_{t-1} - \mu_{t-1}^X \end{pmatrix} + \varepsilon_t^Y \qquad (7.6)$$

and computing the dynamic multipliers, i.e.

$$Y_t - \mu_t^Y = \mathbf{V}(L) \begin{pmatrix} F_{t-1} \\ G_{t-1} \\ X_{t-1} - \mu_{t-1}^X \end{pmatrix} + \varepsilon_t^Y, \qquad (7.7)$$

where $\mathbf{V}(L) = (\mathbf{I} - \mathbf{D}_{YY}(L))^{-1} \left(\mathbf{\Lambda}^Y \mathbf{\Phi}^Y(L) \quad \mathbf{\Xi}^Y \mathbf{\Psi}^Y(L) \quad \mathbf{D}_{YX}(L)\right)$.

The latter is equivalent to the impulse response analysis carried out from the reduced form VMA representation, and is appropriate when the focus is on the impact of a change in a given forcing variable, say US GDP, independently of its underlying economic cause (i.e. a given structural shock), on the Y_t block. The F-VAR model is estimated by means of a consistent and efficient iterative procedure, featuring the Granger and Jeon (2004) robust approach, yielding median estimates for all the parameters of interest, obtained through simulation with 1000 replications (see Bagliano and Morana, 2010 for details).

3.   THE DATA

We use seasonally adjusted quarterly macroeconomic time series data, over the period 1980:1 through 2009:1, for 14 euro area member states (Austria, Belgium, Finland, France, Germany, Greece, Ireland, Italy, Luxembourg, the Netherlands, Portugal, Slovakia, Slovenia and Spain), the US, and 16 additional advanced economies (Australia, Canada, the Czech Republic, Denmark, Hong Kong, Iceland, Israel, Japan, New Zealand, Norway, Singapore, South Korea, Sweden, Switzerland, Taiwan, the United Kingdom), 5 additional advanced emerging economies (Brazil, Hungary, Mexico, Poland, South Africa), and 14 secondary emerging economies (Argentina, Chile, China, Colombia, India, Indonesia, Malaysia, Morocco, Pakistan, Peru, Philippines, Russia, Thailand, Turkey), i.e. a total of 50 countries.[2]

The data set for euro area member countries consists of real GDP, the CPI all-items index, real bank loans to the private sector relative to GDP, the real short-term interest rate (either a 3-month interbank rate or a 3-month Treasury Bill rate, depending on availability), and real house and stock prices. Due to lack of data availability, housing prices have not been considered for Austria, Belgium, Greece, Luxembourg, Portugal, Slovakia, and Slovenia. A similar dataset has also been employed for the remaining non-US countries (house prices are only available for few additional OECD countries, i.e. Australia, Canada, Japan, New Zealand, Denmark, Norway, Sweden, Switzerland, and the UK). All these variables are included in the Y_t vector.

Differently, the dataset for the US is larger and composed of real GDP, civilian employment, real private consumption, real private investment, fiscal deficit to GDP, current account deficit to GDP, CPI all-items index, three-month Treasury Bill real rate, 10-year Federal government securities real rate, real house prices, the real effective exchange rate, real share prices (S&P500). A few financial variables have also been included, in order to monitor the impact of the financial crisis; in particular, the economic/financial fragility index and the excess liquidity index proposed in Bagliano and Morana (2010).[3]

All the above variables enter in the vector X_t. In order to keep the US-euro area spillover analysis manageable, and consistent with previous work on the Great Recession, only a sub-set of US macroeconomic and financial factors has been selected for the computation of dynamic multipliers, namely GDP growth, excess liquidity, house and stock prices and an economic/financial fragility indicator.[4] Finally, also the crude oil price and primary commodities price shocks (excluding energy), computed following Hamilton (1996), have been considered and included in the vector F_t. In order to account for feedback effects from the world economy to the US economy, a single common non-US GDP growth factor, accounting for about 20% of total variance, has been extracted from the GDP growth series of the 37 countries for which data are available since 1980:1.[5] This factor is included as the only element in the G_t vector.

As the econometric model is set in a stationary representation, data have been transformed accordingly;[6] in particular, on the basis of the KPSS test (Kwiatkowski et al., 1992; Becker et al., 2006).

Weak stationarity, in deviation or not from a non-linear deterministic trend component, modelled by means of the Gallant (1984) flexible functional form, *i.e.* $\mu_t = \mu_0 + \mu_1 t + \mu_2 \sin(2\pi t/T) + \mu_3 \cos(2\pi t/T)$, was assumed for the levels of the long-term and short-term real interest rates, the US current account to GDP ratio, the US public deficit to GDP ratio, and for the growth rates of all the remaining series. These deterministic terms are included in vector μ_t.[7]

4. US ECONOMIC AND FINANCIAL SHOCKS AND EURO AREA CONVERGENCE DYNAMICS

The ordering of the variables in the econometric model is country-by-country and standard, from relatively 'slow' to relatively 'fast' moving variables. Then, the X_t vector for the US is ordered as follows: employment growth, real GDP growth, the Federal Deficit/GDP ratio, real private consumption growth, real private investment growth, the current account/GDP ratio, the CPI inflation rate, the excess liquidity index, the real three-month Treasury bills rate, the real ten-year Government Bonds rate, real house price returns, real effective exchange rate returns, real stock price returns, the financial fragility index. Similarly, the ordering for the Y_t vector, concerning the non-US countries, is: real GDP growth, CPI inflation, real excess credit growth, the real short-term rate, real house price returns (when available), and real stock price returns.

The dynamic specification of the econometric model has been selected by means of the BIC information criterion, pointing to an optimal first order F-VAR system. Assuming an own-variable diagonal structure for the corresponding elements of the $\mathbf{D}(L)$ matrix for the non-US countries diagonal ($\mathbf{D}_{YY}(L)$), the euro area block then counts 77 equations, each containing 13 parameters, of which 1 is for the lagged own variable, 5 are for the lagged US series, 3 for the lagged F_t and G_t series, and 4 for the deterministic component (including a constant, a linear trend and two non-linear components, as described in the data section); similarly, for the remaining elements in the vector Y_t. Differently, the 14 equations corresponding to the US block X_t contain 21 parameters each, of which 14 are for the lagged US series, 3 for the lagged F_t and G_t series, and 4 are for the deterministic component. The full system therefore counts 278 equations.

The impact of the US economic and financial shocks on euro area convergence dynamics is assessed by means of the properties of the cross-sectional distributions of the dynamic multipliers, measuring the response of euro area variables to a unitary change in the US variables included in (7.7) at two forecasting horizons, namely 2-quarter (short-term) and 12-quarter (medium-term). This is consistent with the fact that a different degree of shock persistence in each country may lead a symmetric shock to have different effects across countries. The results reported in Table 7.1 and Figures 7A.1-7A.5 refer to the case of a unitary increase in the US variables. The effects of a unitary contraction in these variables, which is the case of interest for some of them (output growth, for instance), can be read from the table and plots by reversing the sign of the dynamic multipliers and associated statistics.

4.1. The Effects of US Financial Shocks

In a boom-bust credit cycle interpretation of the recent crisis (see e.g. Bagliano and Morana, 2010), asset prices misalignments in the US housing and stock markets would have initially been fuelled by the availability of excess liquidity and low interest rates.[8] The ballooning US trade deficit likely also contributed to the latter dynamics, as huge capital inflows were redirected from the Treasury and stock markets to the housing market. Then, expected but not materialised housing price appreciation have led the predatory lending mechanism to break down and a generalised decline in asset prices and tight credit conditions, as financial institutions were forced into deleveraging and recapitalisation.[9] Due to the strong integration of US and euro area (EA) financial markets (Giannone et al., 2009; Morana, 2010), and the leading role of the US economy, the US financial cycle has affected financial markets in the EA economy as well. In particular, the spillover of the US financial crisis to the EA and the rest of the world is likely to have taken place through housing prices (see Bagliano and Morana, 2010; Beltratti and Morana, 2010), as well as through excess liquidity and stock market dynamics.

Results concerning the impact of US financial shocks over our investigated sample (1980-2009) on the EA convergence process are collected in Table 7.1 (columns 2 through 5) and Figures 7A.2 through 7A.5, presenting descriptive statistics and corresponding box plots of the cross sections of dynamic responses of selected EA variables (GDP growth, inflation rate, real excess credit growth (the rate of change of real loans to GDP), real house price returns and real stock returns to various US disturbances over the 2- and 12-quarter time horizons. Several results are remarkable.

First, concerning the effects of the US financial shocks on real convergence, from Table 7.1 it can be noted that neither US excess liquidity, nor US housing or stock prices, or US economic/financial fragility, have a sizable impact on the median of the EA output growth distribution, neither in the short nor the medium term. Yet, in two cases, i.e. US housing prices and economic/financial fragility, the mean impact is sizable, and stronger in the short (−0.2%, −0.34%) than in the medium term (−0.15% and −0.26%).

Table 7.1 Descriptive statistics for the cross-section of dynamic responses after 2 quarters and 12 quarters for euro area variables: mean, standard deviation, first, second (median) and third quartile, index of skewness and kurtosis

EA variables		US variables									
		GDP		Excess liquidity		House prices		Stock prices		Fragility index	
Responses after		2q	12q	2q	12q	2q	12q	2q	12q	2q	12q
GDP	mean	0.336	0.264	-0.081	-0.057	-0.198	-0.152	-0.007	-0.005	-0.340	-0.256
	std. dev	0.554	0.415	0.287	0.217	0.623	0.472	0.068	0.052	1.098	0.830
	Q1	0.050	0.050	-0.110	-0.090	-0.120	-0.095	-0.005	-0.005	-0.450	-0.340
	Q2	0.130	0.110	0.010	0.010	-0.030	-0.020	0.001	0.001	-0.050	-0.050
	Q3	0.300	0.260	0.050	0.045	0.005	0.005	0.010	0.010	0.012	0.012
	skewness	2.061	2.053	-2.378	-2.377	-2.777	-2.776	-1.931	-2.076	-2.169	-2.165
	kurtosis	6.650	6.686	7.869	7.906	9.613	9.603	7.425	7.665	7.579	7.557
Inflation	mean	-0.029	-0.042	-0.009	-0.023	-0.003	-0.004	0.006	0.008	0.039	0.076
	std. dev	0.055	0.066	0.069	0.111	0.022	0.037	0.010	0.010	0.088	0.147
	Q1	-0.082	-0.113	-0.032	-0.055	-0.025	-0.032	0.001	0.001	-0.030	-0.036
	Q2	-0.010	-0.026	-0.011	-0.032	-0.005	-0.008	0.003	0.004	0.031	0.034
	Q3	0.005	0.008	0.022	0.028	0.012	0.022	0.004	0.007	0.085	0.159
	skewness	-0.901	-0.431	-1.260	-1.546	0.183	-0.091	2.159	1.491	0.301	0.408
	kurtosis	2.709	1.584	5.053	5.850	1.830	2.015	6.638	3.755	2.539	2.406

Table 7.1 (continued)

EA variables						US variables						
		GDP		Excess liquidity		House prices		Stock prices		Fragility index		
Responses after		2q	12q	2q	12q	2q	12q	2q	12q	2q	12q	
Credit	mean	1.260	1.145	-0.939	-0.954	1.170	1.188	-0.083	-0.099	1.995	1.815	
	std. dev	3.941	3.435	3.337	2.925	3.707	3.313	0.367	0.319	3.953	3.100	
	Q1	-0.145	-0.135	-0.850	-1.115	-0.235	-0.250	-0.160	-0.175	0.010	-0.010	
	Q2	0.280	0.340	-0.160	-0.200	0.100	0.090	-0.060	-0.080	0.670	0.840	
	Q3	0.620	0.590	0.170	0.175	0.660	0.700	0.000	0.005	1.520	1.615	
	skewness	2.864	2.737	-2.598	-2.411	2.698	2.562	-0.939	-0.983	2.172	1.931	
	kurtosis	9.972	9.497	9.000	8.173	9.357	8.760	5.944	5.499	6.781	5.896	
House prices	mean	0.020	-0.141	-0.257	-0.407	0.417	0.486	0.024	0.027	-0.219	-0.201	
	std. dev	0.876	1.694	0.632	0.967	0.760	0.654	0.046	0.067	0.503	0.986	
	Q1	-0.605	-1.360	-0.945	-1.287	0.038	0.080	-0.015	-0.035	-0.672	-1.202	
	Q2	-0.025	-0.055	-0.260	-0.695	0.085	0.185	0.014	0.015	-0.365	-0.405	
	Q3	0.550	0.797	0.055	0.153	0.253	0.542	0.033	0.070	-0.005	0.008	
	skewness	-0.812	-0.976	-0.279	-0.027	1.510	1.242	0.643	-0.273	0.186	0.540	
	kurtosis	2.401	2.632	1.486	1.192	3.561	3.044	2.151	1.390	1.393	1.903	

Table 7.1 (continued)

	mean	21.78	25.30	11.81	13.86	24.09	26.59	0.543	0.464	-6.764	-7.649
	std. dev	20.05	22.16	15.43	20.09	16.73	18.37	1.903	2.143	16.17	19.29
Stock	Q1	8.555	9.905	2.265	2.680	10.39	11.09	-0.750	-1.020	-20.80	-19.40
prices	Q2	17.60	19.30	7.080	6.950	23.40	21.60	0.630	0.690	0.390	0.420
	Q3	26.05	29.10	13.85	14.20	28.85	37.60	1.475	1.760	1.095	1.445
	skewness	1.343	1.072	0.861	1.038	0.469	0.395	-0.453	-0.852	-1.025	-1.159
	kurtosis	4.640	3.348	2.685	2.919	2.020	1.763	2.433	2.865	2.357	2.843

Moreover, US financial factors do have an impact on the second and third moments of the EA output growth distribution, with a sizable increase in both dispersion (0.29% through 1.1% in the short term, apart from stock prices) and skewness (−2 through −2.8 in the medium term).

Second, concerning the effects of US financial factors on nominal convergence, it can be noted that, apart from the medium-term impact of US excess liquidity and economic/financial fragility dynamics on the dispersion of the EA inflation rate cross-sectional distribution (0.11% and 0.15%, respectively), no sizable effects on first, second and third order moments of the inflation rate distribution can be noted.

Finally, concerning the impact of US financial factors on financial convergence within the EA, much richer interactions, of similar size in the short and medium term, can be noted. For instance, mean credit growth is sizably affected by US excess liquidity (−0.95%), housing prices (1.19%) and economic/financial conditions (2%); the median impact on the other hand is somewhat smaller (−0.2%, 0.09% and 0.84%, respectively); the impact on EA credit growth dispersion is also sizable (2.9% through 3.3%), as well as its impact on skewness (−2.4 through to 2.6). Similar findings hold for EA house price returns, as US excess liquidity, house prices and economic/financial fragility conditions fairly largely affect both the mean (−0.41%, 0.49%, −0.21%, respectively), median (−0.69%, 0.19%, −0.41%) and dispersion (0.97%, 0.65% and 0.99%) of the EA housing price distribution, while the impact on skewness is more attenuated. Differently, US financial factors, stock returns included, are important for both the first and second moments of the distribution of EA stock returns, while their impact on skewness is more modest; for instance, the mean (median) impacts are 13.9%, 26.7%, 0.46%, and −7.65% (6.95%, 21.6%, 0.69%, and 0.42%) for US excess liquidity, house prices, stock prices and economic/financial fragility conditions. The impact on dispersion is also large (20.1%, 18.4%, 2.14%, 19.3%).

Overall, US financial factors appear to be important determinants of euro area financial conditions, coherent with the strong integration of financial markets between the two countries: destabilising US financial conditions may have then contributed to destabilising euro area financial markets. In particular, US excess liquidity, house and stock prices, may have contributed to keep momentum in the euro-area stock markets during the boom phase of the credit cycle, yet contributing to a market crash during deleveraging. Similarly, US house prices would have contributed to the cyclical phase in euro area house prices. The interactions across financial markets are complex, involving not only first moments, but also second and third moments.

4.2. The Effects of US GDP Shocks

There are different mechanisms that can explain how the US crisis originated in the financial sector then became an economic crisis, as both tight credit conditions and falling asset prices (wealth and Tobin's Q effects) may have constrained aggregate demand.[10] A present value model, relating future developments in dividends and rents to output dynamics, can also account for second round effects, linking the slowdown in real activity to asset price deflation. According to the results reported in Bems et al. (2010) and Levchenko et al. (2010), external demand can be singled out as one of the key mechanisms through which the slowdown in US economic activity has been transmitted to the world economy.[11]

Results concerning the implications of US economic disturbances (captured in our framework by GDP shocks) for the convergence process in the euro area are collected in Table 7.1 (first column) and Figure 7A.1. As for the effects of US recessions on the real convergence within the EA, it can be noted that a contraction in US GDP may lead to mean and median negative responses of EA GDP growth. The impact is in both cases inelastic, with a stronger point impact in the short term (−0.34% and −0.13%) than in the medium-term (−0.26% and −0.11%); dispersion is also larger in the very short-term (0.55%) than in the medium-term (0.42), while skewness is sizable, but similar at both horizons (about −2). Hence, the evidence does point to a role of the slowdown in US economic activity in the explanation of current real divergence in the EA. Yet, apart from Greece (result not reported), cyclical responses still appear to be synchronised.[12] The divergence effect also appears to be slightly attenuated in the medium term, due to a smaller dispersion. Moreover, concerning the effects of US recessions on EA nominal convergence, the evidence does not support any direct linkage between the state of the US business cycle and inflation dynamics in the EA. In fact, neither first, nor second or third moments of the cross-sectional inflation distribution do seem to have been influenced.

Finally, concerning the effects of the contraction in US GDP on EA financial convergence, while for housing prices only the dispersion of the cross-sectional distribution seems to have been affected in both the short and medium term (0.88% and 1.69%, respectively), more sizable effects can be detected for credit growth and stock returns. In both cases a contraction in US GDP is associated with negative mean and median responses, stronger in the medium term (−0.34% for credit; −19.3% for stock returns) than in the short term. The impact on dispersion and skewness is also notable for both stock returns (20%, −1.07) and credit growth (3.94%, −2.74). Hence, euro area financial convergence may have been affected by the slowdown in US GDP growth, particularly in the credit and the stock markets.

5. CONCLUSIONS

The aim of the chapter is to assess whether the US economic and financial crises may have had some effect on the process of real and nominal convergence in the euro area. The current chapter addresses this issue by investigating the linkages between the US and the euro are countries for a large set of real and financial variables over the 1980-2009 period. In addition to 14 euro area member countries and the US, 35 additional countries, covering advanced and major emerging countries, have been included in the econometric model, set in the factor vector autoregressive (F-VAR) framework.

The findings of the chapter indeed point to a likely contribution of US real and financial factors to real divergence in the euro area. In fact, a slowdown in US economic activity may not only lead to a contraction in the first moment of euro area GDP cross-sectional distribution, but also to an increase in second and third moments. US financial factors may also contribute to the increase in dispersion and skewness of the euro area output growth distribution, but are less likely to affect the first moment of the distribution. Differently, neither real nor financial US factors are likely to have affected the process of nominal convergence in the euro area during the current crisis, given the near independence of the euro rate inflation distribution from the US real and financial cyclical dynamics.

Both real and financial US factors are found to be important for euro area financial convergence, coherent with the strong economic and financial integration for the two areas and the leading role of the US economy: destabilising US financial conditions may then have contributed to destabilise euro area financial markets. In particular, US excess liquidity, house and stock prices, would have contributed to euro area stock market fluctuations, while US house prices would have contributed to euro area house prices' cyclical dynamics. Moreover, the downturn in US GDP growth would have contributed to the contraction in euro area stock prices, as well as to the increase in volatility and downside risk for both house and stock prices.

Overall, the interactions between US and EA real and financial markets appear to be complex, involving not only first moments, but also second and third ones.

APPENDIX 7A

Figures 7A.1 to 7A.5

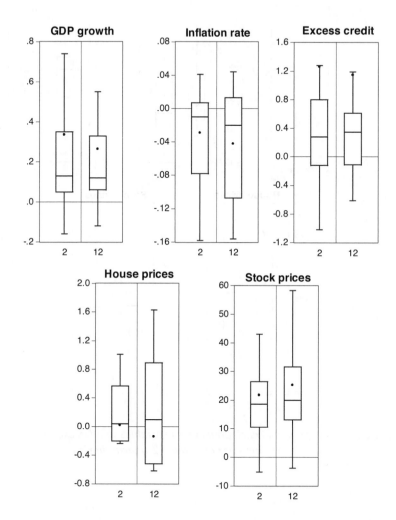

Figure 7A.1 Responses of euro area macro variables to a US output 1% increase at 2- and 12-quarter horizons

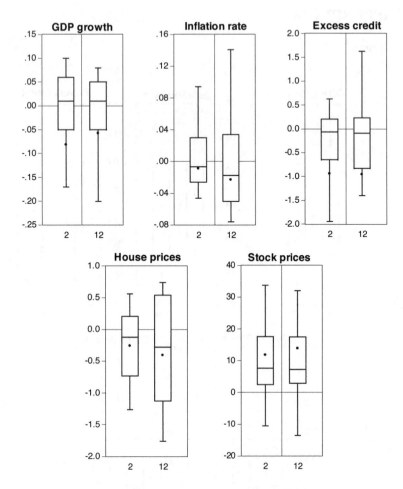

Figure 7A.2 Responses of euro area macro variables to a US excess
liquidity 1% increase at 2- and 12-quarter horizons

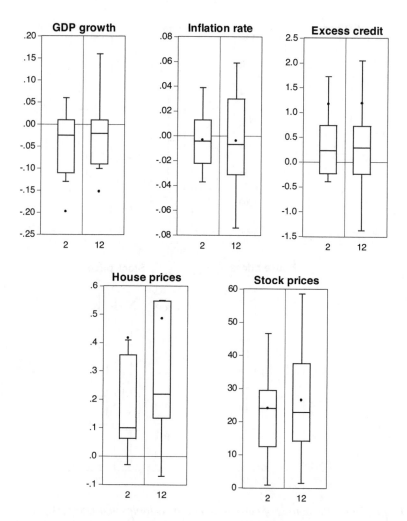

Figure 7A.3   Responses of euro area macro variables to a US house prices 1% increase at 2- and 12-quarter horizons

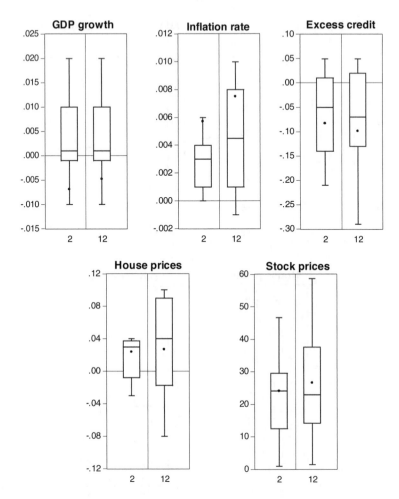

*Figure 7A.4   Responses of euro area macro variables to a US stock prices
1% increase at 2- and 12-quarter horizons*

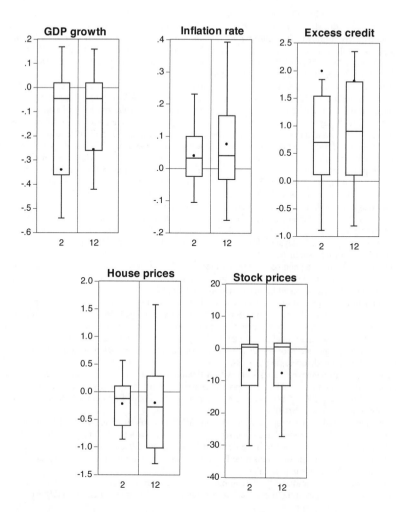

Figure 7A.5   Responses of euro area macro variables to a US financial fragility index 1% increase at 2- and 12-quarter horizons

NOTES

1. For instance, Aguiar-Contraria and Soares (2009) find that Germany, Austria, France, Spain, the Netherlands, Belgium and Luxembourg would form the euro-core, while Portugal, Greece, Italy and Finland are in the periphery. Yet, the evidence in favour of an upward trend is weak at most. See also Mink et al. (2007).

2. US data are from FRED2; OECD countries data are from OECD *Main Economic Indicators*, integrated with IMF *International Financial Statistics* (bank loans series); data for the other countries are from IMF *International Financial Statistics*; house price series for OECD countries are taken from a non-official OECD database (see http://www.olis.oecd.org/olis/ 2006doc.nsf/linkto/ECO-WKP%282006%293). The authors are grateful to P. Donati, S. Ejerskov, P. Benczur and M. Jensen for help with some of the data.
3. The economic/financial fragility index is computed as the first principal component extracted from the TED spread, the AGENCY spread, and the BAA-AAA corporate spread, providing an overall measure of credit/liquidity risk, stress in the mortgage market and risk appetite. The excess liquidity index is computed as the first principal component extracted from the M2 to GDP ratio and the total loans and leases at commercial banks to GDP ratio.
4. For instance, Bagliano and Morana (2010) find that the trade channel is the likely key transmission mechanism of the US economic crisis to the rest of the world, while US housing and stock prices and excess liquidity would have all contributed to the spillover of the US financial crisis to foreign countries. See also Bems et al. (2010) and Levchenko et al. (2010).
5. That is, the largest 18 OECD countries (Austria, Belgium, Denmark, Finland, France, Germany, Ireland, Italy, the Netherlands, Norway, Spain, Sweden, Switzerland, the UK, Australia, Canada, Japan and New Zealand), and a selection of the Latin American countries (Argentina, Brazil, Chile, Mexico, Peru), Asian countries (China, Hong Kong, Korea, Taiwan, Indonesia, Malaysia, Philippines, Singapore, Thailand, India, Pakistan, Turkey) and African countries (South Africa).
6. Of the 14 euro area member countries, there are 7 countries for which 6 macroeconomic series are available, yielding 42 equations; for the other 7 only 5 macroeconomic series are available. This yields 35 additional equations, in a total of 77.
7. Details are not included for reasons of space, but are available upon request from the authors.
8. Recent empirical evidence for the US point to a positive linkage between excess liquidity and house and stock prices, and to a negative linkage between interest rates and asset prices, with the latter being stronger than the former. See Bagliano and Morana (2010) for details.
9. See also Bagliano and Morana (2010) for significant interactions between housing and stock prices during the deleveraging process.
10. The empirical evidence is consistent with a linkage between asset prices and aggregate demand, pointing to an inelastic response of real activity, particularly for housing prices (Chirinko et al., 2004; Case et al., 2005; Carroll et al., 2006; Bagliano and Morana, 2010; Beltratti and Morana, 2010).
11. Levchenko et al. (2010) report a contraction in US imports of about 40% relatively to the level that would otherwise have occurred in a no-crisis environment. Moreover, according to Bems et al. (2010), real world trade declined 15% between 2008Q1 and 2009Q1. 27 percent of the fall in US GDP was transmitted to foreign countries through a demand spillover, affecting durable goods in particular.
12. The negative correlation of the Greek business cycle with the euro area business cycle is a well established fact in the literature. See for instance Bower and Guillemineau (2006).

REFERENCES

Adam, K., T. Jappelli, A. Menichini, M. Padula and M. Pagano (2002), 'Analyse, Compare, and Apply Alternative Indicators and Monitoring Methodologies to Measure the Evolution of Capital Markets Integration in the European Union', Report to the European Commission, available at http://ec.europa.eu/internal_market/ economic-reports/docs/ 020128_cap_mark_int_en.pdf.
Aguiar-Contraria, L. and M.J. Soares (2009), 'Business Cycle Synchronization across the Euro Area: a Wavelet Analysis', University of Minho, mimeo.

Angeloni, I. and M. Ehrmann (2004), 'Euro Area Inflation Differentials', *ECB Working Paper Series*, no. 388.

Bagliano, F.C. and C. Morana (2009), 'International Macroeconomic Dynamics: a Factor Vector Autoregressive Approach', *Economic Modelling*, **26**, 432-444.

Bagliano, F.C. and C. Morana (2010), 'The Great Recession: US Economic Dynamics and its Spillover to the World Economy', Università del Piemonte Orientale, mimeo.

Becker, R., W. Enders and J. Lee (2006), 'A Stationarity Test in the Presence of an Unknown Number of Smooth Breaks', *Journal of Time Series Analysis*, **27**, 381-409.

Beltratti, A. and C. Morana (2010), 'International House Prices and Macroeconomic Fluctuations', *Journal of Banking and Finance*, **34**, 535-545.

Bems, R., R.C. Johnson and K.-M. Yi (2010), 'Demand Spillovers and the Collapse of Trade During the Great Recession', *IMF Working Paper Series*, no. 10/142.

Bower, U. and C. Guillemineau (2006), 'Determinants of Business Cycle Synchronisation across Euro Area Countries', *ECB Working Paper Series*, no. 587.

Busetti, F., L. Forni, A. Harvey and F. Venditti (2007), 'Inflation Convergence and Divergence within the European Monetary Union', *International Journal of Central Banking*, **3**(2), 95-121.

Camacho, M., G. Perez-Quiros and L. Saiz (2005), 'Are European Business Cycles Close Enough to be Just One?' *CEPR Working Paper Series*, no. 4824.

Carroll, C.D., M. Otsuka and J. Slacalek (2006), 'How Large is the Housing Wealth Effect? A New Approach', *NBER Working Paper Series*, no. 12746.

Case, K.E., J.M. Quigley and R.J. Shiller (2005), 'Comparing Wealth Effects: the Stock Market versus the Housing Market', *Advances in Macroeconomics*, **5**(art. 1), 1-33.

Cavallero, A. (2010), 'The Convergence of Inflation Rates in the EU-12 Area: a Distribution Dynamics Approach', Univeristà del Piemonte Orientale, mimeo.

Chirinko, R.S., L. de Haan and E. Sterken (2004), 'Asset Price Shocks, Real Expenditures, and Financial Structure: a Multicountry Analysis', De Nederlandsche Bank, Working Paper, no. 14/04.

de Haan, J., R. Inklaar and R. Jong-a-Pin (2008), 'Will Business Cycles in the Euro Area Converge? A Critical Survey of Empirical Research', *Journal of Economic Surveys*, **22**, 234-273.

Fratzscher, M. (2002), 'Financial Markets Integration in Europe: on the Effects of EMU on Stock Markets', *International Journal of Finance and Economics*, **7**, 165-193.

Gallant, R. (1984), 'The Fourier Flexible Form', *American Journal of Agricultural Economics*, **66**, 204-208.

Giannone, D., M. Lenza and L. Reichlin (2009), 'Business Cycles in the Euro Area', *ECB Working Paper Series*, no. 1010.

Granger, C.W. and Y. Jeon (2004), 'Thick Modelling', *Economic Modelling*, **21**, 323-343.

Guiso, L., M. Haliassos and T. Jappelli (2003). 'Households Stockholding in Europe, Where do We Stand and Where do We Go?', *Economic Policy*, **36**, 123-170.

Hamilton, J. (1996), 'This is What Happened to the Oil Price Macroeconomy Relationship', *Journal of Monetary Economics*, **38**, 215-220.

Honohan, P. and P.R. Lane (2003), 'Divergent Inflation Rates in the EMU', *Economic Policy*, **18**, 357-394.

Kwiatkowski, D., P.C.B. Phillips, P. Schmidt and Y. Shin (1992), 'Testing the Null Hypothesis of Stationarity against the Alternative of a Unit Root', *Journal of Econometrics*, **54**, 159-178.

Levchenko, A.A., L.T. Lewis and L.L. Tesar (2010), 'The Collapse of International Trade during the 2008-2009 Crisis: in Search for the Smoking Gun', *NBER Working Paper*, no. 16006.

Mink, M., J.P.A.M. Jacobs and J. de Haan (2007), 'Measuring Synchronicity and Co-movement of Business Cycles within an Application to the Euro Area', *CESifo Working Paper Series*, no. 2112.

Montoya, L.A. and J. de Haan (2008), 'Regional Business Cycle Synchronization in Europe?', *International Economics and Economic Policy*, **5**, 123-137.

Morana, C. (2010), 'Realized Mean-variance Efficient Portfolio Selection and Euro Area Stock Market Integration', *Applied Financial Economics*, **20**, 989-1001.

Morana, C. and A. Beltratti (2002), 'The Effects of the Introduction of the Euro on European Stock Markets', *Journal of Banking and Finance*, **26**, 2047-2064.

8. A Euro Peg System as an Alternative for the Chinese Exchange Rate Regime?

Kang-Soek Lee

1. INTRODUCTION

The US crisis of 2007-2009 triggered a global financial crisis, which then turned into a serious recession in the world economy. The international monetary system is also experiencing a very substantial disturbance: the US dollar is losing its status as the international monetary reference. The situation is also slowing down the growth of major emerging countries, such as China, which in fact enjoyed exchange rate stability combined with an undervalued renminbi during more than a decade and a half.

Given the growing importance of China in the world economy as well as in the international monetary system, its foreign exchange rate policies matter in two aspects: (1) the perceived undervaluation of the renminbi; (2) the fixity of the dollar-renminbi exchange rate.

On the one hand, there is an ongoing debate on whether the renminbi is undervalued or not, among policy-makers and in the exchange rate literature. Many economists, including Frankel (2006, 2009), Coudert and Couharde (2007), Roubini (2007), Cline and Williamson (2008), Goldstein and Lardy (2008), Zhang and Wan (2008) and Das (2009) argue that the renminbi is excessively undervalued (up to almost 50%), while Wang (2004) and Funke and Rahn (2005) conclude that the renminbi is undervalued but only to some limited extent (around 15%). But on the contrary, according to some other researchers, such as Cheung et al. (2007), McKinnon (2007) and Yajie et al. (2007), there is little evidence that the renminbi is undervalued. On the whole, even though there is no complete consensus on the undervaluation of the renminbi, it is generally acknowledged that the weak renminbi generated, and continues to generate, trade imbalances all over the world, allowing China to finance its rapid growth.

On the other hand, many recent studies try to answer the question whether the dollar peg is suited to China's current economic conditions. Some authors, such as Frankel (2006), Kaplan (2006) and Roubini (2007) argue that China should abandon its dollar peg, because the renminbi needs to appreciate in order to ease inflationary pressure and China should achieve adjustment in the real exchange rate via flexibility in the nominal exchange rate. Some other economists however, such as McKinnon and Schnabl (2004), Sun and Ma (2005) and McKinnon (2007), underline the monetary rationale for China using the dollar peg, both to prevent unduly low interest rates and deflationary traps and to stabilise its domestic price level.

But, from a global point of view, it is important to note that China's dollar standard has also been depriving the American economy of one of the most important macroeconomic adjustment mechanisms: foreign exchange rate flexibility. In fact, the dollar has a potential downward trend on the international currency markets due to the worsening economic conditions in the US, while the renminbi has a potential upward trend. But the fixity of the dollar-renminbi exchange rate neutralises these two opposite trends and keeps their values vis-à-vis all other currencies relatively stable. In other words, the depreciation of the dollar, necessary to improve the American economic conditions, is limited by the 'already' undervalued renminbi. Given the dollar-renminbi exchange rate fixity, this implies that the dollar's depreciation would lead to a further undervaluation of renminbi that international markets would no longer be able to absorb. Furthermore, China's dollar peg combined with its growing role in the US economy in terms of trade and investment now makes Mundell's incompatibility triangle applicable even to the biggest country in the world. It means that this absence of a macro-adjustment mechanism exacerbated the US financial crisis and the global recession, which in turn decelerated Chinese growth. This is what can be called 'the Chinese boomerang effect', implying that China's current exchange rate policies are not efficient anymore, even for its own economy. In this sense also, China may need to abandon the dollar peg.

However, China cannot abandon so easily its dollar standard, at least for two reasons. First, the renminbi would risk appreciating sharply if it were allowed to float freely immediately and completely, which would hamper Chinese export-driven growth. A second reason may refer to the value of the huge Chinese foreign exchange reserves, which are denominated mostly in US dollars. Given that the downward trend of the dollar is for the moment counterbalanced by the upward trend of renminbi, the dollar would likely drop sharply if China abandoned its dollar standard. In short, China would risk losing a lot in the value of its international reserves if it abandoned the dollar peg before diversifying its reserves. These drawbacks led to what can be called 'the Chinese exchange rate dilemma', which may explain a somewhat confused line of the exchange rate policy announced by Chinese policymakers: for example, they proposed the use of an SDR instead of the dollar,[1] but have finally chosen to maintain the dollar standard.

Faced with this dilemma, China seems to have only one option for the moment: making a very progressive change in its foreign exchange rate policy, despite international pressures towards a re-evaluation of renminbi or a move to a floating exchange rate regime. Such a progressive change would at least allow China to maintain exchange rate stability and avoid disturbing the world economy again with (this time) a sudden drop of the dollar.

Anyway, China will not be able to continue keeping its dollar standard forever. As mentioned before, the American economy is blocked in a vicious cycle because of the absence of a macroeconomic adjustment mechanism, while China is already experiencing some serious boomerang effects from its foreign exchange rate regime. In this context, China may ultimately abandon its dollar peg and try to cut in this way the Gordian knot of its foreign exchange policy dilemma.

So, should China really abandon the dollar standard? If yes, what could be the most likely alternatives for its exchange rate regime? In this chapter, we try to answer these questions using a macro-structural economic shock approach as an assessment tool.

This chapter is organised as follows. Section 2 describes the exchange rate regime assessment methodology. Section 3 examines China's dollar standard. Section 4 considers a euro peg system. Section 5 concludes.

2. AN EXCHANGE RATE REGIME MISMATCH INDICATOR

2.1. Macro-structural Economic Shock Symmetry as a Prerequisite for a Fixed Exchange Rate Regime: the Chinese Case

In general, optimum currency area theories consider economic convergence as a prerequisite for a fixed exchange rate system. Otherwise, exchange rate variability would have to absorb asymmetric shocks. Supposing that countries are affected by asymmetric shocks, traditional OCA approaches however consisted in looking for other adjustment mechanisms than a flexible exchange rate, such as high labour mobility (Mundell, 1961), sufficient economic openness (McKinnon, 1963) or pronounced production diversification (Kenen, 1969). The application of different criteria, however, often gives different results and interpretations. One might for example argue that the labour market in China is 'insufficiently' flexible and that its economy is 'insufficiently' open to international markets. So, in the particular case of this country, one might possibly say that it is exchange rate variability that must absorb asymmetric shocks. A successful insertion of the Chinese economy in a fixed exchange rate context could, however, possibly be defended in the Kenen approach: maybe important 'asymmetric' shocks do not even occur, e.g. because of 'sufficient' diversification. It is therefore of interest to examine whether shocks that have occurred have indeed affected the US, EU and Chinese economies in a sufficiently 'symmetric' way. To do this we need a method to deduce the unobserved structural shocks from observed regression errors of the model that is estimated.

Instead of looking for the existence of different adjustment mechanisms as in the extended literature of traditional OCA theories, Bayoumi and Eichengreen (1994), for instance, examine 'directly' the (asymmetric or symmetric) nature of economic shocks. In this chapter we consider aggregate economic shocks in demand and supply – we use the term 'macro-structural economic shocks' – as generated by a structural vector autoregression (SVAR) model such as developed by Blanchard and Quah (1989). The series of economic shocks obtained in this way are then assumed to be white noise processes – i.e., these shock series are not correlated between them and thus represent independent sources of disturbance (e.g., technological progress, economic crises, natural disasters, economic policy shocks, etc.). They obviously differ from the estimated residuals from a standard VAR system, which stand for the unexplained part of the variables included in the model, such as GDP or price level.

Once the 'macro-structural economic shock' series have been obtained for each country in question, we will measure the degree of symmetry or asymmetry in a bilateral approach (China-US and China-EU), using correlation coefficients.

Before determining the bilateral characteristics of macro-structural economic shocks, the following section describes the SVAR model used in this paper to generate the required shock series relative to China, the US and the European Union.

2.2. A SVAR Model Approach for Generating Macro-structural Economic Shock Series

In general, the SVAR model combines economic theories with the standard 'atheoretical'[2] VAR approach in order to determine the dynamic response of endogenous variables to various white noise (independent) disturbances. These disturbances are also called underlying disturbances, exogenous shocks or structural shocks. The SVAR model imposes in fact a certain number of theoretical restrictions on the estimated reduced form model (where the endogenous variables are a function of the estimated and thus observable residuals e_t) in order to identify the underlying structural model (where the endogenous variables are function of white noise and thus initially non-observable underlying disturbances ε_t). The theoretical identification restrictions can be relevant to either a short-run relationship (in the Sims-Bernanke approach[3]) or a long-run relationship (in the Blanchard-Quah approach[4]), depending on whether the exogenous or structural shocks are considered as a temporary or permanent disturbance. Once the identification of the model is achieved in any of the above approaches, it is 'mathematically' possible to generate the structural shock series. But because of short-run dynamic uncertainties in the economy, the Blanchard-Quah approach is often preferred.[5]

We use the approach of the latter in order to generate aggregate supply (AS) shock series and aggregate demand (AD) shock series relative to China and its major economic partners. To this end, our model contains two key macroeconomic (endogenous) variables: real GDP and the Consumer Price Index (CPI).

For each of the three geographic entities we estimate the following standard VAR of order k with two stationary endogenous variables:

$$\mathbf{A}(L)\, X_t = e_t \tag{8.1}$$

with $\quad X_t = \begin{bmatrix} \Delta GDP \\ \Delta CPI \end{bmatrix}_t$, $\; e_t = \begin{bmatrix} e_{\Delta GDP} \\ e_{\Delta CPI} \end{bmatrix}_t$ and $\mathbf{A}(L) = \sum_{i=0}^{k} \mathbf{A}_i L^i$,

where X is the vector of the endogenous variables (in the first difference), e is the vector of the estimated residuals in the standard VAR system and Δ and L are the usual difference and lag operators, respectively. We have $\mathbf{A}_0 = \mathbf{I}$ and $var(e_t) = \Omega$. $e_{\Delta GDP}$ is the series of (observed) residuals of ΔGDP (serially uncorrelated but correlated with $e_{\Delta CPI}$) and $e_{\Delta CPI}$ is the series of (observed) residuals of ΔCPI (serially uncorrelated but correlated with $e_{\Delta GDP}$).

This model can be also written in a moving average form:

$$X_t = \mathbf{B}(L)e_t \; , \tag{8.2}$$

where $\mathbf{B}(L) = \mathbf{A}(L)^{-1}$ and $\mathbf{B}(L) = \sum_{i=0}^{k} \mathbf{B}_i L^i$. It holds that $\mathbf{B}_0 = \mathbf{I}$.

In this reduced form, the endogenous variables are function of the residuals e_t that can be easily estimated by the OLS method.

But, if the endogenous variables are expressed as a function of white noise structural shocks ε_t, we have

$$X_t = \mathbf{C}(\mathrm{L})\varepsilon_t \quad , \tag{8.3}$$

where we normalise so that var$(\varepsilon_t) = \mathbf{I}$.

We have: $\varepsilon_t = \begin{bmatrix} \varepsilon_{AS} \\ \varepsilon_{AD} \end{bmatrix}_t$ and $\mathbf{C}(\mathrm{L}) = \sum_{i=0}^{k} \mathbf{C}_i \mathrm{L}^i$.

ε is the white noise vector of the exogenous structural disturbances (called in this paper 'macro-structural economic shocks'), ε_{AS} is the series of (unobserved) aggregate supply shocks (also called AS-shocks), and ε_{AD} is the series of (unobserved) aggregate demand shocks (also called AD-shocks). $\mathbf{A}_i$, $\mathbf{B}_i$ and $\mathbf{C}_i$ are square 2×2 matrices of coefficients.

In order to deduce the unobserved structural shocks ε from the observed regression errors e, it is sufficient to know the matrix $\mathbf{C}_0$. This follows from the fact that, contemporaneously, the effect of the stochastic innovations $\mathbf{B}_0 e_t = e_t$ by necessity have to coincide with the effect of the white noise structural shocks $\mathbf{C}_0 \varepsilon_t$:

$$e_t = \mathbf{C}_0 \varepsilon_t \equiv \mathbf{S} \varepsilon_t \text{ for every value of } t .$$

This means that the identification of $\mathbf{C}_0$ will allow us to identify and generate the series of ε_t. Then, because $\mathbf{\Omega} = ee' = (\mathbf{S}\varepsilon_t)(\mathbf{S}\varepsilon_t)' = \mathbf{S}\mathbf{I}\mathbf{S}'$, we obtain

$$\mathbf{C}_0 \mathbf{C}_0' = \mathbf{\Omega} \quad . \tag{8.4}$$

To identify $\mathbf{C}_0$ we need four restrictions because $\mathbf{C}_0$ contains four unknown elements. Combined with the assumption of orthogonality and unit variance of the structural shocks ε_t, equation (8.4) provides three restrictions. We need now only one additional restriction to exactly identify $\mathbf{C}_0$. To do this, we use economic theory.

In the Blanchard-Quah sense, the theoretical restriction is not imposed directly on the matrix $\mathbf{C}_0$. In fact, as the VAR system is estimated in first-difference form, the effects of a shock on the level of a variable in the long run is represented by the sum of all coefficients of the structural shocks with lags. If $\mathbf{C}_S$ refers to the matrix of these sums in the long run, we can say that $\mathbf{C}_S = \mathbf{C}_0 + \mathbf{C}_1 + \mathbf{C}_2 + ... + \mathbf{C}_k$, where k is the number of lags. If a shock j has no long-run effect on the level of a variable i (Blanchard and Quah's assumption), it means that $\mathbf{C}_S\{i,j\} = 0$. We, specifically, suppose that aggregate demand shocks do not have any impact on real GDP variation in the long run. This restriction implies $C_S\{1,2\} = 0.$[6]

In the Blanchard-Quah sense, C_S meets the following condition:

$$B_S \Omega B_S' = C_S C_S' \quad , \tag{8.5}$$

where B_S and Ω are both obtained in the reduced form of the VAR system. Let us now define a new lower triangular matrix H as the Choleski decomposition of $B_S \Omega B_S'$. As C_S is also a lower triangular matrix, resulting from the theoretical restriction, we can say that

$$C_S = H \quad . \tag{8.6}$$

And because equations (8.4), (8.5) and (8.6) imply that $B_S \Omega B_S' = B_S C_0 C_0' B_S' = C_S C_S' = HH'$, we have that $B_S C_0 = C_S = H$. Since B_S and H are known, we can write

$$C_0 = B_S^{-1} H \quad . \tag{8.7}$$

Once C_0 is identified in this way, the time series of macro-structural economic shocks (ε_{AS} and ε_{AD}) can be easily generated using their relationship with the series of residuals, i.e. $\varepsilon_t = C_0^{-1} e_t$.

2.3. Exchange Rate Fixity and Shock Symmetry Measured by Correlation Coefficients

When macro-structural economic shock series estimated for each country are examined, the similarity of economic conditions between two countries is represented by the symmetry of these shocks as measured by correlation coefficients. For example, a high AD shock correlation between China and the US will indicate that the two countries are experiencing symmetric AD shocks and that their demand-side economic conditions are 'sufficiently' similar to be compatible with a fixed exchange rate regime.

On the other hand, correlation coefficients between exchange rates can be used to characterise the exchange rate regime between two countries. In this chapter, we compute correlation coefficients between the euro-renminbi exchange rate and the euro-dollar rate for the China-US link, while the China-Eurozone link is examined by correlation between the dollar-renminbi rate and the dollar-euro rate. In other words, the fixity (or stability) of the dollar-renminbi (resp. euro-renminbi) exchange rate will be measured by correlation between their exchange rates vis-à-vis the euro (resp. the dollar) (as the most important third party currency).

It is important to note that, although both analyses (the China-US peg issue and the possible Chine-EMU peg alternative) use basically the same exchange rate information (only two out of the three possible bilateral exchange rates are logically independent), both analyses are performed independently.

Given that our series, especially the exchange rate series, do not follow a normal distribution, we use Spearman's rank-ordered correlation defined as $\rho = 1 - 6 \sum (d_i^2)/(n(n^2 - 1))$ where d_i represents the difference between two ranks of pair values of each variable examined, while n shows the number of observation pairs. The significance level is then tested by the t-statistic $t = \rho(n-2)^{0.5}/(1-\rho^2)^{0.5}$ which follows a Student distribution with $n - 2$ degrees of freedom, under the null hypothesis of zero correlation.

Furthermore, instead of estimating only one correlation coefficient covering the whole observation period, we use a sliding-window correlation approach in order to examine the evolution of shock symmetry and changes in foreign exchange rate policies. We obtain 28-quarter correlation coefficients, sliding quarter by quarter, from 1986Q1 to 2009Q4. Thus, the first correlation coefficient computed (labelled as 1992Q4) refers to the period from 1986Q1 to 1992Q4, while the last one (labelled as 2009Q4) the period from 2003Q1 to 2009Q4. This dynamic approach allows us to easily observe the evolution of both shock symmetry and exchange rate fixity.

2.4. Definition of the Exchange Rate Regime Mismatch Indicator

Once exchange rate fixity and shock symmetry have been measured by the correlation coefficients ρ_{FIX} (exchange rate fixity) and ρ_{SYM} (structural shock symmetry), we compute the exchange rate regime mismatch indicator μ defined as the difference between the two: $\mu = \rho_{FIX} - \rho_{SYM}$.

The indicator μ may have any value between −2 and 2, and shows the sign and degree of mismatch between exchange rate regime and economic conditions. For example, a positive (negative) value will indicate that exchange rate fixity or stability is more (less) pronounced than structural shock symmetry. However, it is important to note that by definition of the indicator, different combinations of exchange fixity and shock symmetry can yield a same value of the indicator. In order to distinguish between different situations, it may be interesting to use a 'fixity-symmetry point' that shows exact values of both exchange rate fixity and shock symmetry. Any combination point can be shown on a plane with exchange rate fixity on the vertical axis and shock symmetry on the horizontal axis. The bisector in such a plane represents a 'perfect match curve' joining together all perfectly balanced fixity-symmetry combinations.

In this framework, a higher absolute value of the indicator shows a stronger mismatch. We can then distinguish three categories of indicator value:

- A zero value means that exchange rate regime matches perfectly economic conditions. In this case, the fixity-symmetry point will be on the perfect match curve.
- A positive value means that nominal exchange rate fixity is excessive compared to macro-structural economic shock symmetry. In this case, the fixity-symmetry point will be on the upper-left side of the perfect match curve. Given economic conditions, exchange rate policies should then consist in reducing nominal fixity (changes toward a floating exchange rate system) in order to reinforce the efficiency of their exchange rate regime.
- A negative value means that nominal exchange rate fixity is less important than macro-structural economic shock symmetry. In this case, the fixity-symmetry point will be on the lower-right side of the perfect match curve. Given economic conditions, exchange rate policies should then consist in consolidating nominal exchange rate stability (changes toward a fixed exchange rate system) in order to reinforce the efficiency of their exchange rate regime.

3. WOULD CHINA ABANDON THE DOLLAR PEG?

China opened its economy to international markets in the early 1980s. At that time, the exchange rate was about 2 renminbi per dollar. Due to a progressive devaluation of its currency until the end of 1993, it began to achieve a significant economic growth. In January 1994, China suddenly adopted a hard dollar peg with a massive devaluation of the renminbi (1 USD = 8.27 CNY). Then, it maintained the hard dollar peg for more than a decade (January 1994-July 2005). After about three years of a closely controlled dollar-renminbi exchange rate system, China came back to the hard dollar peg since August 2008. China's primary motivation for such exchange rate policies is still, of course, to promote international trade (exports), the main engine of its economic growth. China seems to have successfully taken advantage of exchange rate stability and recorded a high growth for more than fifteen years.

But today, especially in this difficult world economic environment, does China's dollar standard fit its economic conditions? As mentioned before, there is no consensus on this issue. We try here to answer this question by applying the exchange rate regime mismatch approach to the China-US link. To this end, we estimate first AS and AD shock series relative to China and the US, using the SVAR model previously presented with quarterly data on real GDP and CPI for the period between 1986Q1 and 2009Q4.[7] Preliminary tests indicate that each of these variables is characterised as I(1) and are not co-integrated with each other. Figure 8A.1 in the appendix describes the estimated AS and AD shock series for China, the US and the Eurozone.

From these estimated series and using 28-quarter sliding-window correlation, we can measure China-US shock symmetry, the evolution of which is shown in Figure 8.1. According to the results, structural shocks were not symmetric between China and the US prior to 1994. But when China adopted the dollar peg in 1994, AS shock symmetry (which was even asymmetric with a negative value of ρ_{SYM}, around −0.12 for the period between 1988 and 1994) was quickly and significantly strengthened (around 0.48 for the period between 2003 and 2009). On the contrary, AS-shock symmetry (which was weakly symmetric with a limited positive value of ρ_{SYM}, around 0.13 in the period between 1988 and 1994) was not significantly toned up later on, which could be explained by lingering differences in terms of economic development (including, for example, a dissimilar level of production technology).

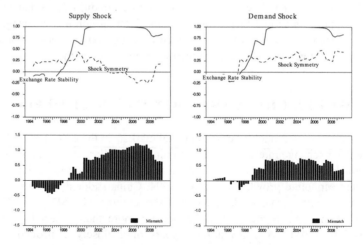

Note: As we use a 28-quarter correlation coefficient, the shock symmetry labelled as 1994Q4, for example, refers to the period from 1988Q1 to 1994Q4; Estimation in Rats v6.20. Data source: IFS-IMF.

Figure 8.1   Evolution of symmetry-fixity and mismatch indicator, China-US (1988-2009)

Regardless of AS shock asymmetry, our finding that demand shock symmetry rose sharply at the beginning of the dollar peg and increased progressively until 2006, is compatible with arguments based on the endogeneity theory proposed by Frankel and Rose (1998). That is, the fixed exchange rate regime contributes to the fulfilment of the prerequisite for its own adoption by increasing macro-structural economic shock symmetry between China and the US. Furthermore, as China effectively achieved its growth target during that period, mainly due to its exports boosted by exchange rate stability, the dollar-standard exchange rate policies were fully justified.

However, demand shock symmetry began to decline abruptly in 2006 despite the quasi-fixity of the dollar-renminbi exchange rate. In addition, supply shock symmetry, which had begun a downward turn already in the early 2000s, continued to decline until 2007. Even though the symmetry of those shocks has slightly increased since 2008 until recently, the dollar-renminbi exchange rate fixity is still too high. This result, combined of course with an excessive value of μ, does not support the current Chinese exchange rate arrangement.

In fact, even those arguments that could support the fixity of the dollar-renminbi exchange rate based on the endogeneity theory may not condone such a high value of the mismatch indicator shown during the last ten years (around 1 for the supply side and around 0.6 for the demand side). Furthermore, apart from the early period of the dollar standard (1994-2000), when the exchange rate fixity effectively strengthened both AS and AD shock symmetry, there was no 'endogenous' effect on macro-structural economic conditions. Between 2000 and 2009, supply shock symmetry even decreased significantly, while demand shock symmetry stagnated. In addition, it is important to note that during 2007-2009, both supply and demand shock symmetry were increasing while the exchange rate fixity was decreasing. These findings suggest that China's dollar-standard system is no longer suited to its macro-structural economic conditions.

But, even though this exchange rate regime mismatch is not an immediate problem for China, two key characteristics of its exchange rate regime (the exaggeratedly undervalued renminbi and its fixity vis-à-vis the dollar) are creating the exchange rate dilemma and the boomerang effects that China is facing today.

These underlying problems, combined with the dollar-standard system's pronounced mismatch, might lead China to make changes in its exchange rate policies, although the dilemma would possibly force China to put off the changes.

It is important to note that were China to make changes in its exchange rate regime, it would anyhow prefer to maintain a weak value of the renminbi as long as it continues to finance its economic growth by exports. In addition, given that the renminbi risks appreciating quickly under a floating exchange rate regime, China would like somehow to preserve exchange rate stability. In this sense, there is no immediate possibility that China would adopt a floating exchange rate regime. But there are some possible alternative systems that would allow China to maintain a weak value of the renminbi and preserve exchange rate stability.

4. A EURO PEG SYSTEM FOR CHINA?

If China abandoned the dollar peg system, which exchange rate regime would it adopt? As mentioned before, this country is likely to choose a system that would allow it to maintain a weak value of the renminbi under a fixed exchange rate system. There could be several types of alternative that could satisfy these conditions, including a euro peg system and an Asian currency union. We shall examine the first one here.

The European Union of 27 countries is the leading economic block in terms of economic size, greater than the US. In addition, the EU has already overtaken the US in trade with China.[8] Furthermore, the current euro-renminbi exchange rate (1 EUR = more than 9 CNY) is even more attractive than the dollar-renminbi exchange rate (1 USD = 8.27 CNY) at which China had fixed its currency to the dollar in 1994. These pragmatic aspects are likely to prompt China to seriously consider the possibility of adopting a euro peg system.

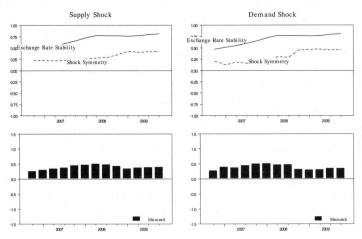

Note: As we use a 28-quarter correlation coefficient, the shock symmetry labelled as 2009Q4 for example stands for the period from 2003Q1 to 2009Q4. Estimation in Rats v6.20. Data source: IFS-IMF.

Figure 8.2   Evolution of symmetry-fixity and mismatch indicator, China-Eurozone (1999-2009)

In order to examine if such a system fits Chinese economic conditions, we can apply the mismatch approach to the China-eurozone link, using quarterly data on real GDP and CPI covering the period from 1999Q1 to 2009Q4 (data source: *International Financial Statistics*, IMF). Figure 8A.1 in the appendix describes the estimated AS-AD shock series. Figure 8.2 shows respectively the mismatch indicators and fixity-symmetry combinations. We find that both euro-renminbi exchange rate stability and structural shock symmetry are growing, while the mismatch indicator shows a positive value during the period examined, meaning that euro-renminbi exchange rate stability is greater than the shock symmetry between China and the eurozone. This result suggests that a euro peg system is at first sight not suited to the bilateral economic relationship between China and the eurozone.

However, compared to the China-US shock symmetry prior to 1994, this finding may not be that discouraging to China: despite a more pronounced shock asymmetry, China adopted the dollar peg system in 1994, which then increased shock symmetry and even justified the exchange rate fixity. Furthermore, if the limited stability of the euro-renminbi exchange rate, probably resulting from the fixity of the dollar-renminbi exchange rate, is followed even by a somewhat enhanced shock symmetry, a euro peg system would be likely to be consolidated through the endogeneity approach. In this sense, and as long as the fixed exchange rate system can be helpful to its economic growth, a euro peg system should not be an excluded, as an option for China.

In fact, even though our empirical results do not directly support the idea of a euro peg system for China, we consider that there is a possibility that China adopts it when abandoning the dollar peg system, possibly for the pragmatic reasons mentioned above (economic size, importance as a trade partner).

If ever China fixes the renminbi to the euro, for example at 1 EUR = 9 CNY, the eurozone or the EU would experience the same difficulties as the US: (1) Europe would record higher trade deficits; (2) the euro would appreciate excessively due to the upward trend of the renminbi combined with the downward trend of the dollar; (3) Europe would 'finance' Chinese growth through trade and investment. China would maintain this system until it could finance its own growth through domestic consumption.

5.   CONCLUSION

China is facing some boomerang effects and an exchange rate dilemma, both resulting from its dollar standard with a significantly undervalued renminbi. This situation is likely to lead China to make changes in its exchange rate policies. But this country would be able to abandon the dollar standard only if it found an alternative allowing it to preserve its exchange rate stability, combined with a weak value of renminbi. It seems that one of the most plausible alternative exchange rate systems for China is a euro peg system. All the conditions that China is likely to impose could be met by this alternative.

Within a macro-structural economic approach, we tried to determine in this paper if the dollar standard or a possible euro peg system would fit Chinese economic characteristics today. Our empirical results are in line with Frankel (2006), Roubini (2007) and Cline and Williamson (2008) suggesting that the Chinese dollar standard might no longer be consistent with its economic conditions, even in the light of endogeneity theory. On the other hand, our findings indicate that macro-structural shocks to China and the eurozone are not symmetric enough either to support at this stage a euro peg system for China.

But compared to the period when China adopted the dollar peg in 1994, the adoption of a euro peg system could be founded on the expected self-fulfilment process based on endogeneity theory. Furthermore, several pragmatic aspects seem to make a euro peg system more attractive to China: (1) Europe is the largest economic block in the world; (2) Europe is the leading trade partner of China; (3) the current value of the euro is higher than that of the dollar in 1994.

Despite all these attractive characteristics of a euro peg system for China, there is very little debate on this subject in the literature. China continues to confirm its preference for the dollar standard and promises only a very gradual change. But it is possible that what is officially announced differs from what China has in mind. The switch to a euro peg system could certainly be one of the options China might envisage. This possibility may explain the findings of Frankel (2009) that the renminbi basket had switched a substantial part of the dollar's weight onto the euro.

APPENDIX 8A

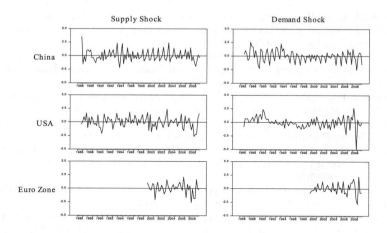

Note: Estimation in Rats v6.20. Data source: IFS-IMF.

Figure 8A .1 AS shocks and AD shocks to China, US and Eurozone (1986-2009)

NOTES

1. In 2009, Zhou Xiaochuan, China's central bank governor, said: 'the SDR serves as the light in the tunnel for the reform of the international monetary system [...] and the world should consider the SDR as a super-sovereign reserve currency.'
2. In a standard VAR system, economic theories are used only in choosing the variables to be included in the model. Furthermore, there is no explicit theoretical consideration in the ordering of the variables in the standard VAR approach, while the identification of the model and the results are quite sensitive to the ordering. This also makes any economic interpretation of the 'statistical' results problematic.
3. Cf. Sims (1986) and Bernanke (1986).
4. Cf. Blanchard and Quah (1989).
5. Cf. Galí (1992, 1999), Lastrapes (1992), Bayoumi and Eichengreen (1994, 1996), Clarida and Galí (1994), Lee and Chinn (1998), Rogers (1998), Corsetti et al. (2003), Lucas (2003), Mody and Taylor (2003), Buckle et al. (2007), Canova et al. (2007), Kano (2008), Zhang and Wan (2008), Voss and Willard (2009) and Forni and Gambetti (2010).
6. Note that AD shocks are not supposed to affect real GDP in the long run, but may have an impact in the short run. In other words, even though we suppose $C_S\{1,2\} = 0$, we may have $C_0\{1,2\} \neq 0$.
7. Data source: *International Financial Statistics*, IMF.
8. Chinese trade in 2008: exports to EU 20.5% + US 17.7%; imports from EU 11.7% + US 6%. (Source: WTO).

REFERENCES

Bayoumi, T. and B. Eichengreen (1994), 'One Money or Many? Analyzing the Prospects for Monetary Unification in Various Parts of the World', *Princeton Studies in International Finance*, no.76, pp.1-39.

Bayoumi, T. and B. Eichengreen (1996), 'Is Asia an Optimum Currency Area? Can it Become One? Regional, Global and Historical Perspectives on Asian Monetary Relations', *CIDER Working Papers*, no. C96-081.

Bernanke, B.S. (1986), 'Alternative Explanations of the Money-Income Correlation', *Carnegie-Rochester Conference Series on Public Policy*, **26**, 49-99.

Blanchard, O.J. and D. Quah (1989), 'The Dynamic Effects of Aggregate Demand and Supply Disturbances', *American Economic Review*, **79**, 655-73.

Buckle, R.A., K. Kim, H. Kirkham, N. McLellan and J. Sharma (2007), 'A Structural VAR Business Cycle Model for a Volatile Small Open Economy', *Economic Modelling*, **24**, 990-1017.

Canova, F., M. Ciccarelli and E. Ortega (2007), 'Similarities and Convergence in G-7 Cycles', *Journal of Monetary Economics*, **54**, 850-878.

Cheung, Y.W., M.D. Chinn and E. Fujii (2007), 'The Overvaluation of Renminbi Undervaluation', *Journal of International Money and Finance*, **26**, 762-785.

Clarida, R. and J. Galí (1994), 'Sources of Real Exchange Rate Fluctuations: How Important are Nominal Shocks?', *Carnegie-Rochester Conference Series on Public Policy*, **41**, 1-56.

Cline, W.R. and J. Williamson (2008), 'Estimates of the Equilibrium Exchange Rate of the Renminbi: Is There a Consensus and If Not, Why Not?', in M. Goldstein and N.R. Lardy (eds), *Debating China's Exchange Rate Policy*, Washington D.C.: Peterson Institute for International Economics, pp.131-168.

Corsetti, G., L. Dedola and S. Leduc (2003), 'International Risk-sharing and the Transmission of Productivity Shocks', *Federal Reserve Bank of Philadelphia Working Paper*, no. 03-19.

Coudert, V. and C. Couharde (2007), 'Real Equilibrium Exchange Rate in China: is the Renminbi Undervalued?', *Journal of Asian Economics*, **18**, 568-594.

Das, D.K. (2009), 'The Evolution of Renminbi Yuan and the Protracted Debate on its Undervaluation: an Integrated Review, *Journal of Asian Economics*, **20**, 570-579.

Forni, M. and L. Gambetti (2010), 'The Dynamic Effects of Monetary Policy: a Structural Factor Model Approach', *Journal of Monetary Economics*, **57**, 203-216.

Frankel, J.A. (2006), 'On the Renminbi: the Choice between Adjustment under a Fixed Exchange Rate and Adjustment under a Flexible Exchange Rate', *CESifo Economic Studies*, **52**, 246-275.

Frankel, J.A. (2009), 'New Estimation of China's Exchange Rate Regime', *NBER Working Paper*, no. 14700.

Frankel, J.A. and A.K. Rose (1998), 'The Endogeneity of the Optimum Currency Area Criteria', *Economic Journal*, **108**, 1009-1025.

Funke, M. and J. Rahn (2005), 'Just how Undervalued is the Chinese Renminbi?', *World Economy*, **28**, 465-489.

Galí, J. (1992), 'How well does the IS-LM Model Fit Post-war US Data?', *Quarterly Journal of Economics*, **107**, 709-738.

Galí, J. (1999), 'Technology, Employment, and the Business Cycle: do Technology Shocks Explain Aggregate Fluctuations?', *American Economic Review*, **89**, 249-71.

Goldstein, M. and N.R. Lardy (2008), 'China's Exchange Rate Policies: an Overview of some Key Issues', in M. Goldstein and N.S. Lardy (eds), *Debating China's Exchange Rate Policy*, Washington D.C.: Petersen Institute for International Economics, pp. 1-60.

Kano, T. (2008), 'A Structural VAR Approach to the Inter-temporal Model of the Current Account', *Journal of International Money and Finance*, **27**, 757-779.

Kaplan, S.B. (2006), 'The Political Obstacles to Greater Exchange Rate Flexibility in China', *World Development*, **34**, 1182-1200.

Kenen, P.B. (1969), 'The Theory of Optimum Currency Areas: an Eclectic View', in R.A. Mundell and A.K. Swoboda (eds), *Monetary Problems of the International Economy*, Chicago: University of Chicago Press, pp. 41-60.

Lastrapes, W.D. (1992), 'Sources of Fluctuations in Real and Nominal Exchange Rates', *Review of Economics and Statistics*, **74**, 530-539.

Lee, J.W. and M.D. Chinn (1998), 'The Current Account and the Real Exchange Rate: a Structural VAR Analysis of Major Currencies', *NBER Working Papers*, no. 6495.

Lucas, R.E. (2003), 'Macroeconomic Priorities', *American Economic Review*, **93**, 1-14.

McKinnon, R.I. (1963), 'Optimum Currency Areas', *American Economic Review*, **53**, 717-725.

McKinnon, R.I. (2007), 'Why China should Keep its Dollar Peg: a Historical Perspective from Japan', *International Finance*, **10**, 43-70.

McKinnon, R.I. and G. Schnabl (2004), 'The East Asian Dollar Standard, Fear of Floating, and Original Sin', *Review of Development Economics*, **8**, 331-360.

Mody, A. and M.P. Taylor (2003), 'The High-yield Spread as a Predictor of Real Economic Activity: Evidence of a Financial Accelerator for the United States', *IMF Staff Papers*, **50**, 373-402.

Mundell, R.A. (1961), 'A Theory of Optimum Currency Areas', *American Economic Review*, **51**, 657-665.

Rogers, J.H. (1998), 'Monetary Shocks and Real Exchange Rates', *FRB International Finance Discussion Papers*, no. 612.

Roubini, N. (2007), 'Why China Should Abandon its Dollar Peg', *International Finance*, **10**, 71-89.

Sims, C.A. (1986), 'Are Forecasting Models Usable for Policy Analysis?', *Quarterly Review*, **10**, 2-16.

Sun, H. and Y. Ma (2005), 'Policy Strategies to Deal with Revaluation Pressures on the Renminbi', *China Economic Review*, **16**, 103-117.

Voss, G.M. and L.B. Willard (2009), 'Monetary Policy and the Exchange Rate: Evidence from a Two-country Model', *Journal of Macroeconomics*, **31**, 708-720.

Wang, T. (2004), 'Exchange Rate Dynamics', in E. Prasad (ed.), *China's Growth and Integration into the World Economy*, IMF Occasional Paper No. 232, pp. 21-28.

Yajie, W. H. Xiaofeng H. and A.S. Soofi (2007), 'Estimating Renminbi (RMB) Equilibrium Exchange Rate', *Journal of Policy Modeling*, **29**, 417-429.

Zhang, Y. and G. Wan (2008), 'Correcting China's Trade Imbalance: Monetary Means will not Suffice', *Journal of Policy Modeling*, **30**, 505-521.

9. Inflexibilities and Trade Imbalances: Evidence from Europe

Helge Berger and Volker Nitsch

1. INTRODUCTION

Imbalances in bilateral trade relationships have recently become an issue of growing concern. For many countries, the difference between the value of shipments to and from a particular partner has risen sizably in recent years. More notably, large bilateral imbalances appear to increasingly dominate some countries' overall trade balance. For the United States, for example, the trade deficit with China has increased from virtually zero in 1985 to 227 bn US dollar in 2009, thereby accounting for about 45% of the overall trade deficit of the US of 501 bn US dollar.[1] Italy's trade deficit with Germany has risen by factor 5 within a decade; it now even exceeds the country's total trade deficit.[2]

While there is no economic reason to assume that a bilateral trade relationship should necessarily be balanced, the emergence of large and persistent trade imbalances is often interpreted as prima facie evidence of underlying rigidities or distortions. For example, protectionist measures can bias trade in favour of a particular country. Similarly, distortionary policies could delay a country's external adjustment to shocks. Also, fixed or managed exchange rates may slow corrections of the real exchange rate.[3]

In this chapter, we examine the association between inflexibilities and trade imbalances in more detail. More precisely, we compare the effects on trade of three types of rigidities: 1) a fixed nominal exchange rate, 2) inflexibilities on the labour market, and 3) rigidities on product markets. All these rigidities may have an effect on patterns of trade, both independently and jointly. For instance, the lack of an adjustable nominal exchange rate supposedly poses a particular problem within a currency union that also operates a single and unrestricted market for goods and services, such as the euro area. In this case, the permanently fixed nominal exchange rate forces real exchange rate adjustment through relative price levels alone, which can be difficult in the presence of rigidities in national goods and labour markets.

Following Berger and Nitsch (2010), we analyse the formation of the European Economic and Monetary Union as an experiment to study the effects of a currency union on trade imbalances. With the adoption of a common currency, 11 European countries irrevocably fixed their bilateral exchange rates on 1 January 1999. In addition, we use measures of employment protection legislation and product market regulation as proxies for inflexibilities on the labour and product markets. Our sample covers trade between a set of 18 European countries, some of which have adopted the euro as their common currency, over the period from 1985 to 2008.

Previewing our main results, we find that trade imbalances – measured as the fraction of deficits and surpluses in total bilateral trade – are indeed considerably larger for country pairs that face various types of rigidities. Moreover, since we also control for pairwise fixed effects, our analysis indicates that the larger imbalances are not (only) the result of enduring asymmetries in trade competitiveness between a given pair of countries.

The remainder of the chapter is organised as follows. Section 2 describes the empirical methodology and the data. Section 3 presents the results. Finally, we summarise our findings in a brief concluding section that also provides some policy conclusions.

2.   METHODOLOGY AND DATA

Our variable of interest is the bilateral trade balance between a reporter country r and a partner country p, defined as the difference between r's exports to p and r's imports from p in a given year t. To account for differences in the importance of a trade relationship, both across partners and over time, we normalise the trade surplus or deficit by the total value of bilateral trade:[4]

$$TradeBalance_{rpt} = (Exports_{rpt} - Imports_{rpt})/(Exports_{rpt} + Imports_{rpt})$$
$$(9.1)$$

Since we proxy for exchange rate stability by using dummy variables for the presence of a fixed exchange rate (e.g., euro area membership), we focus on the magnitude (not the sign) of the trade imbalance.[5] That is, we estimate variants of the regression

$$\left| TradeBalance_{rpt} \right| = \alpha + \beta_1 FEXR_{rpt} + \beta_2 EPL_{rpt} + \beta_3 PMR_{rpt}$$
$$\left\{ + \sum_t \phi_t T_t \right\}\left\{ + \sum_{rp} \phi_{rp} RP_{rp} \right\} + \varepsilon_{rpt} \quad , \qquad (9.2)$$

where the regressand is the absolute value of the normalised trade balance, *FEXR* is a dummy variable that takes the value of one if there was no change in the nominal exchange rate (e.g., because both trade partners are members of the euro area) and zero otherwise, *EPL* is the average level of employment protection in both countries, *PMR* is the average level of product market regulation, and ε is the disturbance term. We also include various combinations of fixed effects. In our baseline specification, we use common time fixed effects {*T*} to control for joint variations in trade imbalances over time. We also allow pair-wise imbalances to consistently deviate from the sample average by adding pair-specific fixed effects {*RP*}.

In line with previous work on the effects of EMU on trade (Berger and Nitsch, 2008), our analysis focuses on a homogeneous set of 18 European countries. The approach has the advantage of including countries that either share the European Union's institutional framework or are closely associated with it. The sample comprises the 15 countries that were member of the EU at the time of the introduction of the euro (eleven of which adopted the currency from the beginning, followed by Greece in 2001), plus Iceland, Norway and Switzerland. We analyse the period from 1985 to 2008.

Our key source of data is the International Monetary Fund's *Direction of Trade Statistics* from which we obtained nominal values of bilateral exports and imports on an annual basis. Since country *r*'s trade balance with *p* is typically not identical to *p*'s inversely-signed trade balance with *r* (e.g., because of different statistical valuation methods for exports and imports), we analyse the full sample of bilateral imbalances.[6] Our trade data set is augmented with a set of institutional variables. The data are taken from the OECD, which aggregates detailed indicators that proxy the intensity of various aspects of product and labour market regulation into summary indicators of strictness of regulations, with larger values implying less flexibility. These indicators are consistent across time and countries.[7] Variables and sources are described in detail in the appendix.

Figure 9.1 graphs the evolution of absolute trade imbalances in our sample over time. Two observations stand out. First, the sample average trade imbalance consistently exceeds the median imbalance, indicating that the distribution could be dominated by a few disproportionately large imbalances between country pairs. Indeed, some bilateral trade relationships are characterised by one-directional trade flows and, thus, high imbalances, especially for small countries (such as Iceland, Ireland, and Greece).[8] Second, median and mean imbalances display an increase in imbalances since the mid-1990s. Taken at face value, this pattern is consistent with the hypothesis that a fixed exchange rate regime is associated with larger trade imbalances.

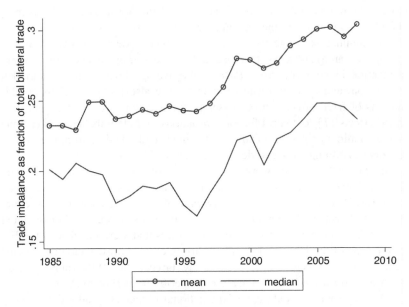

Notes: The figure graphs the absolute difference between a country's exports and imports
with a partner as a fraction of total bilateral trade (exports plus imports) for a sample
of 18 European countries. Data are taken from the IMF's Direction of Trade
Statistics.

Figure 9.1   Bilateral trade imbalances over time

To analyse this issue in more detail, Figure 9.2 shows the trade balances of
various groups of countries over the same period. Specifically, we distinguish
between trade relationships for which exchange rates were fixed with the
introduction of the euro (intra-EMU trade) and trade pairs for which nominal
exchange rates remained flexible (i.e., trade between EMU countries and
non-members, as well as trade between non-members). Interestingly, the
finding of growing imbalances applies most strongly to trade between EMU
member countries, while trade between non-members displays no clear tendency over time. Trade imbalances between EMU member countries and
non-members show a similar but less pronounced increase. A possible explanation is that the external value of the euro, while flexible for the euro area as
a whole, cannot adjust to individual (and possibly opposing) member country
needs.

Figure 9.3 contains corroborating graphical evidence for this hypothesis.
The figure plots, separately for each EMU member country, the difference
between the largest bilateral trade surplus and deficit with a non-member in
our sample. For most countries, the spread between the most positive and the

most negative trade imbalance has indeed been increasing over the last few years, possibly reflecting a growing divergence in trade competitiveness.

Finally, we examine the relationship between market flexibility and the trade balance – a link emphasised by Blanchard (2007) and others. Figure 9.4 is a set of scatter plots of the trade balance against both cross-country differences in employment protection and product market regulation for individual years, covering the period of available data. The graphs clearly illustrate that higher relative levels of labour or product market flexibility are associated with higher bilateral trade surpluses (or lower deficits). Also, the association has apparently become stronger over time, especially for country pairs in which both partner countries adopted the euro (marked with a filled circle).

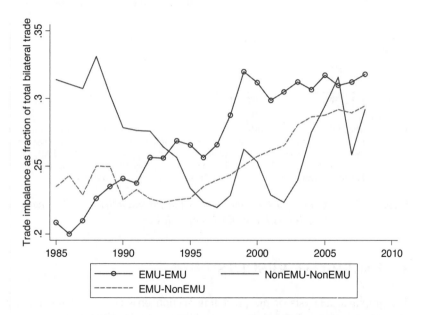

Notes: The figure graphs the average absolute difference between a country's exports and imports with a partner as a fraction of total bilateral trade (exports plus imports) for various groups of country pairs. Data are taken from the IMF's Direction of Trade Statistics.

Figure 9.2   Bilateral trade imbalances by group of country pairs

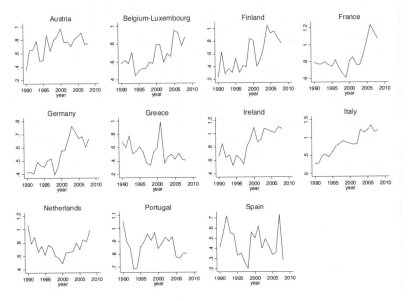

Notes: The figure graphs the difference between the maximum and the minimum trade imbalance (defined as a country's exports and imports with a partner as a fraction of total bilateral trade) of the EMU member country with one of the six non-EMU members in the sample (Denmark, Iceland, Norway, Sweden, Switzerland, the United Kingdom). Data are taken from the IMF's *Direction of Trade Statistics*.

Figure 9.3   Spread of trade imbalances (surplus/deficit) of EMU member countries with non-EMU countries

3.   EMPIRICAL RESULTS

The graphical analysis of the preceding section provides an interesting and illustrative picture of the dynamics in bilateral trade imbalances after currency union formation. We now test for the effect of inflexibilities on trade imbalances more formally. We begin with a specification in which the indicators for the presence of a certain type of inflexibility enter the regression separately as explanatory variable.

Table 9.1 presents results. The first four columns on the left of the table tabulate estimation results for the most parsimonious specification of equation (9.2), a regression of the absolute value of bilateral trade imbalances on the restrictiveness measure of interest and a comprehensive set of year fixed effects.

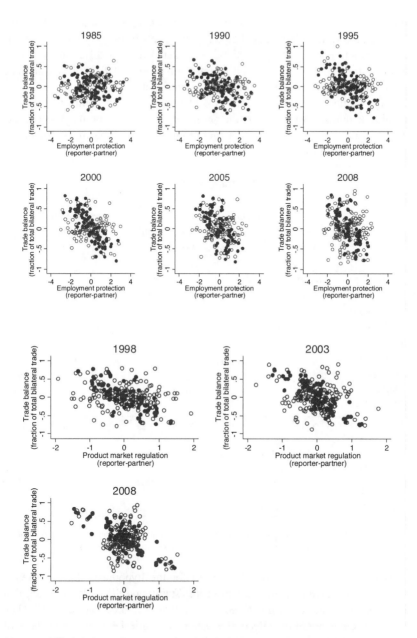

Note: Filled circles mark country pairs where both partners are/become EMU members.

Figure 9.4   Trade imbalances and regulation: employment protection and product market regulation

As shown, the results strongly confirm the association between EMU membership and trade imbalances. The estimated β coefficient on the EMU variable is positive and, with a t-statistic of 2.1, significantly different from zero at the 5 percent level. The point estimate of about 0.018 implies that trade imbalances between euro area member countries are on average about 2 percentage points larger than for the rest of the sample. In contrast, when we include a dummy variable for the presence of a fixed (or unchanged) exchange rate other than euro area membership, the estimated coefficient is negative and significant.

Table 9.1　　*Inflexibilities and trade imbalances*

	Plain OLS				Pair-wise fixed effects			
	1985-2008	1985-2008	1985-2008	1998, 2003, 2008	1985-2008	1985-2008	1985-2008	1998, 2003, 2008
EMU	0.018				0.027			
	(0.009)				(0.005)			
Other fixed exchange rate		-0.057				0.008		
		(0.018)				(0.009)		
Employment protection			0.035				-0.001	
			(0.004)				(0.007)	
Product market regulation				0.222				0.093
				(0.026)				(0.031)
Common time fixed effects?	Yes	Yes	Yes	Yes	Yes	Yes	Yes	Yes
Pair-wise fixed effects?	No	No	No	No	Yes	Yes	Yes	Yes
Number of observations	6518	6256	6472	816	6518	6256	6472	816
Adj. R^2	0.01	0.01	0.02	0.09	0.74	0.73	0.74	0.83

Note:　　OLS regression. Dependent variable is the absolute trade imbalance as a fraction of total bilateral trade. Robust standard errors are reported in parentheses.

This finding appears to provide support for the hypothesis that a currency union is fundamentally different from just stabilising the exchange rate; that is, a currency union is a much more restrictive exchange rate regime.[9] Also, the coefficient possibly reflects the pattern of trade between some pairs of highly integrated economies with small imbalances and stable exchange rates (e.g., the former DM bloc). Analysing a much longer sample period, Berger and Nitsch (2010) find a positive effect of exchange rate stability on trade imbalances. The next two columns report the estimation results for inflexibilities on the national labour and product markets. In each case, the coefficient is significantly positive, indicating that country pairs with more rigid markets experience larger trade imbalances. Given our very crude measure for the presence of inflexibilities (by simply averaging the restrictiveness measures for the reporter and the partner country in a given year), we consider these results as particularly encouraging.

The final four columns of Table 9.1 seek to further generalise these results. The columns present analogous estimates for specifications in which we add a comprehensive set of pair-wise fixed effects. With this extension, we control for any pair-wise specific differences in trade imbalances over the sample period so that the coefficient on the restrictiveness measure now captures only the time variation in imbalances. For EMU membership, the estimated coefficient not only remains positive and significant, but increases considerably in magnitude to 0.027. This suggests that euro area member countries have experienced an increase in their bilateral trade imbalances with other euro area members by an average of about 3 percentage points since the adoption of the common currency, which appears large compared to a sample mean of about 0.3. For other measures of inflexibilities, the results become considerably weaker with this extension. The β-coefficients for the measures of exchange rate stability and employment protection legislation both lose significance completely and even change signs. As a result, the baseline estimates for these indicators were apparently driven by persistent differences in the variable of interest and the trade imbalance across country pairs. The estimated coefficient on product market regulation falls in magnitude, but remains different from zero at any conventional measure of statistical significance.

We now compare the effect of various types of inflexibilities by sequentially adding the restrictiveness measures to our regression. Table 9.2 presents the results. Again, we tabulate results for two different estimators. The upper panel contains estimates using simple ordinary least squares (OLS); the lower panel applies a panel fixed effects estimator.

Column 1 of Table 9.2 basically confirms our previous findings. The effect of EMU membership on trade imbalances is significantly positive, while the analogue for other situations of an unchanged exchange rate is significantly negative. For both coefficients, the estimates are almost similar in magnitude and significance to their independent effect reported in Table 9.1. In column 2, we add our measure of employment protection. Again confirming previous findings, the estimated coefficient on this indicator takes a significantly positive sign, suggesting that countries with more rigid labor markets face larger trade imbalances.

With this extension, however, the effect of EMU membership becomes economically and statistically small. Finally, we add our measure of product market regulation. This effect clearly appears to dominate all other effects of inflexibilities. The coefficient is not only significantly positive and economically large; also, all other coefficients lose significance. Part of the explanation may be different sample sizes. Since the product market measure is only available for three years (1998, 2003, 2008), the number of observations for regressions where this measure is included is considerably smaller. The remainder of the table shows, however, that our previous estimation results remain essentially unchanged when the smaller subsample is analysed. In sum, product market regulation wins the horse race of the effect inflexibilities on trade imbalances.

Table 9.2   Inflexibilities and trade imbalances: plain OLS

	1985-2008	1985-2008	1998, 2003, 2008	1998, 2003, 2008	1998, 2003, 2008	1998, 2003, 2008
EMU	0.020	0.005	-0.011	0.010	0.032	0.032
	(0.009)	(0.009)	(0.020)	(0.021)	(0.020)	(0.020)
Other fixed exchange rate	-0.056	-0.064	-0.015	-0.054	-0.041	
	(0.018)	(0.017)	(0.044)	(0.041)	(0.036)	
Employment protection		0.033	-0.016	0.047		
		(0.004)	(0.018)	(0.015)		
Product market regulation			0.245			
			(0.032)			
Number of observations	6256	6212	812	812	816	816
Adj. R^2	0.01	0.03	0.09	0.02	0.01	0.01

Note: OLS regression. Dependent variable is the absolute trade imbalance as a fraction of total bilateral trade. Robust standard errors are reported in parentheses. Year fixed effects are included but not reported.

Table 9.3 shows that this finding is robust to a perturbation that applies a pair-wise fixed effects estimator. As before, the effect of employment protection legislation on trade imbalances is insignificant as soon as we control for average differences in trade imbalances over the sample period. Similarly, the estimated EMU effect turns out to be generally stronger for this specification, except for the sub-sample for which data on product market regulation is available. Most notably, however, product market regulation keeps its strong and statistically significant effect on trade imbalances. There is a consistent finding that countries with rigid product markets display on average larger trade imbalances.

Table 9.3   Inflexibilities and trade imbalances: pair-wise fixed effects

Period	1985-2008	1985-2008	1998, 2003, 2008	1998, 2003, 2008	1998, 2003, 2008	1998, 2003, 2008
EMU	0.026	0.025	-0.014	-0.024	-0.015	-0.015
	(0.006)	(0.006)	(0.016)	(0.015)	(0.015)	(0.015)
Other fixed	0.011	0.011	0.005	0.005	0.002	
exchange rate	(0.009)	(0.009)	(0.027)	(0.026)	(0.026)	
Employment		-0.001	-0.039	-0.044		
Protection		(0.007)	(0.021)	(0.021)		
Product market			0.087			
regulation			(0.033)			
Number of observations	6256	6212	812	812	816	816
Adj. R^2	0.73	0.74	0.83	0.83	0.82	0.82

Note: OLS regression. Dependent variable is the absolute trade imbalance as a fraction of total bilateral trade. Robust standard errors are reported in parentheses. Year and pair-wise fixed effects are included but not reported.

4.   CONCLUSION

Although bilateral trade relationships need not necessarily be balanced, the emergence of large and persistent trade imbalances between a pair of countries may reflect underlying policy tensions or rigidities. In this chapter, we add to evidence that shows that imbalances in trade among euro area member countries have indeed widened markedly after the introduction of the common currency (Berger and Nitsch, 2010). In addition to possible distortions introduced by a fixed exchange rate, we examine the effects of other inflexibilities on trade imbalances, both independently and jointly. Applying very crude pair-wise measures to capture regulation of adjustment, we find that policy and market institutions affect external balances. Countries with relatively less flexible labour and product markets tend to display larger trade imbalances. Moreover, the effect of product market regulation on trade imbalances dominates that of other rigidities, including the effect of euro area membership on trade imbalances.

Our findings imply both bad and good news for policymakers. The bad news is that irrevocably fixed nominal exchange rates do come at the cost of larger and more permanent trade imbalances. The good news is that these imbalances are not completely unavoidable. With a fixed exchange rate, trade imbalances are all the smaller and their adjustment to shocks all the faster, the more flexible the national labour and product markets are.

APPENDIX 9A

Table 9A.1   Data Description

Variable	Description	Source	Period
Trade balance	(Exports–Imports) / (Exports+Imports)	IMF, *Direction of Trade Statist- ics*	1985-2008
EMU	Dummy for common membership in euro area (time-variant)		1985-2008
Other fixed ex- change rate	Dummy for exchange rate volatility < 0.1 in a given year		1985-2008
Employment protection	Strictness of employment protection	OECD	1985-2008
Product market regulation	Product market regulation	OECD	1998, 2003, 2008

NOTES

1. The figures are taken from the U.S. Census Bureau (http://www.census.gov/foreign-trade/balance).
2. See Eurostat's *External and Intra-EU Trade: A Statistical Yearbook*; the publication is available at http://epp.eurostat.ec.europa.eu/cache/ITY_OFFPUB/KS-GI-10-001/EN/KS-GI-10-001-EN.PDF . Italy's trade deficit with Germany has increased from 2.7 bn euro in 1999 to 13.7 bn euro in 2008, when Italy reported an overall deficit of 11.5 bn euro.
3. In the United States, the trade deficit with China is widely attributed to the Chinese policy of pegging its currency to the US dollar. Within the European Monetary Union (EMU), it is frequently claimed that, with fixed exchange rates, differences in national economic policies have a direct effect on trade patterns.
4. Given our interest in the symmetry of trade relations, normalising by total trade is the natural choice (rather than, for instance, normalising by country size). Larger magnitudes of the variable of interest indicate greater imbalances in bilateral trade.
5. In principle, we could also use a measure of bilateral exchange rate variability (such as the standard deviation of monthly exchange rate changes). It is unclear, however, whether the effect of flexible exchange rate flexibility on trade is linear. While moderate adjustments may help lowering imbalances, large exchange rate fluctuations may be associated with greater imbalances.
6. Restricting the sample to only one observation per country pair requires a decision on which observation to analyse and which to ignore. In our sensitivity analysis, we experimented with a number of approaches and found most results to be reasonably robust. For example, including only one observation per country pair while dropping any observations where pair-wise balances differ by more than 10 percentage points between the two reporting countries delivers results quite similar to those tabulated below.

7. The indices range from 0 (least restrictions) to 6 (most restrictions). The data are described in detail at http://www.oecd.org/document/36/0,3343,en_2649_34323_35790244_1_1_1_1,00. html.
8. The introduction of fixed country-pair effects will limit the possible effect of outliers on our econometric results below.
9. See, for instance, Rose (2000).

REFERENCES

Berger, H. and V. Nitsch (2008), 'Zooming Out: The Trade Effect of the Euro in Historical Perspective', *Journal of International Money and Finance*, **27**, 1244-1260.

Berger, H. and V. Nitsch (2010), 'The Euro's Effect on Trade Imbalances', *IMF Working Paper*, 10/226.

Blanchard, O. (2007), 'Current Account Deficits in Rich Countries', *NBER Working Paper*, 12925.

Rose, A.K. (2000), 'One Money, One Market: The Effect of Common Currencies on Trade', *Economic Policy*, **30**, 7-45.

10. Global Imbalance, Excess Liquidity and Financial Risk in China

Zongxin Qian

1. INTRODUCTION

As a manifestation of global economic imbalance, China has accumulated huge international reserves. At the end of 2001, China's total foreign reserve was only 212.165 billion USD. By the third quarter of 2009, this number had increased to 2.27 trillion USD. The accumulation of foreign reserves has had a significant effect on China's money supply. Two recent papers (Zhang and Pang, 2008; Zhang, 2009) argue that the accumulation of international reserves has created excess liquidity in China. Furthermore, they argue that this excess liquidity has been driving China's CPI inflation since 1998. In this chapter, we argue that their empirical results are questionable. Excess liquidity created by excessive accumulation of international reserves has not significantly affected China's CPI inflation dynamics. However, it has significant effects on China's financial markets and imposes a noteworthy financial risk to the Chinese economy. The CCER Macro Group of Peking University (2008) finds that excess liquidity has a significant effect on China's stock market price. As a complementary study, in this chapter we therefore focus on the relationship between excess liquidity and boom-bust cycles in China's real estate market. This is particularly important for financial stability in China as the development of the real estate market depends heavily on external finance.[1]

We proceed as follows: section 2 re-evaluates the effect of excess liquidity on China's CPI inflation rate. Section 3 investigates the effect of excess liquidity on the boom-bust cycles in the real estate market. Section 4 discusses the potential financial risk created by the excess liquidity-real estate cycle correlation. Section 5 concludes.

2.   EXCESS LIQUIDITY AND CHINA'S CPI INFLATION RATE

2.1. The Empirical Results of Zhang and Pang (2008) and Zhang (2009)

Zhang and Pang (2008) and Zhang (2009) measure excess liquidity by means of the following definition of this concept:

$$excess_t = \frac{M2_t}{NGDP_t + NGDP_{t-1} + NGDP_{t-2} + NGDP_{t-3}}$$

where $M2_t$ is the broad money aggregate, $NGDP_t$ is the quarterly nominal GDP level. Their test equation is:

$$\pi_t = \beta_0 + \beta_1 \pi_{t-1} + \beta_2 excess_t + u_t \quad , \tag{10.1}$$

where π_t is the CPI inflation rate, u_t is a serially uncorrelated error term. The estimation results from equation (10.1) by those authors reveal that excess liquidity has significantly increased China's inflation rate over the period 1998-2007. There is, however, some doubt on the validity of this result.

Recent literature shows that the inflation rate is an I(0) variable (Culver and Papell, 1997; Basher and Westerlund, 2008). Hence *excess* should also be an I(0) variable for equation (10.1) to be balanced. By definition *excess* is the ratio of money supply to nominal GDP. Since both money supply and nominal GDP are usually I(1) variables, *excess* will be an I(0) variable only when money supply and nominal GDP are co-integrated. However, there is no guarantee that this is true. We will put this to statistical tests in section 2.2.3. In this subsection, we discuss the theoretical possibility that equation (10.1) is not valid in a deeper sense.

Let us assume that in the long run there is no excess liquidity and the following quantity theory of money holds: $M/Py = k$. Define excess liquidity as the deviation of M/Py from its long-run level k. Hence the variable *excess* defined by Zhang and Pang (2008) and Zhang (2009) would better be called liquidity, rather than excess liquidity. The variables *excess* and $excess_t - k$ are perfectly and positively correlated in the special case that k is a constant. *excess* can in that case be used as the measure of excess liquidity and equation (10.1) is valid. However, if k is a non-stationary stochastic process, *excess* will also be non-stationary and equation (10.1) will be unbalanced.

Given the assumption that $excess_t \equiv M_t / P_t y_t = k_t$ in the long run, we now have that $excessgr_t = g_k$ (where *excessgr* is the growth rate of M/Py and g_k is the growth rate of k), is an alternative measure of excess liquidity since liquidity will deviate from its long-run level whenever $excessgr = g_k \neq 0$. Because *excessgr* can be stationary even when *excess* is not, we may replace *excess* by *excessgr* in equation (10.1) and re-estimate the model.

2.2. Robustness of Zhang and Pang's (2008) and Zhang's (2009) Empirical Results

2.2.1. A measure of China's CPI inflation rate

The Chinese statistics authority publishes two versions of monthly CPI index: one sets price level in the same month of last year equal to 100 (let's denote it by CPI1), the other sets price level in the last month equal to 100 (we denote it by CPI2). Zhang and Pang (2008) and Zhang (2009) used CPI1 to construct a measure of China's quarterly inflation rate. The problem of using such a measure is that it will overestimate inflation persistence in equation (10.1). The reason is that the CPI1 index of two consecutive periods contains price information of overlapping periods. For example, CPI1 of the second quarter of 1998 contains price information from the second quarter of 1997 to the second quarter of 1998 while CPI1 of the first quarter of 1998 contains price information from the first quarter of 1997 to the first quarter of 1998. There are overlapping price information for three quarters. Therefore even if there is no inflation persistence, using CPI1 to measure the inflation rate will find inflation persistence in equation (10.1). When the estimate of inflation persistence is biased, the estimate of our parameter of interest β will also be biased.

To avoid this problem we propose another way to measure the inflation rate in China. We first construct a CPI index from CPI2. The Chinese statistics authority provides CPI2 growth rate data from February 1995, and CPI2 level data from January 2001. Based on these data, we can calculate a CPI index with the price level of January 1995 equal to 100. Then we interpret the CPI index of the last month of each quarter as the price index of that quarter. The price index obtained is seasonally unadjusted. We use the Census X12 method to filter out the seasonal changes and so get the seasonally adjusted index P_t. Using the traditional definition of inflation in the literature ($\pi_t = \log P_t - \log P_{t-1}$), we finally get the quarterly inflation rates of China.

Figure 10.1 shows the time path of China's quarterly inflation rate based on our calculation. It successfully captures the major inflation peaks (1994Q1 and Q3, 2003Q4 and 2008Q1) since the start of China's price liberalisation reform (around 1992). It also captures the deflation periods after the Asian financial crisis.

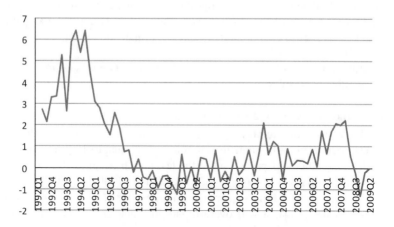

*Figure 10.1   China's quarterly CPI inflation rate, 1992Q1-2009Q2
(in percent)*

2.2.2. Re-estimated results for equation (10.1)

In this subsection, we re-estimate equation (10.1) with our new quarterly inflation rate data.[2] Following Zhang and Pang (2008) and Zhang (2009), we use the IFS data for M2 and NGDP to construct their measure of excess liquidity. Since the NGDP data in the current IFS database starts from the first quarter of 1999, our sample period is slightly different from those two previous studies. More specifically, our sample covers the period from the first quarter of 1999 to the second quarter of 2009.

Table 10.1   Estimation results for equation (10.1)

	π_{t-1}	$\Delta\pi_{t-1}$	$excess_t$	$const.$	$\overline{R}^2$	P_{auto}
Coefficient	0.603***	-0.360**	0.021*	-0.032*	0.261	0.487
(S.E.)	(0.167)	(0.144)	(0.011)	(0.018)		

Note: ***, **, * denote significance levels at 1%, 5%, 10% level respectively. P_{auto} denotes the P-value of the LM autocorrelation test up to two lags.

Table 10.1 summarises the estimation results. The qualitative results are similar to previous studies. Consistent with Zhang and Pang (2008) and Zhang (2009), we find that 'excess liquidity' has a significantly positive effect on China's inflation rate, though the significance level is now lower than the level found in those previous studies. A notable difference is that, because CPI1 contains overlapping price change information in two consecutive periods, our estimate for inflation persistence is lower than in the previous studies, which confirms our argument that using CPI1 to measure inflation will overestimate inflation persistence.

2.2.3. The potential problem with equation (10.1)

In section 2.1 we argued that if *excess* is not an I(0) variable, equation (10.1) may not be balanced. In this subsection, we put this to a formal test. Table 10.2 summarises the unit root tests results of π and *excess*.

Table 10.2   Unit root tests

	π		*excess* (no deterministic trend)		*excess* (with deterministic trend)	
	ADF test	Phillips-Perron test	ADF test	Phillips-Perron test	ADF test	Phillips-Perron test
Test Statistics	-2.340	-4.246	-2.342	-1.723	-2.414	-1.756
1% Critical Value	-3.610	-3.610	-3.621	-3.615	-4.227	-4.219
5% Critical Value	-2.939	-2.939	-2.943	-2.941	-3.537	-3.533
10% Critical Value	-2.608	-2.608	-2.610	-2.609	-3.200	-3.198

Note: Lag orders in the ADF tests are chosen by means of the Schwartz Information Criterion.

We follow the literature (Culver and Papell, 1997; Basher and Westerlund, 2008) and assume there is no deterministic trend but a constant in the test equation for inflation. Since it is difficult to see whether there is a deterministic trend in *excess*, we report test results with and without deterministic trend in the test equation.

Both ADF and Phillips-Perron tests fail to reject the unit root hypothesis of excess, which suggests it is an I(1) variable. Although the ADF test fails to reject the unit root hypothesis of the inflation rate, the Phillips-Perron test rejects the unit root hypothesis of inflation rate at the 1% level. Considering the limited power of unit root tests in small samples, the rejection of the unit root hypothesis of inflation rate by the Phillips-Perron test suggests that inflation rate is actually an I(0) variable in this period. When π is an I(0) variable and excess is an I(1) variable, equation (10.1) is not balanced. One way to fix this problem is by replacing excess by its growth rate in equation (10.1). Following our discussion in section 2.1, this is also desirable from a theoretical point of view. Table 10.3 presents the regression results with excess liquidity growth.

Table 10.3   *Estimation results of the model for inflation and excess liquidity growth*

	π_{t-1}	$\Delta\pi_{t-1}$	$excessgr_t$	const.	$\overline{R}^2$	P_{auto}
Coefficient	0.661***	-0.333*	0.036	0.001	0.171	0.481
(S.E.)	(0.238)	(0.176)	(0.062)	(0.002)		

Note: ***, **, * denote significance at 1%, 5%, 10% level respectively. P_{auto} denotes the P value of the LM autocorrelation test up to two lags. *excessgr_t* denotes the growth rate of *excess_t*.

The results in Table 10.3 suggest that excess liquidity growth has no significant effect on China's inflation rate. This reveals that the key finding by Zhang and Pang (2008) and Zhang (2009) is indeed questionable.

Another way to look at this is to test whether there is a co-integration relation between China's price level and the level of excess liquidity. Table 10.4 summarises the co-integration test results based on a bivariate VAR of P_t and *excess_t*. Both trace and maximum eigenvalue tests find no co-integration between the two variables. This again suggests that excess liquidity is not the key driving force of China's inflation dynamics.

Table 10.4   *Co-integration tests for CPI and the excess liquidity measure*

	Rank Test	Maximum Eigenvalue Test
Test Statistics	9.709	8.285
5% Critical Value	15.494	14.264

Note: Lag order of the VAR is selected as 1 according to the Schwartz Information Criterion. We include a constant term in the test VAR because there is an obvious time trend in the data.

3.   EXCESS LIQUIDITY, BOOM-BUST CYCLES IN THE REAL ESTATE MARKET AND FINANCIAL RISK

3.1.   The Measurement of Boom-Bust Cycles in the Real Estate Market

The Chinese Statistics Authority publishes each month the 'national real estate climate index' (denoted by *rs_sum*). It is a composite measure of the development in the Chinese real estate market in the form of a weighted average of six disaggregated indices: an investment index of real estate development (*rs_invest*), an index of capital source (*rs_finance*), of land space development (*rs_land*), of floor space of buildings under construction (*rs_construct*), of vacant floor space of commercial buildings (*rs_vacant*), and a sale price index of houses (*rs_price*). All these indices are seasonally adjusted. Price adjustments are also applied to reveal real changes. We adopt *rs_sum* as our aggregate measure of boom-bust cycles in the real estate market.

The Chinese Statistics Authority also publishes a quarterly 'climate index of real estate enterprises' (*rs_enterprise*). This index reflects the business status of the real estate enterprises. It is made according to the surveyed judgments and expectations of real estate entrepreneurs. We take this as an alternative measure of boom-bust cycles in the real estate market.

3.2. Excess Liquidity and Aggregate Measures of Boom-Bust Cycles in the Real Estate Market

As we have indicated already, the real estate sector in China is highly leveraged, so it is natural to expect that its boom-bust cycles are closely related to the changes in the money supply. In this subsection, we investigate the relationship between excess liquidity and aggregate measures of boom-bust cycles in the Chinese real estate market. Table 10.5 presents the regression results of the growth rate of our two measures of boom-bust cycles in the real estate market on the lagged excess liquidity measure. It is revealed that changes in excess liquidity are positively correlated to real estate market development and that this correlation is significant.

Table 10.5   Excess liquidity and the real estate market: aggregate single equation regressions

Dependent variable	rs_sumgr_t	$rs\_enterprisegr_t$
$excessgr_{t-1}$	0.236***	0.918*
	(0.069)	(0.545)
Const	-0.002	-0.002
	(0.003)	(0.010)
$\overline{R}^2$	0.174	0.206

Note: ***, **, * denote significance at 1%, 5%, 10% level respectively. HAC standard errors are in parentheses. *rs_sumgr*, *rs_enterprisegr* and *excessgr* denote the growth rate of the corresponding variables in levels. The sample span prior to lag adjustment is 2000Q1-2009Q2.

In order to control for a potential endogeneity bias, we also estimate two bivariate VARs between the growth rate of excess liquidity and the growth rate of the measure of boom-bust cycles in the real estate market. The results are summarised in Table 10.6.[3] These results confirm the finding of the single equation regressions that excess liquidity is significantly correlated to the development of the real estate market.

Table 10.6   Excess liquidity and the real estate market: aggregate VAR analysis

VAR($rs\_sumgr, excessgr$)

$$rs\_sumgr_t = -0.001 + 0.448 \; rs\_sumgr_{t-1} + 0.243 \; excessgr_{t-1}$$
$$\quad\quad\quad (0.002) \quad (0.138^{***}) \quad\quad\quad\quad\quad (0.071^{***})$$

$$\overline{R}^2 = 0.351$$

VAR($rs\_enterprisegr, excessgr$)

$$rs\_enterprisegr_t = -0.002 + 0.136 \, rs\_enterprisegr_{t-1} + 0.901 \; excessgr_{t-1}$$
$$\quad\quad\quad\quad (0.0008) \quad (0.178) \quad\quad\quad\quad\quad\quad\quad (0.288^{***})$$

$$\overline{R}^2 = 0.196$$

Note: Standard errors are in parentheses. ***, **, * denote significance at 1%, 5%, 10% levels respectively. *rs_sumgr*, *rs_enterprisegr* and *excessgr* denote the growth rates of the corresponding variables in levels. Lag orders of the VARs are selected according to the Schwartz Information Criterion.

3.3. Excess Liquidity and Disaggregate Measures of Boom-Bust Cycles in the Real Estate Market

The analysis in the previous subsection focuses on aggregate measures of boom-bust cycles in the real estate market. In this subsection, we investigate the correlation between excess liquidity and disaggregated indicators of the development of real estate market. As we did in subsection 3.2, we use both single equation regressions and VARs in order to check for the robustness of the results (summarised in Table 10.7 and Table 10.8 respectively).[4]

Table 10.7   Excess liquidity and the real estate market: disaggregate single equation regressions

Dependent variable	$rs\_investgr_t$	$rs\_financegr_t$	rs_landgr_t	$rs\_constructgr_t$	$rs\_vacantgr_t$	$rs\_pricegr_t$
$excessgr_{t-1}$	0.197***	0.534***	0.250**	0.307***	-0.053	0.170
	(0.054)	(0.127)	(0.106)	(0.108)	(0.136)	(0.211)
$\overline{R}^2$	0.053	0.247	0.031	0.134	-0.025	0.010

Note: ***, **, * denote significance at 1%, 5%, 10% level respectively. HAC standard errors in parentheses. Variables with 'gr' are growth rates of the original variables.

Table 10.8   Excess liquidity and the real estate market: disaggregate VAR analysis

Dependent variable	$rs\_investgr_t$	$rs\_financegr_t$	rs_landgr_t	$rs\_constructgr_t$	$rs\_vacantgr_t$	$rs\_pricegr_t$
$excessgr_{t-1}$	0.231**	0.473***	0.268*	0.287**	0.188	0.194
	(0.114)	(0.160)	(0.162)	(0.118)	(0.236)	(0.148)
$\overline{R}^2$	0.088	0.251	0.127	0.175	0.350	0.013

Note: ***, **, * denote significance at 1%, 5%, 10% levels respectively. Standard errors are in parentheses. Variables with 'gr' are growth rates of the original variables. The lag order of the VARs are selected according to the Schwartz Information Criterion.

Both single equation and VAR results suggest that an acceleration of excess money supply growth significantly accelerates the growth of investment in real estate and land. It also significantly accelerates the construction of buildings. These results are not surprising given that the housing price is much higher than its unit cost. When profit is high, the developers will increase investment in land and real estate whenever financial constraint becomes looser. The results in Tables 10.7 and 10.8 suggest that the financial constraints faced by the developers are indeed looser when excess liquidity increases.

The following case illustrates the degree of profitability of the Chinese real estate sector. As a measure of social welfare, the local government of Beijing provides low-price apartments to families whose income is below a certain threshold. By regulation, the price of those low-price apartments should be cost plus 'reasonable profit', which assures 'reasonable' profitability for the developers. Let us consider the building called 'Xi Cheng Jia Yuan', the apartments of which are low-price. Its regulated price is 6,500 yuan per square metre. The following table lists the average per square metre prices of unregulated apartments in the surrounding buildings.[5]

Table 10.9   Unregulated apartment prices of the buildings surrounding 'Xi Cheng Jia Yuan'

Name of Building	Shan Shui LAVIE	Guan Ju Yi Hao	Guo Ao Cun	Run Ze Jia Yuan	Yuan Yang Wan He Cheng	Ao Dong No.18	Rong Hua Shi Jia	Beijing Hua Mao Cheng	Run Ze Yue Xi
Price per square meter (yuan)	29,000	27,000	39,000	42,000	45,000	35,000	40,000	27,000	25,000

Source: http://data.house.sina.com.cn/bj3715/jiage.

The price ratio of the unregulated price to the regulated price ranges from 3.85 to 6.92. This indicates a minimum profit rate of 285%, assuming that those buildings have the same characteristics. Of course, these buildings have in reality different in characteristics. But the price ratios are too high to be explained by them. Therefore, this case suggests that the Chinese real estate market is highly profitable, the developers having strong incentives to increase investment whenever the financial constraints become looser.

Both single equation regressions and VARs suggest also that the growth of excess liquidity does not have a significant effect on the changes in vacant floor space of commercial buildings. This indicates that looser monetary conditions do not encourage the purchase of houses for the purpose of living. With constant demand, increased supply should lower the price. Hence a positive correlation between the real estate price and excess liquidity implies that the latter also increased the demand for real estate. Since this increase in demand is not driven by the purpose of home using, it is very likely that it is driven by speculation.

The finding that the positive correlation between real estate price and excess liquidity is insignificant runs counter to the popular argument that excess liquidity has contributed to the creation of a bubble in the Chinese real estate market. This is because the rising speculative demand is absorbed by increasing supply. This does not, however, mean that excess liquidity has no impact on the riskiness of investment in the real estate market. There is indeed evidence that a bubble does exist in China's real estate market (see section 4)

Even though excess liquidity has not contributed to the creation of the bubble, it could increase the financial loss when the bubble bursts. The supply of real estate increases to meet the increase in demand caused by excess liquidity. This prevents the creation of a speculative bubble. On the other hand, when excess liquidity would be eliminated, speculative demand will decrease. Hence there will be excess supply and the real estate price may fall dramatically. The real estate developers and the financial system that finances them will suffer the loss from the price collapse.

4.   POTENTIAL FINANCIAL RISK

Our econometric analysis so far suggests that there is a significant link between accumulation of foreign reserves, excess liquidity and development of the Chinese real estate market. Since capital inflows are major sources of excess liquidity in China (Zhang, 2008), the investment growth of the real estate sector is directly and indirectly financed by capital inflows. The question is whether this is sustainable. Two factors are channelling foreign money into China's real estate market. The first one is high profitability in the

Chinese real estate market. The second one is the expectation of yuan appreciation.

Is the high housing price sustainable? The rent-price ratio of the Chinese real estate market has kept decreasing since 2002 and reached 1:500 in major Chinese cities by April 2010. In some cities, this ratio even reached 1:800.[6] At the same time, however, the vacant space rate is very high. In 2008 the vacant space rate reached 9.50% nationwide and 16.64% in Beijing (Wang and Chen, 2009). Both the decreasing rent-price ratio and the high vacant space rate in the real estate market indicate that the real estate price is increasingly deviating from its fundamental value. This is largely driven by market speculation and therefore is not sustainable.

Foreign direct investment (FDI) attracted by high profitability in the Chinese real estate market is not the only way in which foreign capital inflows affect the financing of investment into the Chinese real estate market. The following equation shows the regression results of the non-FDI growth rate of real estate investment in China on excess liquidity. An increase in excess liquidity apparently not only increases funds raised from FDI but also increases funds from other sources.

$$rs\_financegr_t^{nonFDI} = \underset{(0.006^{***})}{0.063} + \underset{(0.213^{***})}{0.521} \ excessgr_{t-1}$$

$$\overline{R}^2 = 0.123$$

Since late 2002, there has been a pressure on the Chinese currency to appreciate. This pressure, together with China's mandatory exchange settlement and sales system, has released a large amount of capital inflows into the domestic money supply. The above regression results suggest that a large part of that extra money has entered the real estate market. Is this indirect money from foreign capital inflows sustainable? The answer cannot be 'yes' in the long run since China's twin surplus and accumulation of foreign reserves are parts of the global economic imbalance. As argued by Martin Feldstein (2008), even if governments are reluctant to take actions to reduce this global economic imbalance, market forces will adjust automatically in the long run. If the Chinese government does not take action sufficiently early to prevent the excess liquidity-financed over-expansion of the real estate sector, it may have to suffer a much higher cost when the adjustments of global imbalance eventually let themselves be felt. The Chinese real estate sector is a highly indebted sector. Therefore, if its over-expansion finally leads to a collapse, the financial system has to suffer the loss.

5. CONCLUSION

As a manifestation of global economic imbalance, China has accumulated huge international reserves. The accumulation of foreign reserves has substantially increased China's money supply, leading to an over-supply of liquidity in the Chinese economy. Zhang and Pang (2008) and Zhang (2009) argue that excess liquidity created by foreign reserve accumulation has affected China's inflation dynamics. However, their econometric approach is problematic. In this chapter, we show that excess liquidity has not significantly affected China's CPI inflation rate. Rather, a large amount of the oversupply of money has entered the real estate market through direct FDI and other channels.

Excess liquidity financing the expansion of the Chinese real estate sector poses a potential financial risk in China for two reasons. First, the high real estate price is increasingly deviating from its fundamental value. Second, the growth of excess liquidity itself is not sustainable. The direction of international capital flows may indeed change in the future due to the inevitable adjustments to global economic imbalance. Continuing to let the excess liquidity finance the real estate sector expansion could lead to a future collapse of that market. Because the Chinese real estate sector is highly dependent on external finance, its fall will generate a huge loss for the Chinese financial sector.

Since 14 April 2010, the Chinese government has therefore introduced a series of policies to fight speculation in the real estate market and bring down the speed of the real estate price increase. However, the effectiveness of these policies in the long run is still not clear. More importantly, if China keeps accumulating foreign reserves in a disequilibrium context, excess supply of money will persist. If this excess supply were not to enter the real estate market, it may enter other asset markets and nurture bubbles there. Therefore, it would be wise for the Chinese government to take actions to deal with its current and capital account imbalances as soon as possible, before the more painful market-forced adjustments take place.

NOTES

1. On average, real estate developer's own funds account for less than 17% of the funds they invest.
2. In order to control for autocorrelation, we add lags of the first difference of inflation to equation (10.1). The order of the lags is determined by the Schwartz Information Criterion.
3. For simplicity of illustration, the equations for *excessgr* are not reported.
4. Only estimates of the interested coefficient and standard error are reported.

5. These are average prices of apartments in the same building in April (by 14 April 2010).
6. Data published by the China Central Television (CCTV).

REFERENCES

Basher, S. and J. Westerlund (2008), 'Is there Really a Unit Root in the Inflation Rate? More Evidence from Panel Data Models', *Applied Economics Letters*, **15**, 161-164.

Culver, S. and D. Papell (1997), 'Is there a Unit Root in the Inflation Rate? Evidence from Sequential Break and Panel Data Models', *Journal of Applied Econometrics*, **12**, 436-444.

Feldstein, M. (2008), 'Resolving the Global Imbalance: the Dollar and the U.S. Saving Rate', *Journal of Economic Perspectives*, **22**, 113-125.

Wang, J. and S. Chen (2009), 'The Specific Reasons of China's Real Estate Price Increase and Policy Suggestions', *Economic Review* (in Chinese), **12**, 122-125.

Zhang, C. (2009), 'Excess Liquidity, Inflation and the Yuan Appreciation: What can China Learn from Recent History?', *The World Economy*, **32**, 998-1018.

Zhang, C. and H. Pang (2008), 'Excess Liquidity and Inflation Dynamics in China: 1997-2007', *China and the World Economy*, **16**, 1-15.

PART III

The Euro Perspective in East and Central
Europe after the Crisis

11. How has the Financial Crisis Affected the Eurozone Accession Outlook in Central and Eastern Europe?

John Lewis

1. INTRODUCTION

All new EU member states are obliged to join the EMU in the context of the 'acquis communautaire'. In particular, entry is conditional on meeting the five well-known Maastricht convergence criteria. The speed and strategy with which a member state seeks to fulfil these is entirely up to the country concerned. Up to now, recently acceded member states have followed quite different accession paths. Slovenia and Slovakia have already joined, the Baltic states are in post-euro version of the Exchange Rate Mechanism (ERM-II) with a view to joining, whilst the other states have yet to join ERM-II.[1]

The goal of this chapter is to examine how the current financial crisis has affected the task of meeting the Maastricht Criteria in the eight Central and Eastern European Countries (CEECs) that (as of 2010) have not joined the Eurozone:[2] Bulgaria, the Czech Republic, Estonia, Hungary, Latvia, Lithuania, Poland and Romania.

In general, the CEE region has been hit more sharply by the crisis than Western Europe. Between 2008 and 2010 cumulative GDP growth was close to minus 10 percent across the whole region, exchange rates have come under pressure, and three countries – Hungary, Romania and Latvia – have implemented IMF programmes. Overall, the crisis led to worsening fiscal positions, higher interest rates on government debt, and lower inflation. This stands in sharp contrast to the situation faced by most CEECs prior to the crisis. Back then, the major policy challenge appeared to be managing strong real exchange rate appreciation without violating the inflation or exchange rate criteria, whereas the fiscal and interest rate criteria seemed for the most part either already fulfilled or at least relatively straightforward to meet.

In this chapter I try to identify the channels by which the crisis has affected deficits, debts, interest rates and inflation and provide some numerical estimates for the magnitude of these effects in each CEEC. In particular, to what extent are the observed budget deficits structural or cyclical, and how has the crisis changed the assessment of the relative size of these two factors? On debt ratios, how much harder has it become for governments to stabilise their debt ratios, and to what extent does this pose a risk to complying with the debt criterion? For inflation, how much of the observed decline in inflation can be attributed to the fall in output gaps, and how much reflects exchange rate or other effects? Lastly, what is the relative contribution of exchange rate risk and default risk to rising bond spreads in the region?

The main findings are as follows. On the deficit side, large headline deficits in CEE are in mostly structural rather than cyclical in origin, and hence governments cannot rely solely on economic recovery to bring deficits below the reference value. Further, large revisions in potential output have led to a much more negative assessment of the pre-crisis structural position than was evident on the basis of 2007 data. On debt, higher interest rates, lower economic growth and lower inflation have increased the debt stabilising primary surplus by between 1 and 3% of GDP. For most countries, however, low starting levels mean that the debts remain below the reference value. Nevertheless, Hungary has moved considerably further away from the reference value, and Latvia and Poland face a challenge to keep their debt ratios below 60% of GDP in two years' time. If economic conditions remain poor, substantial fiscal adjustments would be necessary to get levels back down to the reference value.

In terms of inflation, the deteriorating output gap accounts for a 6-8 percentage point fall in inflation in the Baltic states, and a fall of 1-3 percentage points in the Central European economies. For the Baltics large negative output gaps and the relatively high price levels compared to real GDP levels are likely to generate downward pressure on inflation rates for some years to come, although price convergence effects may generate pressure the other way.

On long-term interest rates, perceived exchange rate risk has added between 0 and 2 percentage points to bond yields, and ratings downgrades add between 0 and 1.5 percentage points. However, the combined size of these effects falls some way short of the observed rise in interest rates in many other countries.

Related Literature

A good deal of the earlier work on the challenges faced by CEECs was focussed on the challenges posed by trend appreciation of the real exchange rate for compliance with the exchange rate and inflation criteria.[3] Several authors argued that the strategy of inflation targeting coupled with a steady appreciation of the nominal exchange rate – as opposed to a hard fix – was likely to prove the best way to accommodate the real exchange rate appreciation and fulfil both criteria. However, this strand of research focussed on how to manage longer-term underlying trends, and largely abstracts from cyclical considerations or the effects of large shocks. This chapter therefore seeks to add to the literature by quantifying empirically the effects of the crisis on inflation.

On the fiscal side, Hughes Hallett and Lewis (2007) analysed debt dynamics for CEECs and concluded that in general the debt criterion did not pose much of an obstacle, given the low initial debt levels and strong growth performance expected as part of the convergence process. However, recent developments may call this finding into question since debt ratios are now higher than in 2007 and the growth outlook is much less benign. Consequently, this chapter makes a contribution by updating the literature and analysing how debt dynamics have changed since the onset of the crisis.

Several papers have looked at various forms of Phillips curves for CEECs. Mihajlov et al. (2009) find an important role for the external factors, and for the most part find that domestic output gaps also play a role. Masso and Staehr (2005), for the Baltic states, find a much stronger role for external factors and find that internal output gaps have little effect. A similar result was obtained for the Baltics by Dabušinskas and Kulikov (2007). This chapter seeks to extend the literature and quantify the effects of the crisis on inflation.

The literature on the determinants of bond spreads in CEECs is still in its infancy. Two papers that have looked at this issue (Ebner, 2009; Nickel et al., 2009) have concluded that variables which are traditionally used explain bond spreads in the euro area appear to perform much less well when applied to CEE. However, both papers use pre-crisis data. Accordingly, this chapter adds to the existing work by investigating whether the pricing of risk in CEE by market participants has been altered by the crisis.

The chapter is organised as follows. Section 2 deals with the fiscal criteria, section 3 with inflation and exchange rate criteria and section 4 with the interest rate criterion. Section 5 concludes.

2. FISCAL CRITERIA

2.1. The Deficit Criterion

The Maastricht Treaty specifies the deficit criterion as a general consolidated government budget deficit of less than 3% of GDP. Prior to the crisis, all CEECs, bar Hungary, had a deficit below this reference value. However, as Figure 11.1 shows, fiscal balances have deteriorated sharply since 2007:

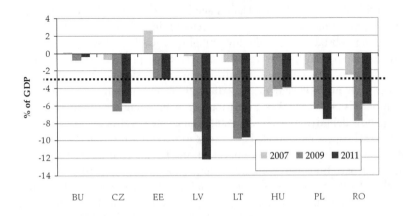

Source: *European Economy*, November 2009.

Figure 11.1   Deficit ratios 2007-2009

The financial crisis has affected public finances in several ways. Firstly, the sharp fall in output has led to a corresponding fall in government revenues and a rise in spending via the operation of automatic stabilisers. Secondly, some governments have undertaken discretionary measures – either to stimulate the economy, or to consolidate deteriorating public finances. Thirdly, the financial crisis has led to substantial downward revisions in estimates of potential output, causing large re-assessments of the structural state of public finances. Unlike in Western Europe, direct costs in terms of financial rescue packages have been rather limited, inter alia because most banks in the region were foreign owned.[4]

To decompose automatic and discretionary components of fiscal policy, I utilise the same method as the European Commission. This is based on the following definition:

$$CAB_{it} = Bal_{it} - Sensitivity_i * Gap_{it} \ .$$ (11.1)

The EC estimates budgetary sensitivities for each country, which are assumed to be time invariant. Multiplying these sensitivities by the output gap (*Gap*) gives an estimate of the cyclical component. The cyclically adjusted balance (*CAB*) is then defined as the overall balance (*Bal*), minus the estimated cyclical component.[5]

Multiplying their estimates of budgetary sensitivities by the change in the output gap, gives an estimate of the cyclical contribution to public finances; the change in *CAB*, gives a measure of the change in discretionary policy. These are calculated over the period 2007-2010, which for most countries appears to represent the peak and trough in terms of the output gap. For levels, 2010 data are used.

Table 11.1   Automatic versus discretionary fiscal policy, 2007-2010

	Change 2007-2010			Level 2010		
	Auto. Δgap* sensitivity	Disc. ΔCAB	Total	Cyclical gap* sensitivity	Struc'l CAB	Total Bal
BU	-4.0	2.8	-1.3	-2.2	1.0	-1.2
CZ	-3.5	-1.4	-4.8	-1.1	-4.5	-5.5
EE	-6.1	0.3	-5.8	-2.7	-0.4	-3.2
LV	-7.6	-4.5	-12.0	-3.0	-9.3	-12.3
LT	-6.2	-2.1	-8.2	-2.9	-6.3	-9.2
HU	-3.6	4.3	0.8	-2.2	-2.1	-4.2
PL	-1.9	-3.7	-5.6	-0.9	-6.6	-7.5
RO	-4.0	-0.4	-4.3	-1.3	-5.5	-6.8

Source: European Economy, November 2009, author's own calculations.

The left-hand side of the table shows the changes in the period 2007-2010. On the automatic side, the deteriorations in the output gap have typically knocked between four and six percentage points off the overall budget balance. In general, the largest deteriorations in the output gap have occurred in countries with relatively low automatic stabilisers (and vice versa). The picture is far more varied when it comes to the discretionary components. Latvia, Lithuania and Poland have seen a marked loosening in their fiscal stances whereas Estonia and Romania have held their *CAB*s broadly constant.[6] Fiscal stance has tightened considerably in Bulgaria and Hungary.

The right-hand side shows the situation in levels in 2010. For all countries, bar Bulgaria and Estonia, the budget deficit is some way beyond the 3%

reference value. Splitting this up into cyclical and structural components, the analysis shows that even though countries are experiencing large negative output gaps, for the majority of countries the primary source fiscal problems is structural rather than cyclical. This can be seen most clearly for the Czech Republic, Poland and Romania, where cyclical factors account for less than one fifth of total deficit. Latvia and Lithuania have larger cyclical components, but these are accompanied by substantial structural deficits. On the basis of the current figures, only Bulgaria and Estonia can claim that their fiscal deficits are largely cyclical in nature.

This decomposition has important implications for prospects of future compliance with the deficit criterion. To the extent that a deficit is cyclical, policymakers can simply hold fiscal stance constant and wait for the recovery to improve public finances. On the other hand, eliminating the structural component of the deficit requires specific discretionary measures on the part of policymakers. Aside from the political difficulties of consolidating public finances during a recession, tightening at the bottom, the cycle risks weakening the recovery with possible effects on revenues arising via automatic stabilisers. On the basis of these figures, five of the eight countries will likely face such a difficulty, with only Bulgaria and Estonia being able to rely on an upturn to get the budget deficit below the reference value.

This point is also related to the third channel-revisions to potential output. The crisis has led to large downward revisions in estimates of potential output, which in turn have led to major reassessments of cyclical conditions, and hence estimates of the structural component of public finances. To analyse this effect, I compare different vintages of data for the reference year 2007, from a pre-crisis vintage (the May 2007 edition of *European Economy*) and a post-crisis vintage (the November 2009 edition of *European Economy*). The choice of 2007 as the year is deliberate. If a later year were chosen, data revisions to the *CAB* could also reflect discretionary measures taken in response to the crisis, which were not known to forecasters in 2007.

Using the superscript 'REV' to denote revisions between vintages (i.e. the autumn 2009 figure minus the spring 2007 figure), and noting that the output gap is equal to actual minus potential GDP expression (11.1) can easily be manipulated to yield the following decomposition of revisions in *CAB*:

$$CAB_{it}^{REV} = Balance_{it}^{REV} - Sensitivity_i * (GDP_{it}^{REV} - Potential_{it}^{REV})$$

$$(11.2)$$

Revisions to the balance have a one for one effect on *CAB*, whereas the impact of revising actual and potential GDP is determined by budgetary sensitivity. Notice here that if GDP turns out higher than originally planned but potential output is not revised then the upward revision to the budget balance is exactly cancelled out by the upward revision of the cyclical component, and hence *CAB* is unchanged. Table 11.2 presents a decomposition of these three effects.[7]

Table 11.2   Revisions to estimates of fiscal and cyclical conditions

	2007 Output gap		Effect of potential output revision	Effect of GDP revision	Effect of balance revision	Revision to *CAB*
	May 07	Nov 09	$Potential^{REV}*$ sensitivity	$GDP^{REV}*$ sensitivity	Bal^{REV}	CAB^{REV}
BU	0.7	5.2	-1.8	0.2	-1.9	-3.4
CZ	0.5	6.6	-2.9	0.6	3.2	1.0
EE	0.7	11.1	-3.0	-0.1	-1.1	-4.2
LV	0.8	16.3	-4.2	-0.2	-0.5	-4.8
LT	0.6	12.1	-4.0	0.9	-0.6	-3.6
HU	0.2	3.1	-1.1	-0.3	1.8	0.5
PL	0.4	2.6	-1.5	0.6	1.5	0.7
RO	0.9	8.8	-2.5	0.1	0.7	-1.6

Note: All data refer to the calendar year 2007, 'revision' means the November 2009 figure minus the May 2007 figure; figures may not sum exactly due to rounding.
Source: *European Economy*, authors own calculations.

The second and third columns indicate that there were substantial upward revisions to the output gap, especially in the case of the Baltic states where revisions were into double figures. These gap revisions largely reflect revisions to estimates of potential output rather than to real GDP levels.[8] For the Baltic states and the Czech Republic, revisions to potential output lead to a revision in *CAB* of around 3-4% of GDP. In Bulgaria, Hungary and Poland the effects are in the 1-2% range, with Romania an intermediate case. Effects of GDP revisions are of a smaller magnitude (within the ±1% of GDP range).

Revisions to budget balances vary quite substantially across countries. For the Czech Republic, Hungary and Poland they are large and positive, for the Baltics and Bulgaria they have a negative sign.

In terms of the overall impact on *CAB*, two distinct groups clearly emerge. On the one hand, the Baltics and Bulgaria were subject to substantial downward revisions in the 2007 value of *CAB* after the onset of the crisis. Romania also experienced this, but to a lesser extent. Thus, alongside the effects of falling GDP, these countries were suddenly revealed to have a much weaker structural position in public finances going into the crisis than previously thought. That may partially exonerate policymakers in these countries, since their apparent fiscal weakness did not show up as strongly at the height of the boom.

On the other hand, for central European inflation targetters – the Czech Republic, Hungary and Poland – the opposite is true. The picture that we now have of the structural position of public finances in 2007 is, if anything, slightly more optimistic than the one that was available at the time. In other words, the poor structural position of public finances was also evident in 2007, and hence policymakers cannot blame the poor quality of real time data and the unexpected nature of the crisis for failing to improve structural balances before the crisis arrived.

2.2. The Debt Criterion

The debt criterion requires that government debt be no more than 60% of GDP, or, if is above that level, that it is 'converging at a satisfactory pace'. In practice therefore, assessments of the debt criterion in convergence reports have also included an analysis of likely future trends in debt to GDP ratios.

Worsening public finances have also led to rising debt ratios across the region. As Figure 11.2 shows, this has occurred in all countries and has been most pronounced in Latvia.

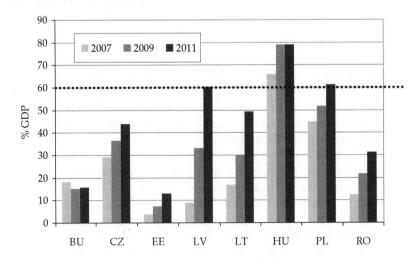

Source: *European Economy*, November 2009.

Figure 11.2   Debt/GDP ratios, 2007-2011

The starting point for the analysis here is the standard debt dynamic analysis. Under the standard assumption of one period bonds, this yields the following equation describing the evolution of the debt to GDP ratio b:

$$b_{t+1} = \left(\frac{1+r}{1+\gamma}\right) b_t - pb_t \quad , \tag{11.3}$$

where r is the real rate of interest, γ is the rate of real GDP growth and pb is the primary balance.

Aside from the deterioration in fiscal balance discussed above, the crisis has also affected the other variables that govern debt dynamics: real interest rates have risen due to increasing nominal rates and falling inflation, whilst growth rates have fallen sharply. That implies that debt dynamics might look quite different in the light of the crisis, which may make the debt criterion more difficult to achieve.

To assess how the crisis has affected the ability of countries to meet the debt criterion, two yardsticks are used. The first one is simply the budget balance required to stabilise the debt ratio at its current value given the prevailing levels of interest rates and economic growth. This is derived by setting $b_t = b_{t+1}$ and re-arranging to yield:

$$pb_t^* = \left(\frac{1+r}{1+\gamma} - 1\right) b_t \quad . \tag{11.4}$$

A numerical value is then obtained by substituting in the current values of debt, real GDP growth and the real interest rate. The implied level of interest payments, rb, is then added to this figure to yield the debt budget balance.

The second yardstick is the budget balance which brings the debt/GDP ratio to 60% in two years time, given prevailing interest rate and growth conditions. For countries with debt ratios above 60%, this represents the balance required to get debt down below the benchmark. For those currently below the benchmark, this figure gives an idea of the maximum deficit compatible with keeping debt at or below 60%.

This is achieved by substituting $b_{t-1} = \left(\dfrac{1+r}{1+\gamma}\right) b_{t-2} - pb_{t-2}$ into (11.3) to yield

$$b_t = \left(\frac{1+r}{1+\gamma}\right)\left(\frac{1+r}{1+\gamma} b_{t-2} - pb_{t-2}\right) - pb_{t-1} \quad . \tag{11.5}$$

On the basis that the primary balance is the same in periods, and that the final debt ratio is 60%, one can then solve for pb^{**}:

$$pb^{**} = \frac{b_{t-2}\left(\dfrac{1+r}{1+\gamma}\right)^2 - 0.6}{\left(1+\dfrac{1+r}{1+\gamma}\right)} \quad .$$
(11.6)

Numerical values are then substituted in, and interest payments added, as before. These benchmarks and the economic variables used to generate them are shown below in Table 11.3 for both before and after the crisis.[9]

Table 11.3   Debt dynamics

	Nominal int. rate	Inflation	Real GDP growth	Debt	Debt stabil'g balance	Bal. to get debt=60% at t+2	Actual balance
2007							
BU	4.0	5.0	6.1	20.9	-2.1	-21.5	2.0
CZ	3.8	4.0	4.9	30.6	-2.5	-16.4	-3.9
EE	4.3	8.2	8.7	2.7	-0.4	-30.6	3.7
LV	4.1	11.0	9.6	8.0	-1.5	-29.2	0.2
LT	4.1	5.1	7.3	18.6	-2.1	-22.8	-0.4
HU	7.1	6.2	2.4	67.1	-5.6	2.7	-6.8
PL	5.2	2.3	6.1	48.4	-3.7	-7.1	-3.4
RO	7.1	9.8	7.7	12.8	-2.1	-25.9	-3.2
2010							
BU	5.4	1.9	0.3	16.2	-0.4	-21.9	-1.2
CZ	4.6	1.3	2.2	40.6	-1.4	-11.0	-5.5
EE	8.2	-3.1	2.4	10.9	0.1	-23.4	-3.2
LV	6.4	-5.0	1.7	48.6	1.6	-3.8	-12.3
LT	5.6	-1.5	-1.5	40.7	1.2	-8.0	-9.2
HU	8.2	2.6	0.3	79.8	-2.3	7.3	-4.2
PL	6.1	1.5	2.9	57.0	-2.5	-3.9	-7.5
RO	7.7	5.3	-0.3	27.4	-1.4	-17.5	-6.8

Note: No real time data available for Romania in May 2007, so November 09 vintage data are used instead; the inflation measure used is the GDP deflator.
Source: *European Economy* May 2007, November 2009; authors own calculations.

The upper panel shows the pre-crisis data. It is evident that the majority of countries were running fiscal policies where the balance comfortably exceeded that required for debt stabilisation. Although the Czech Republic and Romania were running deficits that implied a rising debt ratio, they were well below the levels required to hit 60% within two years. In that time, only

Hungary had a debt ratio above 60% and the debt criterion appeared to represent a challenge for them.

The lower panel depicts the current situation. The left-hand columns show the extent of the sharp deterioration in growth rates and inflation and the rise in nominal rates. The effect of this on debt dynamics can be seen by comparing the 'debt stabilising balance' figures from the two periods. Hardest hit were Hungary, Latvia and Lithuania that experienced a 3 percentage point rise in the balance required to stabilise their debt ratios. For the latter two countries this largely reflects the role of the sharp decline in GDP growth. For Hungary the fall in inflation is the most important channel. Comparing this with the figures for the actual balance, one sees that every single country is now running a bigger deficit than the debt stabilising benchmark, implying that debt ratios are rising. Although Hungary had a debt ratio above 60%, both Poland and Latvia now face challenges to keep debt ratios below 60% in the coming years. Latvia's current budget balance is some 8 percentage points short of the benchmark needed to do so, and Poland's is nearly 4 points short.

To sum up, whilst the crisis did substantially worsen debt dynamics, for the majority of countries this was not sufficient to seriously impair compliance with the debt criterion. Hungary's debt ratio was already above 60% before the crisis, but for Poland, Latvia and Lithuania, one consequence of the crisis has been to render the debt criterion a much more pressing issue.

Quite how exacting the debt criterion will be for these countries depends in part on how the criterion is interpreted. In the 1998 convergence report, a number of countries had debt ratios well above 60%, but they were judged to be 'falling at a satisfactory pace'. If a similar interpretation were applied in the future, then both Hungary and Poland would only need to make a small adjustment beyond that required to meet the deficit criterion. The debt stabilising balance for these countries is –2.3 and –2.5% respectively and thus a deficit ratio of 2% would be sufficient to put debt on a downward trajectory. On the other hand, if these countries were required to get their debt ratios back below 60%, this could prove much more onerous in a low growth, higher interest rate environment.

3. INFLATION AND EXCHANGE RATE CRITERIA

3.1. The Inflation Criterion

The inflation criterion contains two components: a rate of inflation no more than 1.5 percentage points more than the average of the best three performing countries and the requirement that price performance is sustainable.[10] In

practice, past convergence reports have assessed the sustainability requirement by considering both the factors which have led to inflation performance,
as well as a forward looking assessment of the outlook for inflation.

As Figure 11.3 demonstrates, one effect of the crisis has been a substantial
decline in inflation rates in CEE. At the same time, falling inflation rates
across the whole EU have depressed the reference value,[11] but this fall has
been much less pronounced than the fall in CEE inflation rates. This partly
reflects the exclusion of countries with negative inflation from the calculation
of the reference value, but arguably it is also a consequence of the relatively
stronger downturn in CEE.

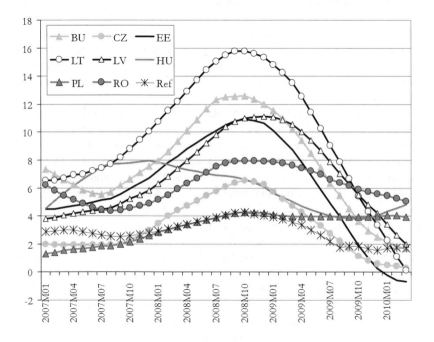

Source: Eurostat, author's own calculations (the inflation measure used is a 12-month moving
average of HICP inflation).

Figure 11.3   Inflation rates, 2007-2009

To estimate the effect of the crisis on inflation rates and to gauge the relative
size of different channels, a Phillips curve relationship between relating inflation to the output gap and several other variables is estimated. A 'poolability'
test indicated that the data for the six 2004 entrants could be pooled together,
but did not accept the addition of Romania and Bulgaria.[12] Therefore the
equation was estimated as a balanced panel for these six countries.

Panel unit root tests did not uncover strong evidence of a unit root, therefore the panel is estimated as a stationary process.[13] The following relationship was estimated using a panel data regression including time and country fixed effects:

$$\pi_{it} = \alpha + \rho \pi_{it-1} + \beta \, gap_{it} + \phi \, exrate_{it-1} + \theta \, conv_{it-1} * balt_{it-1} + u_{it} \, .$$

(11.7)

This specification captures three distinct channels by which the crisis has affected inflation (π). A lagged inflation term is included to capture any backward-looking expectations formation by agents. A positive output gap (*gap*) is associated with higher inflation due to capacity shortages and standard Phillips-curve type mechanisms. To capture the effects of exchange rate changes the trade weighted nominal exchange rate (*exrate*) is included. Given the high openness of the CEE economies, one might expect a depreciation to be associated with higher inflation as import prices rise. Note here that even in countries with fixed exchange rates, this variable can move around, as the anchor currency fluctuates against those of trading partners.

The *conv* variable measures the relative extent of nominal and real convergence. Specifically, it is the relative price level of country i (compared to the eurozone), divided by the relative real GDP level. It is a simple proxy for the level of the real exchange rate with respect to productivity. Its inclusion captures the possibility that countries with fixed exchange rates may have to undergo an internal devaluation to regain competitiveness. This effect would place additional downward pressure on inflation, arising independently of the output gap. Since this should only show up in countries with floating exchange rates, this variable interacts with a dummy variable (*balt*) equal to one for Baltic states and zero for others.

When lagged inflation was included, the coefficient was strongly insignificant, and therefore the variable was dropped. This is equivalent to assuming that inflation expectations are anchored. Other studies have included an expectations term[14] but, given the small number of observations and problems with finding suitable instruments, no explicitly forward looking term is included.

The results are shown in Table 11.4. The results are fairly similar across all three specifications. The simplest specification (I) reveals a significant degree of backward-lookingness, and a strongly significant role of the output gap, which enters with a positive coefficient, as predicted by theory.

Table 11.4   Determinants of inflation

	I	II	III
Lagged inflation	0.485***	0.358***	0.212*
	(0.11)	(0.10)	(0.12)
Output Gap	0.283***	0.256***	0.291***
	(0.06)	(0.07)	(0.07)
Exchange Rate		-0.187***	-0.177***
		(0.04)	(0.05)
Convergence*Baltic			-0.062**
			(0.02)
n	72	72	66
R^2	0.820	0.869	0.872
AIC	4.12	3.82	3.68
FE χ^2	52.21 (0.00)	59.50 (0.00)	59.95 (0.00)
DW	2.28	2.40	2.45

Note: *, **, *** indicate significance at 10, 5 and 1% levels of significance respectively. White standard errors shown in brackets.
AIC is the Akaike Information Criterion, FE χ^2 gives the test statistic for redundant fixed effects, p-value in brackets; DW is the Durbin Watson test statistic.

Adding the exchange rate in specification II yields a significant negative coefficient, implying that a depreciation in the exchange rate is associated with higher inflation. The pass-through coefficient of 0.2 is plausible in the light of other empirical work.[15] Including convergence effects in specification III, interacting with a dummy for the Baltic states, yields a significant negative coefficient, consistent with the above intuition.

Based on these coefficients it is possible to estimate the likely effect on inflation of the crisis of the different channels. These are shown below in Table 11.5, which reports both the variable itself, and the product of the variable and the coefficient. The left-hand part shows the effect on 2010 inflation of the 2010 output gap and exchange rate change.[16] The right-hand part shows the impact of the peak to trough change in the output gap and the relative convergence measure.[17]

The output gap exerts a much stronger downward effect on 2010 inflation in the Baltic states on account of their much larger negative output gap (amounting to some 2.5-3 percentage points). The exchange rate effects differ in sign by country groups. The central European countries have all seen depreciations in their nominal exchange rates, which have generated upward pressure on inflation, which helped to counteract the effects of the output gap fall, whereas the Baltic countries, with their euro anchor, have seen their trade-weighted nominal exchange rate appreciate slightly, further lowering inflation.

Table 11.5   Effects of the crisis on inflation

| | Level effects on 2010 inflation | | | | Peak to trough change | | | |
| | Output gap | | Exchange rate | | Output gap (2007-2010) | | Conv. ratio (2007-2009) | |
	gap	gap* coef	ex	ex*coef	Δgap	Δgap* coef	Δconv	Δconv* coef
CZ	-2.9	-0.8	-3.6	+0.6	-9.5	-2.8	+10.9	0.0
EE	-9.1	-2.6	+1.8	-0.3	-20.2	-5.9	+20.4	-1.3
LV	-10.7	-3.1	+2.1	-0.4	-27.0	-7.9	+30.4	-1.9
LT	-10.8	-3.1	+2.5	-0.4	-22.9	-6.7	+18.2	-1.1
HU	-4.7	-1.4	-8.3	1.5	-7.8	-2.3	+0.9	0.0
PL	-2.2	-0.6	-18.0	+3.2	-4.8	-1.4	-1.3	0.0

Source: European Economy, November 2009, author's own calculations.

Looking at the change from peak to trough, the much larger magnitude of the output gap change in the Baltic countries leads to a much larger effect. The fall of inflation is between 6 to 8 percentage points, whereas for the central European economies the reduction in inflation is in the range of 1.5 to 3 percentage points. Since 2007, output in the Baltic economies has fallen sharply, whereas relative price levels have stayed broadly constant, meaning that relative price levels are now much higher than relative GDP levels. This effect is estimated to lower inflation by just over a percentage point in Estonia and Lithuania, and by almost two points in Latvia. The overall effect of the crisis is a substantial lowering in inflation rates. Given the large negative output gap, and the apparent fragility of the recovery, it appears that the output gap and convergence ratio channels will likely depress inflation for some years to come. On the other hand, a more rapid recovery, or a pick-up in energy price (to which the Baltic HICPs are more sensitive) could exert an upward influence.

3.2. The Exchange Rate Criterion

The exchange rate criterion requires that a country has been a member of ERM-II for two years, keeping within the normal bounds, without severe tensions or devaluation. In practice, this has been interpreted as forbidding a depreciation of more than 2.25% from the central parity, and with a case by case approach to assessing appreciations beyond 2.25%.[18]

The CEECs fall into two groups – those with fixed exchange rates and those with floating exchange rates. Of the former, Estonia and Lithuania are participating in ERM II with a currency board, Latvia is participating in ERM II with a tight peg and Bulgaria has a currency board but is not part of

ERM II. All four have maintained their fixed exchange rate arrangements at an unchanged parity throughout. In that sense, the crisis has not affected the ability of these countries to meet the exchange rate criterion. However, the onset of the crisis has led to some pressure on the fixed exchange rate regimes, which has prompted various countermeasures to enhance the credibility of their fixed exchange rate.

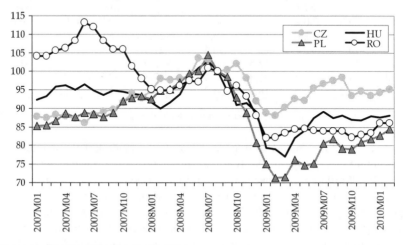

Source: Eurostat, author's own calculations.

Figure 11.4   The exchange rate vis-à-vis the euro (August 2008=100)

The Bank of Estonia concluded a precautionary swap deal with the Riksbank that enabled them to borrow up to 10bn Swedish Krone to bolster liquidity provision under the currency board arrangement. In Latvia, the central bank was forced to consume around 20% of its reserves defending the peg, and in December 2008 the government concluded an agreement with the IMF for a loan of €1.7bn (1200% of its quota), which required various stabilisation measures, including a tightening of fiscal policy by around 7 percentage of GDP.

For the countries with floating exchange rates, the effect of the crisis has been significant depreciations in the nominal exchange rate. Figure 11.4 shows nominal rates normalised around their levels in August 2008.

Prior to the collapse of Lehman Brothers, exchange rates were characterised by a period of appreciation (except for Romania). After this, exchange rates have followed a downward path followed by a partial recovery. However, since none of the four were members of ERM-II, this decline did not have any implications for the exchange rate criterion. Had these countries been in ERM II, substantial policy measures would then have been required to avoid moving below the 2.25% lower band and to prevent a devaluation.

4. THE INTEREST RATE CRITERION

The interest rate criterion is assessed using the long-term interest rate on 10-year government debt. Interest rates must be no more than 2 percentage points more than the average paid by the three countries in the inflation reference group. The economic rationale for this is usually taken to be that low long-term interest rates reflect anchored inflation expectations, limited currency risk and the sustainability of public finances in the member states concerned.

Figure 11.5 plots the evolution of long-term interest rates over the past two and a half years, alongside an imputed reference value. This shows that prior to the onset of the crisis, all of the 2004 intake appeared to meet the interest rate criterion, with Bulgaria and Romania slightly above the reference value. Since the crisis, rates have climbed substantially for all countries, with the exception of the Czech Republic and Poland. However, it is noteworthy that although bond yields in CEE have risen sharply, the reference value has not risen at all, with the consequence that all countries, bar the Czech Republic, currently lie above the reference value.

The interest rate on government bonds is likely to be affected by several risk factors, including expected domestic inflation, the risk of default and the expected movement in the exchange rate vis-à-vis the euro. To capture these effects, a regression of the following form is estimated.

$$lr_{it} = \rho \, lr_{it-1} + \lambda \, rating_{it} + \omega \, exrate_{it-1} + \psi \, inf_{it} + u_{it} \quad , \tag{11.8}$$

where the variable *lr* is the Maastricht convergence criterion measure of 10-year government bond yields. *rating* represents the rating on euro-denominated bonds by Moody's. This should therefore strip out the effect of exchange rate and inflation risk and provide a measure of default risk. It captures a richer information set than simply looking at headline indicators such as deficits, debt and external balance, which the existing literature on CEECs suggest have limited power to explain bond spreads. A one unit change in this variable corresponds to a one notch upgrade/downgrade, a higher value indicates a higher credit rating. *exrate* is the percentage difference between the spot rate and the one year ahead forward rate, where a negative value corresponds to an expected depreciation. This acts as a proxy for perceived devaluation risk. *inf* is expected inflation one calendar year ahead, taken from the relevant issue of *European Economy*. All data are taken at the half-yearly frequency, corresponding to June and December of each calendar year.

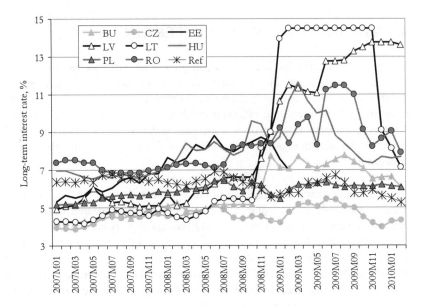

Note: No observations recorded for Estonia beyond November 2009.
Source: Eurostat, author's own calculations.

Figure 11.5   Long-term interest rates

Fixed effects are included by country and per time period. The results of this regression are presented in Table 11.6. Ratings are significant and have the expected negative sign. Thus a one notch downgrade corresponds to a rise in interest rates of around 40 basis points. Similarly, for every percentage point of expected depreciation in the currency, funding costs are raised by around 50 basis points. This may understate the true magnitude of exchange rate risk, since this variable only reflects the expected change over one year, and not over the whole lifetime of the bond. Inflation does not appear to be significant. That may reflect that forecasts are only available one year ahead. Dropping inflation in specification II leads to very similar coefficient estimates.

Estimates for the size of these effects for each country are shown below in Table 11.7. In both cases, these are obtained by multiplying the estimate coefficient by change in each variable from the first half of 2008 to the second half of 2009 for each country.

Table 11.6   Interest rate effects

	I	II
Rating	-0.399*	-0.381*
	(0.20)	(0.20)
ExRate	-0.500***	-0.488***
	(0.13)	(0.11)
Inf	-0.097	-
	(0.12)	
Lagged LR	0.360*	0.396**
	(0.19)	(0.19)
n	88	88
R^2	0.887	0.885
AIC	2.78	2.77
FE χ^2	62.03 (0.00)	61.55 (0.00)
DW	2.10	2.08

Note: *, **, *** indicate significance at 10, 5 and 1% levels of significance respectively. White standard errors shown in brackets. AIC is the Akaike Information Criterion, FE χ^2 gives the test statistic for redundant fixed effects, p-value in brackets. DW is the Durbin Watson test statistic.

Table 11.7   Estimated size of interest rate effects

	Change in exchange rate exp. $\Delta exrate$ coeff.	Exchange rate effect $\Delta exrate*$ coeff.	Change in rating $\Delta rating$ coeff.	Rating effect $\Delta rating*$ coeff.	Actual change in LT rate Δlt coeff.
BU	-3.57	1.71	0	0.00	1.58
CZ	-1.10	0.53	0	0.00	-0.65
EE	-1.53	0.73	0	0.00	N/A
LV	-4.05	1.94	-4	1.52	9.70
LT	-3.56	1.71	-1	0.38	7.82
HU	-0.42	0.20	-2	0.76	-0.71
PL	-0.92	0.44	0	0.00	0.04
RO	-2.63	1.26	0	0.00	0.98

Note: No data available for long-term interest rate in Q42009 for Estonia.
Source: *European Economy*, Author's own calculations.

Looking at the exchange rate effects, it is evident that expected movements in the exchange rates did put upward pressure on bond spreads. In the case of Bulgaria and Romania, these are very close to the actual movement observed in the long-term rate. On the other hand, for Latvia and Lithuania, the exchange rate effect can account for only a fraction of the observed rise in long-term rates. A similar story applies to the effect of ratings. For Latvia and Lithuania they are only a fraction of the rise in bond spreads, and Hungary's interest rate has moved in the opposite direction to that predicted by exchange rate and ratings effects.

A similar point can be made in terms of levels: Bulgaria has the same credit rating as Latvia, yet the latter has 10-year bond yields that are around 800 basis points higher. All in all, variables such as ratings and exchange rate expectations have only a limited power in explaining the observed changes in bond yields. This seems to be a similar conclusion to that reached by Ebner (2009) and Nickel et al. (2009), that traditional variables do not perform particularly well at predicting CEE bond spreads.

5. CONCLUDING REMARKS

Overall, the economic and financial crisis has significantly affected the policy challenges faced by CEEC governments in meeting the Maastricht criteria. Prior to the crisis, the main challenge for CEEC governments seemed to be managing the process of real exchange rate appreciation. Deficits were mostly at or below the reference value, and both debts and long-term interest rates were below the reference value.

Since then much has changed. The deficit criterion has become much more problematic to achieve. As demonstrated in section 2, for most countries the problem is not simply cyclical, but reflects a structural character. Interestingly, for many countries this structural problem only became apparent after the crisis, when large revisions to estimates of 2007 potential output led to a major reassessment of the underlying fiscal position. Concerning debt, higher interest rates, lower economic growth and lower inflation have increased the debt-stabilising primary surplus by several percentage points. For Hungary, Latvia, Lithuania and Poland this is likely to pose an important challenge.

In terms of inflation, section 3 shows that the deteriorating output gap accounts for a 6 to 8 percentage point fall in inflation in the Baltic states, and a fall of 1 to 3 percentage points in the Central European economies. For the Baltics, large negative output gaps, and the relatively high price levels compared to real GDP levels are likely to generate a downward pressure on inflation rates for some years to come, although price convergence effects may generate pressure the other way.

For exchange rates, the crisis has led to significant depreciations for those currencies that float, but as none of these countries were in ERM-II, this did not have direct effects for the exchange rate criterion. The crisis did place some pressure on the fixed exchange rate arrangements, but the parities nevertheless endured. Lastly, there was evidence that expectations of depreciation and worsening credit ratings have served to raise long-run interest rates, but attempts to estimate this empirically could not fully explain the large rises in bond yields seen in some countries. Nevertheless, the significant rises in bond yields seen in most countries since the crisis have made the interest rate criterion more challenging.

NOTES

1. See Dabrowski (2007) for an overview of CEECs' paths towards Eurozone accession.
2. Throughout the chapter the abbreviation CEEC will be used short-hand for these six countries, rather than the broader region.
3. See for example: Jonas and Mishkin (2003), Brooke (2005), De Grauwe and Schnabl (2005), Dobrinsky (2006), Filacek et al. (2006), Darvas and Szapary (2008), Horvath et al. (2009) and Lewis (2009).
4. See Staehr (2010) for a detailed overview of developments in public finances since the onset of the crisis.
5. See European Commission (2005) for details.
6. In the case of Estonia the figure masks considerable intra-year changes. The CAB worsened by around 4 percentage points in 2008, but following a large scale consolidation programme by the government.
7. The implied revisions to level of real GDP were imputed manually. For full details see the working paper version of this chapter.
8. For full details see the working paper version of this chapter.
9. As in Table 11.2, 'real time' data are used for 2007, taken from the May 2007 edition of *European Economy*.
10. The reference value is calculated on the basis of the lowest three positive inflation rates. Past practice has been to exclude negative inflation rates from the calculation of the reference value in convergence reports. For a detailed discussion of the interpretation and application of the inflation criterion, see Lewis and Staehr (2010).
11. The reference value is calculated by taking the lowest three positive inflation rates.
12. This was carried out by estimating a model in which all coefficients were country specific, and then performing a likelihood ratio test on the restrictions implied by the pooled model. The resultant p-value was 0.18. Adding Romania and Bulgaria and repeating test yielded a p-value of 0.01.
13. Furthermore, theory suggests that the output gap cannot have a unit root, and if inflation expectations are to some extent anchored then inflation will not have a unit root.
14. See for example Mihajlov et al. (2009) and Staehr and Masso (2005).
15. See previous note.
16. The relative convergence measure, as a proxy for the real exchange rate, is hard to interpret in levels without some measure of the equilibrium value. It is more easily interpreted in terms of its change (e.g. a rise or fall in the real exchange rate). Therefore it only appears in the table in the section which analyses the peak to trough effect.
17. Relative price level data are only available with a two-year lag, so the 2009 figure was imputed from HICP data for the Eurozone and each country and the change in the nominal exchange rate.
18. See Filacek et al. (2006) for a detailed analysis of the implantation of the exchange rate criterion.

REFERENCES

Brooke, A. (2005), 'The Challenges of EMU Accession Faced by Catching-up Countries: a Slovak Republic Case Study', *OECD Economics Department Working Paper*, no. 444.

Dabrowski, M. (2007), 'EMU Enlargement: A Progress Report', CESifo Forum.

Dabušinskas, A. and D. Kulikov (2007), 'New Keynesian Phillips Curve for Estonia, Latvia and Lithuania', *Bank of Estonia Working Paper*, no. 2007-7.

Darvas, Z. and G. Szapary (2008), 'Euro Area Enlargement and Euro Adoption Strategies', *IHEAS Discussion Paper*, no. 0824.

De Grauwe, P. and G. Schnabl (2005), 'Nominal versus Real Convergence: EMU Entry Scenarios for New Member States', *Kyklos*, **58**, 537-555.

Dobrinsky, R. (2006), 'Catch-up Inflation and Nominal Convergence: the Balancing Act for New EU Members', *Economic Systems*, **30**, 424-442.

Ebner, A. (2009), 'An Empirical Analysis on the Determinants of CEE Government Bond Spreads', *Emerging Markets Review*, **10**, 97-121.

European Commission (2005), 'New and Updated Budgetary Sensitivities for the EU Budgetary Surveillance', mimeo.

Filacek, J., R. Horvath. and M. Skorepa (2006), 'Monetary Policy before Euro Adoption: the Challenges for EU New Members', *William Davidson Institute Working Paper Series*, wp853.

Horvath, R., J. Antal, J. Filacek, J. Frait, V. Kotlan and M. Skorepa (2009), 'Monetary Policy Strategies before Euro Adoption: the Art of Chasing Many Rabbits', *Czech Economic Review*, **3**, 176-198.

Hughes Hallett, A. and J. Lewis (2007), 'Deficits, Debt and the Accession of New Member States to the Euro', *European Journal of Political Economy*, **32**, 316-337.

Jonas, J. and F. Mishkin (2003), 'Inflation Targeting in Transition Economies: Experience and Prospects', *NBER Working Paper*, no. 9667.

Lewis, J. (2009), 'Hitting and Hoping: Meeting the Exchange Rate and Inflation Criteria during a Period of Nominal Convergence', *European Journal of Political Economy*, **28**, 508-524.

Lewis, J. and K. Staehr (2010), 'Maastricht Inflation Criterion: What is the Effect of EU Enlargement?', *Journal of Common Market Studies*, **48**, 687-708.

Masso, J. and K. Staehr (2005), 'Inflation Dynamics and Nominal Adjustment in the Baltic States', *Research in International Business and Finance*, **19**, 281-303.

Mihajlov, A., F. Rumler, and J. Scharler (2009), 'Inflation Dynamics in the New EU Member States: How Relevant Are External Factors?', Working Paper 0913, University of Linz.

Nickel, C., P.C. Rother and J.C. Rülke (2009), 'Fiscal Variables and Bond Spreads: Evidence from Eastern European Countries and Turkey', *ECB Working Paper*, 11101.

Staehr, K. (2010), 'The Global Financial Crisis and Public Finances in the New EU Countries from Central and Eastern Europe', *Working Papers of Eesti Pank*, 2/2010.

12. Portfolio and Short-term Capital Inflows to the New and Potential EU Countries: Patterns and Determinants

Mara Pirovano, Jacques Vanneste and André Van Poeck

1. INTRODUCTION

The present study aims to analyse the patterns and the determinants of inflows of short-term capital in the new and potential EU countries.[1]

The scope of our research is twofold. First, we aim to investigate the trends and patterns of short-term capital inflows in the new and potential EU member countries: in particular, we will examine the extent to which capital inflows in the potential and candidate countries of South-Eastern Europe benefited from the recent EU membership of the Central and Eastern European countries. Secondly, we want to investigate the factors driving short-term capital flows and portfolio flows in the countries of interest adopting a 'push-pull' framework, emphasising the role of government policy and financial sector development in shaping the magnitude and the composition of capital inflows. 'Pull' factors include the internal characteristics of a country that determine its attractiveness to international investors, like macro-economic performance, development of the banking sector and institutional quality. External, or 'push', factors originate outside the boundary of a country: high availability of capital and low interest rates in industrial countries 'push' capital towards developing countries, for diversification or speculative purposes (Montiel and Reinhart, 1999). Distinguishing between push and pull factors is important because it allows us to understand whether capital flows are driven by internal characteristics of a country, which strictly depend on economic policy and institutional development, and hence are under direct control of the country's authorities, or by external factors (and therefore out of the control of the country's authorities).

The rest of the chapter is organised as follows. In section 2 we show the trends and patterns of short-term capital inflows to the new and potential EU member countries in the last two decades. Examining the composition of the inflows of capital, we find that potential member economies are less exposed to short-term capital. Section 3 presents the analysis of the factors driving short-term capital inflows to the countries of interest. First, a brief review of the existing studies is presented. Then, the methodology and the results of our econometric analysis are exposed. Section 4 concludes.

2. CAPITAL INFLOWS TO THE NEW AND POTENTIAL EU COUNTRIES

The countries of Central and Eastern Europe have attracted increasing amounts of capital since the beginning of their transition towards a market economy at the end of the 1980s. The fall of the Berlin Wall and the disruption of the Soviet bloc opened the capital markets of Eastern European countries to international investors seeking new investment opportunities motivated by strategic, speculative or diversification purposes. Capital account liberalisation occurred at a different pace in the ex-Soviet countries, depending on the internal economic conditions and level of macroeconomic development.[2]

After current account convertibility was achieved, as a condition for IMF membership, between 1994 and 1996 and after OECD membership led many countries (Czech Republic, Hungary, Poland, and the Slovak Republic) to liberalise their capital account, EU membership dictated full capital account liberalisation in all the new member countries. International investors, attracted by the prospect of economic restructuring and expectations of future economic growth in the region, injected large amounts of capital. According to the IMF, in 1989 net capital flows in the region as a whole amounted to 535.5 billion US dollars. After a decade, they reached 653.6 billion US dollars and in 2008 that amounted to 2309.1 billion US dollars (certainly influenced by the recent membership in the European Union[3] of the ex-Soviet satellites). Capital flows are classified into three major categories according to the type of traded instruments and duration of the investment.

Foreign direct investment (FDI) implies a long-term relationship between a foreign investor and a domestic firm, and a significant degree of influence of the former on the latter. The foreign investor takes an ownership position in the domestic firm, and contributes essentially to its management. 'Portfolio investment' comprises instruments such as equity and debt securities, generally acquired by small investors with purposes of portfolio diversification. Therefore, foreign portfolio investors usually do not control the domestic firm. The category 'Other Investment' includes all instruments not comprised in the first two categories such as bank loans, transactions in currency and deposits, and trade credits that do not imply a long-lasting relationship or a significant influence of the foreign investor on the recipient of the investment. Figure 12.1 depicts the trends of short-term foreign capital inflows (obtained as the sum of portfolio and other investment liabilities) as a percentage of national GDP in the new and potential EU countries.

Three major facts draw our attention. First, the figure shows that, among the new members, the Baltic countries exhibit a similar increasing trend of short-term capital inflows. These countries never experienced net outflows of short-term capital since the beginning of the 1990s and the magnitude of inflows intensified in the new millennium.

Second, Figure 12.1 reveals a dispersion in the magnitude of short-term inflows to the new member countries of Central Europe. In particular, during the last years of the past century, the Czech and Slovak Republics experienced higher inflows, whereas countries like Bulgaria, Hungary and Poland exhibit lower inflows with even some episodes of capital outflow (in Bulgaria, from 1993 to 1996 and again in 1998; in Poland in 1994 and in 1996; in Hungary, in 1996 and 1997). Slovenia and Romania are situated somewhere in the middle: Romania, in particular, exhibits a small episode of capital outflow at the end of the century. From 2003 on, short-run capital is the increasing in all countries with exception of an abrupt drop in the Slovak Republic in 2006.

Third, the figure reveals a more stable pattern of short-term capital inflow in the potential member countries.[4] Among the set of countries, Croatia exhibits the largest volume of capital inflows, while Macedonia is the only country experiencing a (small) capital outflow in 2002. Moreover, these countries show no tendency towards an increase in capital inflows after 2004 (year in which many Central and Eastern European countries obtained EU membership), revealing that foreign investors were not influenced by the EU enlargement in their investment decisions with respect to Southern European countries. On the other hand, Figure 12.1 reveals significant increases in inflows of short-term capital in the new member states during the years of the run-up to EU membership. Nevertheless, the pattern of short-term capital inflows in the potential members between 2002 and 2007 is very similar to that of the new members between 1998 and 2002 (the pre-accession period): the volume of inflows is, on average, less than 15% of GDP and it exhibits a similar volatility.

The recent financial crisis had a strong impact on capital inflows to the new and potential member countries. IMF projections foresee, for 'emerging Europe' as a whole, a significant reduction in net FDI inflows, and a net outflow of portfolio and other forms of investment in 2009 and 2010 (*World Economic Outlook*, April 2009).

Central and Eastern Europe

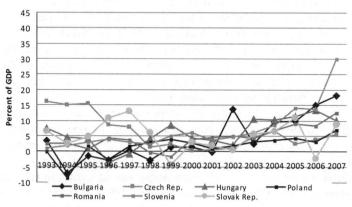

Baltic countries

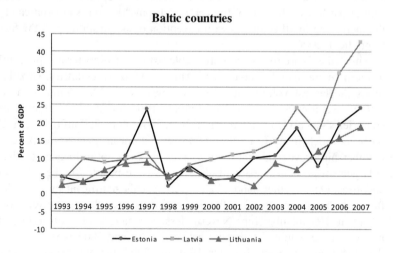

Source: Authors' calculations based on the IFS dataset.

Figure 12.1   Short-term capital inflows as a percentage of GDP: Central and Eastern Europe, Baltic countries and potential new EU members

Potential EU members

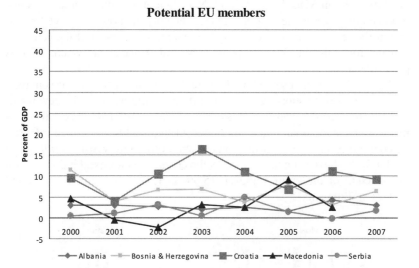

Figure 12.1 (continued)

Figure 12.2 portrays the evolution of the composition of capital inflows in the single countries considered. As we can observe, it is difficult to see a general pattern, because the composition of capital inflows is very country-specific. Some of the member countries such as Latvia, Lithuania (except for an inversion of tendency from 1999 to 2003) and Slovenia exhibit an average predominance of inflows of capital, other than portfolio investment during the whole sample period. Portfolio inflows are, in general, less predominant, except for Hungary, Lithuania in 2000 and 2001, Poland in 2004 and 2005, Slovak Republic in 1993 and 1994 and Slovenia in 1996. Most of the countries exhibit an increase in the share of foreign direct investment inflows between the end of the 20th century and the beginning of the new millennium.

Nevertheless, in most recent years, FDI inflows dominate the scene only in Bulgaria, in the Czech Republic and Hungary. Other investment inflows are predominant in the other countries. The potential new member countries exhibit on average a smaller share of portfolio inflows. Croatia is the country that between 1996 and 2006 received the highest share of portfolio inflows. Foreign direct investment is predominant in Albania, in Macedonia in 2001, 2002 and 2006. In Croatia, FDI took a larger share of total inflows in the first two years of the 1990s and between 1998 and 2001.

Other investment inflows constitute a consistent share of total inflows in all countries, although outflows are registered in Croatia in the beginning of the 1990s and in Macedonia in 2002. Nonetheless we notice, grouping port-folio and other investment in the broader category of short-term investments, that in the recent years this category is predominant in most of the countries (except for Albania, Bulgaria, Hungary and Macedonia, where FDI is preponderant).

All in all, we can observe that the potential member countries are on average less exposed to short-term capital inflows, while many of the new member countries rely heavily on this form of financing. This makes the new member states more vulnerable to the recent financial turmoil: the three Baltic countries (which present the highest share of other investment inflows in total inflows) have been heavily hit by the crisis, and they exhibit the sharpest fall in GDP of the entire region (–15.6% in Estonia, –18% in Latvia and –12.6% in Lithuania).[5]

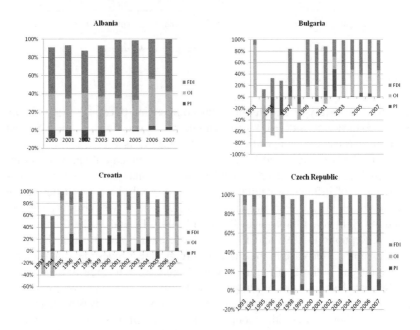

Source: Authors' calculations based on the IFS dataset.

Figure 12.2   Composition of total capital inflows

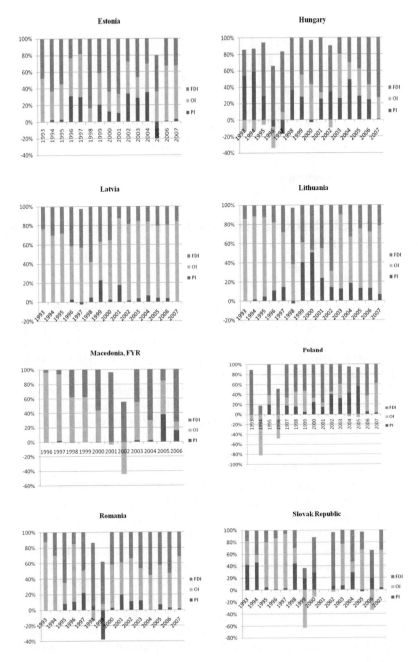

Figure 12.2 (continued)

Figure 12.2   (continued)

3. DETERMINANTS OF SHORT-TERM CAPITAL INFLOWS

3.1. Literature

The majority of studies concerning the determinants of capital inflows adopt the higher-mentioned 'push-pull' framework. Studying the relative importance of push and pull factors is important in that it gives information regarding the potential role of economic policy in shaping the magnitude and the composition of capital flows to a country.

The 'push-pull' framework has been extensively used in the existing empirical literature on the determinants of capital flows to emerging economies. Although no general consensus has been reached as to whether external or domestic factors are more important in explaining capital inflows, the most recent studies suggest that pull variables play a decisive role in the matter.

One of the most well-known studies that highlight the superiority of push variables is by Fernandez-Arias (1996). He approaches the question by developing a model of international portfolio allocation, where country creditworthiness plays an explicit role. Although he confirms that country creditworthiness is a significant factor in explaining capital inflows, he finds that international interest rates are a more important determinant. Therefore, he concludes that push factors dominate domestic ones. In a later study, Taylor and Sarno (1997) use data on portfolio flows from the US to a group of Latin American and Asian countries and conclude that both internal and external factors have equal importance in explaining the inflows of portfolio capital. Subsequent studies started to challenge these views, and point towards an increased importance of domestic factors in explaining portfolio and short-term flows.

Montiel and Reinhart (1999) consider a sample of 15 emerging economies in Latin America, Asia and Africa and estimate a fixed-effect panel in order to identify the effect of two countercyclical policies (namely sterilisation and restriction to capital flows), international interest rates and the development of the domestic capital market. Their results highlight a significant positive effect of sterilised intervention on the volume of total capital flows associated with a rise in the share of short-term capital, suggesting that the policy choices are indeed important in shaping the composition of capital inflows. The effect of capital controls is also a significant explanatory variable, and it is associated with a shift in the composition of total flows towards FDI and long-term debt. Finally, the authors find that indicators of financial market depth are significant and positive in explaining the magnitude of inflows, and that they have a particular importance in explaining portfolio inflows.

In the same wave, Carlson and Hernández (2002) focus on 8 countries that are meant to represent the areas that received the greatest share of capital inflows during the last decade (Asia, Latin America and Central and Eastern Europe), and they test whether policy and real factors affect the share of short-term flows and portfolio equity flows. They use three policy variables, namely the exchange rate regime, capital controls and a measure of sterilisation. The results for short-term debt confirm that high sterilisation leads to higher share of short run debt. Concerning the exchange rate regime, the authors conclude that a dirty float or a free float also increases the share of short-term flows. Finally, higher growth rates tend to decline short-term flows in Asian countries, while it is not significant for the rest of the countries in the sample. Portfolio investments are positively related to domestic GDP growth and to past values of portfolio investments. Moreover, while a floating exchange rate regime significantly reduces the share of portfolio investment and capital controls are not significant, countries that have both capital controls and a fixed exchange rate see their share of inward portfolio investment decline. Observing the results obtained for FDI and for portfolio investment, the authors conclude that the latter react in the same way as the former to policy and real variables, and opposite compared to short-term flows. Therefore, they lay doubt on the conventional wisdom that portfolio investments share the same characteristics of short-term investments.

Another study confirming the importance of pull factors by applying dynamic panel data techniques to a set of developing countries to explain FDI and portfolio inflows has been performed by Amaya and Rowland (2004). These authors included in their analysis pull variables such as market size, macroeconomic variables, indicators of openness and variables concerning government finance, together with a set of push variables pertaining to the US economy. They find that only one push factor, US GDP growth, is significant in explaining portfolio flows, while among the pull factors they find indicators of market size, economic growth and the government debt position to be significant determinants. Their results suggest that portfolio investment tends to favour larger and faster-growing economies that implement prudent fiscal policies. Moreover, the statistical insignificance of lagged values of net portfolio inflows confirms the widespread classification of this type of inflows as 'hot money', i.e. characterised by higher volatility and a lesser degree of persistence.

Domestic factors are found to be important also in explaining international bank lending. Buch and Lusinyan (2002) estimate a panel data model explaining the share of short-term bank lending in total international financing and the share of short-term domestic debt securities in total securities in 60 countries. Among the significant determinants of short-term international bank lending, the authors find factors like market size and development, the importance of inter-bank market and the presence of financial centres while the exchange rate regime and EU membership turn out to be insignificant. Specifically, GDP per capita and the share of M2 over GDP positively influence the share of short-term debt securities: countries with a higher level of development and deeper financial markets will be recipients of higher shares of short-term securities.

Subsequent studies offer significant contributions to the literature by considering the degree of development of the recipient country's institutions. A recent application to a set of 55 countries (including the new EU members and Croatia) is provided by Faria and Mauro (2004). They perform cross-sectional regressions of FDI, portfolio and other short-term liabilities stocks, including as explanatory variables both domestic macroeconomic factors and institutional ones. In particular, primary and secondary school attainment, an institutional quality index and market capitalisation of listed firms are considered. Their results reveal that institutional quality is positively correlated with portfolio equity and FDI, and that high market capitalisation is positively correlated with portfolio equity. They conclude that weak institutions tend to encourage countries to rely on more volatile and crisis-prone sources of financing, while better institutions are associated with higher shares of FDI and portfolio investment.

The empirical literature concerning capital inflows in the new and potential EU members is relatively scarce. Nevertheless, the existing studies point towards the importance of pull variables in explaining inflows of both FDI and short-term capital. Baláž and Williams (2001) analyse the determinants of FDI, portfolio and other short-term inflows for the Czech and Slovak Republics, Poland and Hungary from 1990 to 1997. Their model includes both push (difference between domestic and foreign interest rates) and pull (macroeconomic and population) variables. While the role of government policies and institutions is not investigated, they include the ratio of M2 to

GDP as a proxy for the development of the financial sector. The results of their cross-sectional regression highlight that while FDI investors are less influenced by fluctuations in interest rates and trade balances, these factors are important for investors with a short-term horizon. In particular, for the regression of short-term capital inflows, the ratio of M2 to GDP, the interest rate margin and the inflation rate are the most significant variables. Their results for portfolio inflows reveal a very low explanatory power, and only one variable (per capita GDP) is significant. They attribute this outcome to the heterogeneity of portfolio investors that could have obscured the analysis of the independent variables.[6]

The difficulty of modelling portfolio capital flows in the Central and Eastern European countries has been encountered also by Garibaldi et al. (2001). They perform a dynamic panel estimation of portfolio inflows as a function of inflation, exchange rate regime, market perceptions as captured by 'country risk' ratings, US short-term interest rate, securities market index, international reserves per capita, political stability and security of property. Their results reveal that portfolio inflows are significantly associated only with the development of the financial sector and protection of property rights.

Finally, Lozovy and Kudina (2007) analyse the determinant of portfolio inflows in the CIS countries (among which Bulgaria, Czech Republic, Hungary, Poland, Romania, and Slovakia). They conclude that important determinants of portfolio flows include the domestic deposit interest rate, which exerts a negative impact on the dependent variable, political stability and the quality of institutions. Moreover, indicators of the international economic activity (push factors) are not found to influence portfolio investment inflows.

3.2. Modelling the Determinants of Short-term Capital Inflows

In the following analysis, we pay particular attention to two factors that have been given limited importance in the existing studies on the determinants of portfolio and short-term inflows in the new and potential EU countries.

First, we share the idea developed by Montiel and Reinhart (2000) according to which the policy responses enhanced by a country's authority might contribute to shape both the magnitude and the composition of capital inflows. Therefore, we include in the determinants of capital flows variables that represent countercyclical policies and structural policies such as sterilisation, fiscal policy and strengthening of the banking sector.[7]

Sterilisation policy constitutes an attempt by central banks to prevent capital inflows to exert an expansionary effect on the money supply.[8] It involves increasing the reserves of foreign currency through the selling of government securities in order to keep the monetary base unchanged. Sterilised intervention has the power to avoid monetary expansion and it has the advantage of limiting the intermediation of banks of capital inflows, thereby reducing their vulnerability in the event of a sudden reversal.[9]

Nevertheless, this is a two-edged sword, and has important drawbacks. First of all, it entails the accumulation of foreign assets that typically yield lower interest rates than domestic currency denominated assets. Therefore, the interest rate payments resulting from this kind of manoeuvre could become a burden for the government (quasi-fiscal costs). Secondly, the issuance of government securities leads the interest rate to increase, thereby encouraging new waves of capital (Jang-Yung Lee, 1997). Thirdly, in the event of domestic currency appreciation, domestic authorities are exposed to decreases in the values of their assets.[10] As a proxy for sterilisation policy we construct a sterilisation index based on the ratio of broad money changes to changes in international reserves. In particular, following Carlson and Hernández (2002),[11] the index is constructed as:

$$Sterilisation\, Index = -\frac{M2_t - M2_{t-1}}{IR_t - IR_{t-1}}\ .$$

In case of complete sterilisation, the increase in international reserves does not affect the money supply, therefore the index will be close to zero. If the money supply increases as a consequence of an increase in international reserves, both nominator and denominator of the index will increase. Reversing the sign makes the index easier to interpret: higher values of the index imply higher sterilisation.

In order to assess the role of fiscal policy in shaping the volume and composition of capital inflows, we include the government deficit (as a percentage of GDP) in our model. A tight fiscal policy can effectively help reducing the risks associated with an expansion of aggregate demand, without running into problems characterising sterilised intervention.

We use the ratio of the liquid reserves of banks to assets as an indicator of the strengthening of the banking system: by increasing the amount of liquid reserves, the authorities try to offset the expansion of credit originating from large capital inflows.

Second, when dealing with portfolio investment, we believe that it is very important to consider the development of the domestic financial market as a factor responsible for the attraction of capital flows (Montiel and Reinhart, 2000; Baláž and Williams, 2001). Indeed, as portfolio flows are more volatile and more subject to sudden withdrawals than FDI flows, a sound financial sector ensures that the inward flows are adequately intermediated and efficiently managed. Moreover, if the financial market is not fully developed, the variety of instruments available to foreign investors willing to invest in a country is limited usually to debt instruments (see also Garibaldi et al., 2001). Therefore, to account for the depth of the financial system, we include the variable 'number of listed companies on the domestic stock market'.

The recent empirical literature we reviewed in the previous section found an important role of institutional quality in explaining both FDI and short-term forms of international investment. Although we acknowledge the importance of including such institutional variables in our analysis, we are constrained by data availability. A complete dataset including data on corruption, regulatory quality and rule-of-law has been compiled by Kaufmann et al. (2009). Data are available for the last decade in yearly frequency. Including these variables in our model would however significantly reduce the size of our sample or result in a model where too many series are the result of linear interpolation.

Our model includes push and pull variables present in the majority of studies concerning the determinants of capital inflows. As push variables, we consider the German Treasury Bill rate and German GDP. The pull variables represent macroeconomic fundamentals. In particular, the domestic short-term interest rate (to capture returns on investments), the GDP level (to capture market size), the current account balance (performance of the external sector) and the exchange rate regime are included as independent variables. Finally, we include the degree of privatisation (private sector's share of GDP) as an additional pull variable. The new and potential EU member states of Central and Eastern Europe are characterised by a past in which state ownership was widespread, leaving little or no room for private entrepreneurship. During the transition from central planning to market economy, an increasing amount of industries were privatised, thereby increasing the need of the new private enterprises to attract foreign savings. Following the previous discussion, we model short-term capital inflows and their determinants as follows:

$$CapInf = f(\ Logarithm\ of\ German\ GDP,$$
$$German\ short\text{-}term\ interest\ rate,$$
$$logarithm\ of\ domestic\ GDP,$$
$$domestic\ short\text{-}term\ interest\ rate,$$
$$current\ account\ balance,$$
$$exchange\ rate\ regime,$$
$$sterilisation\ index,$$
$$government\ balance,$$
$$bank\ liquidity,$$
$$number\ of\ companies\ listed\ in\ domestic\ stock\ market,$$
$$privatisation\ ) + u\ .$$

The appendix provides a detailed description of the dataset and the data sources. The equation is estimated for two specifications of the dependent variable: volume of foreign portfolio inflows as a percentage of national GDP, and volume of foreign other investment inflows as a percentage of national GDP. We specify a dynamic linear panel model where the dependent variable is regressed on its own first lag and the set of independent variables.12 The independent variables are treated as strictly exogenous, with the only exception of the sterilisation policy variable. Indeed, we deem the current magnitude of short-term inflows to influence current sterilisation. Therefore we expect this policy variable to be correlated with the current error term.

We implement the Generalised Method of Moments (GMM) estimator proposed by Arellano and Bond (1991), using lagged values of the endogenous variable as instruments for the current values. We do not make the endogeneity assumption for the other policy variable (i.e. fiscal balance) because current fiscal policy is the result of an often long political debate. We therefore do not expect the volume and share of current short-term capital inflows to influence current fiscal policy. We estimate the model for 12 countries,[13] of which 10 are the new EU members of Central and Eastern Europe (Bulgaria, the Czech Republic, Estonia, Hungary, Latvia, Lithuania, Poland, Romania, the Slovak Republic and Slovenia) and two are West-Balkan countries eligible for EU candidacy (Croatia and Macedonia (FYR)). Quarterly data ranging from 1994:1 to 2007:4 on the dependent and independent variables were collected for each country.

3.3. Estimation Results

The results presented in Table 12.1 reveal that the explanatory power of our specification is very different according to the dependent variable considered. In particular, the model explaining the volume of portfolio inflows performs poorly. Only a few variables are significant and their signs correspond to our expectations only in the case of the logarithm of German GDP, whose higher values are associated with larger portfolio inflows. The domestic interest rate, the number of listed companies and the share of private sector in GDP carry a negative sign, while we expected them to increase the inflows of portfolio capital. Given the high correlation between the variables 'listed companies' and 'bank liquidity', we re-estimated the model dropping one of the variables.[14] While the model estimated without the 'bank liquidity' variable performs as the one in Table 12.1, the one without the 'listed companies' variable is slightly different, in that only the variable 'German GDP' is significant and still positive.

Table 12.1 Determinants of short-term capital inflows – Arellano-Bond Dynamic GMM Panel regression (robust standard errors)

	Independent variables	Dependent variable			
		Portfolio inflows (%GDP)		Other (non-FDI) inflows (%GDP)	
		coefficient	t-stat (P-value)	coefficient	t-stat (P-value)
Push	Lagged dependent	-0.0759	-1.33 (0.183)	0.0193	0.31 (0.754)
	GDP Germany	5.9266	2.52** (0.012)	-4.6939	-1.48 (0.139)
	Interest rate Germany	-0.2524	-0.89 (0.372)	0.1411	0.43 (0.667)
Pull	GDP	-4.1675	-1.92* (0.055)	17.143	3.48*** (0.000)
	Interest rate	-0.0102	-1.84* (0.066)	0.0423	2.95*** (0.003)
	CA balance	-0.0429	-0.97 (0.330)	-0.3166	-4.59*** (0.000)
	Exchange rate regime	0.7348	0.85 (0.395)	2.8948	2.62*** (0.009)
	Sterilisation	-0.0060	-0.64 (0.522)	0.0070	1.01 (0.315)
	Government balance	-0.1464	-1.16 (0.245)	0.1250	0.66 (0.512)
	Bank liquidity	0.0030	0.16 (0.872)	0.0528	2.41** (0.016)
	Listed companies	-0.0007	-3.69*** (0.000)	0.0099	1.70* (0.088)
	Privatisation	-0.0739	-1.70* (0.089)	-0.0450	-0.46 (0.644)
number of observations		479		479	
Wald χ^2		43.51 (0.000)		49634.71 (0.000)	
Sargan test		471.51 (0.4328)		484.225 (0.2814)	
autocorrelation test:					
1st order		-2.180 (0.0292)		-2.463 (0.0137)	
2nd order		-0.344 (0.7303)		0.085 (0.9322)	

Note: Significance code: *** significant at the 0.01 level; ** significant at the 0.05 level; * significant at the 0.1 level.

These results seem to suggest that high availability of capital in external economies (and in this particular case with Germany, which is the European country with the strongest commercial and financial links with Eastern Europe) pushes portfolio inflows to the new and potential members. As for pull factors, they either do not significantly explain portfolio inflows or they decrease them.

The results for other capital inflows (including bank loans, transactions in currency and deposits, and trade credits) are more satisfying in terms of overall significance of the explanatory variables. In particular, pull variables such as the domestic short-term interest rate and the logarithm of domestic GDP significantly increase the inwards volume of short-term capital. Our results also reveal the significance of the current account balance in shaping the volume of other short-term inflows. In particular, the coefficient is negative, meaning that this type of capital inflow tends to diminish with a better external performance. This result is not surprising, given that trade credits are a component of other inflows. Also, the exchange rate dummy is positive and significant: international investors interested in short-term investment pay attention to issues related to exchange rate risk when directing their capital towards transition economies. A fixed exchange rate insures investors against a sudden and unexpected decrease in the value of their investments. A more liquid banking sector (characterised by a high ratio of reserves to assets) contributes to attract greater volumes of short-term capital. This is mainly due to the fact that a more liquid banking system reduces the risk of a liquidity crisis that could compromise the profitability of investments. If we interpret higher bank reserve requirements as a policy choice in order to contain the expansion of domestic credit, the significant and positive coefficient in our regression suggests that by increasing the volume of short-term inflows expansion of domestic credit is likely to increase. Nevertheless, as this explanatory variable was not considered as endogenous in our analysis, its causal relation with the dependent variable might be biased by possible endogeneity.[15]

Our results reveal that neither of the policy variables is significant. Moreover, looking at the signs of the coefficients, we notice that, while in the regression of portfolio inflows both variables carry a negative sign, in the model explaining other inflows both estimated coefficients are positive. Moreover, the institutional indicator concerning the development of the financial sector is significant and positive, while the degree of privatisation is not significant.

Overall we notice, on the one hand, how macroeconomic indicators significantly explain other capital inflows, while they are not significant in the regressions for portfolio inflows. On the other hand, we expected a significant impact of push factors on other inflows, while in fact the level of German GDP is significant for the regression of portfolio inflows and not for other inflows.

Our empirical analysis of portfolio and other forms of capital inflows lead us to formulate the following conclusions. First, our findings suggest that portfolio and other investment flows (bank loans, trade credits, transactions in currency and deposits and other short-term capital) are very different in nature and can hardly be grouped under the same denominator. Not only do they exhibit different patterns both within and across countries, but also they do not share the same determinants. Second, the lack of explanatory power of our model of portfolio inflows suggests the inadequacy of a model based on macroeconomic data.

This finding can be interpreted in two ways. It could be a signal that aggregate data are not able to capture the risk and expected profitability dimensions international investors look at before making their investment decisions. A useful direction for further research might therefore be towards the analysis of the characteristic of firms located in the countries of interest, recipient of foreign portfolio investment. Anyway, this will require the collection of good quality firm-level data on portfolio investment. A second interpretation would connect the overall insignificance of macroeconomic variables in explaining portfolio inflows with their unresponsiveness to macroeconomic fundamentals. If investment decisions are driven by speculative and diversification purposes, these will hardly be captured in macroeconomic data. Moreover, herding and non-rational behaviour could be significant determinants. Third, given the insignificance of the macroeconomic policy variables, it emerges that a country's authorities do not have much power to shape capital inflows. Therefore, more effort should be put into building an adequate financial system, capable of efficiently managing capital and protect the economy from destabilising speculative behaviour. In this fashion sudden withdrawals, currency and banking crises can be avoided or, in case they occur, their consequences on the real economy can be mitigated.

4. CONCLUSION

In this chapter we analyse the patterns and the determinants of portfolio and short-term capital inflows in the new and potential EU member states of Central and South Eastern Europe. Our main findings are the following.

First, the analysis of the evolution of portfolio and short-term inflows shows heterogeneity and variability among the new EU members, while the potential and candidate countries exhibit a more similar and stable pattern. In particular, there is a general tendency towards an increase in short-term capital inflows in all the new member states from 2003 onwards. This tendency is not present in the potential member countries. This seems to indicate that EU membership of their neighbouring countries did not lead to spillovers in capital inflows. As for the composition of capital inflows, we conclude that, grouping portfolio and other investment in the broader category of short-term investments, this category is predominant in most of the countries (except for

Albania, Bulgaria, Hungary and Macedonia, where FDI is preponderant). All in all, we can observe that the potential member countries are on average less exposed to short-term capital inflows, while many of the new member countries rely heavily on this form of financing.

Second, our analysis of the determinants of capital inflows to the new and potential EU members, leads us to conclude the following. Firstly, our findings suggest that portfolio and other investment flows (bank loans, trade credits, transactions in currency and deposits and other short-term capital) are very different in nature and can hardly be grouped under the same heading. Secondly, the lack of explanatory power of our model of portfolio inflows suggests the inadequacy of a model based on macroeconomic data. This could be a signal that aggregate data are not able to capture the risk-return trade-off international investors look at before making their investment decisions. Another explanation might be that portfolio inflows are unresponsive to macroeconomic fundamentals. Thirdly, given the insignificance of the macroeconomic policy variables, it emerges that national authorities do not have much power to shape capital inflows. Therefore, more effort should be put into building an adequate financial system, capable of efficiently managing capital and protect the economy from destabilising speculative behaviour. In this fashion sudden withdrawals, currency and banking crises can be avoided or, in case they occur, their consequences on the real economy can be mitigated.

Useful directions for further research involve the analysis of the determinants of short-term capital inflows to the new and potential EU members, using a microeconomic approach. On the one hand, analysis of firm level data would assist in explaining the link between portfolio inflows and the expected profitability of firms, transparency and efficiency of management. On the other hand, the lack of correlation between portfolio inflows and macroeconomic fundamentals found in our model could be examined from the perspective of behavioural finance. This would enable the detection of possible herding behaviour and speculative and diversification purposes of international investors. Finally, focusing on the policy perspective and on the current financial crisis, further research will be needed in order to analyse the reactions of international capital markets to the policy responses enacted by the single countries to stabilise the economy, as soon as data will be available.

APPENDIX

Data sources

Variable Name	Description	Source
Portfolio inflow volume	Foreign net portfolio inflows as a percentage of national GDP	IMF, International Financial Statistic Database (IFS). Lines 78bgd[16] and 99b..zf
'Other inflow' volume	Foreign net other inflows as a percentage of national GDP	IMF, *IFS*. Lines 78bid and 99b..zf
GDP	Logarithm of the dollar value of national GDP	IMF, *IFS*. Computed from lines 99b..zf
Short-term interest rate	3-month Treasury Bill rate. When not available, the deposit rate is used	IMF, *IFS*. Line 60c (Treasury bill rate) Line 60l (Deposit rate)
Current account balance	Current account balance as a percentage of national GDP	IMF, *IFS*. Line 78ald
Exchange rate regime dummy	1 = fixed; 0 = flexible	The classification of exchange rate regimes has been drawn from Dirk Effenberger (2004) for the years 1994-2002, and from IMF (Classification of Exchange Rate Arrangements and Monetary Frameworks, www.imf.org/external/np/mfd/er)
Sterilisation index	Ratio of the change in broad money (dollar value) to the change in international reserves, multiplied by –1.	IMF, *IFS*. Series codes: M2: 91859MB.ZF... Foreign exchange: 918.1D.DZF...
Government balance[17]	Government revenue minus expenditure	EBRD, *Transition Report* (2008)
Bank liquidity[17]	Banks liquidity to assets ratio	World Bank, *World Development Indicators* (WDI) (2007)
Listed companies[17]	Number of companies listed on the domestic stock market.	World Bank, *World Development Indicators* (WDI) (2007)
Private sector share[17]	Private sector share in total GDP	World Bank, *World Development Indicators* (WDI) (2007)

NOTES

1. The new member countries are: Bulgaria, the Czech Republic, Estonia, Hungary, Latvia, Lithuania, Poland, Romania, the Slovak Republic and Slovenia. The potential member countries of South-Eastern Europe are: Albania, Croatia, Macedonia, Montenegro and Serbia. Among them, Croatia and Macedonia are official candidates for EU membership.
2. See Arvai (2005) for a discussion on capital account liberalisation in the new member states.
3. The Czech Republic, Estonia, Hungary, Latvia, Lithuania, Poland, the Slovak Republic and Slovenia joined the EU in 2004. Bulgaria and Romania joined in 2007.
4. Due to limited data availability, we had to restrict our analysis to seven years and to exclude Montenegro.
5. *The Economist*, May 16th 2009, p. 33.
6. Baláž and Williams (2001), p. 10.
7. We do not consider capital controls because this policy tool is not available to the new EU member countries, as the Maastricht Treaty requires full liberalisation of the capital account.
8. See Jang-Yung Lee (1997) for a detailed discussion on the use of sterilisation policy.
9. López-Mejía (1999).
10. For a discussion of domestic implications of sterilised intervention and foreign currency accumulation, see Mohanti and Turner (2006).
11. Carlson and Hernández (2002) construct the index using the change in the dollar value of net domestic assets instead of using the change in broad money, in order to capture the degree to which the authorities contract domestic credit in order to prevent an expansion of the monetary base. However, data on net domestic assets are not available for some of the countries in our sample and, when they are, they cover only a limited time span.
12. We refer to Verbeek (2008) for a discussion of the issues related to dynamic panel data estimation.
13. Albania, Bosnia and Herzegovina and Serbia and Montenegro were excluded from the analysis due to lack of data availability on the chosen time period. Data for these countries were available starting from the beginning of the 21st century, reducing the common sample to less than 20 (quarterly) time observations. As dynamic panel estimation requires at least two lags of each variable in order to estimate the equation for each time period, restricting the sample would result in a less efficient and precise estimation.
14. The results are not reported, but are available upon request.
15. Anyway, the results do not change by running the same regression controlling for endogeneity of the liquidity variable.
16. Note that this category excludes investments by residents in foreign countries. Portfolio (and Other) investments liabilities, not including exceptional financing, represent net inflows of foreign capital in the reporting economy. A plus sign means that there has been a net inflow of foreign capital, while a minus sign means that foreign capital has been repatriated. The chosen category also excludes current transfers.
17. These figures were only available at annual frequency. Therefore they have been linearly interpolated into quarterly observations.

REFERENCES

Amaya, C.A. and P. Rowland (2004), 'Determinants of Investment Flows into Emerging Markets', Banco de la Republica de Colombia, *Borradores de Economia* no. 313.

Arellano, M. and S. Bond (1991), 'Some Tests of Specification for Panel Data: Monte Carlo Evidence and an Application to Employment Equations', *Review of Economic Studies*, **58**, 277-297.

Arvai, Z. (2005), 'Capital Account Liberalization, Capital Flow Patterns and Policy Responses in the EU's New Member States', *IMF Working Paper*, WP/05/213.

Baláž, V. and A.M. Williams (2001), 'Capital Mobility in Transition Countries of Central Europe: Macroeconomic Performance Factors and Structural Policies', *Ekonomický Časopis*, **2001**(1), Institute of Economic Research of the Slovak Academy of Science.

Buch, C.M. and L. Lusinyan (2002), 'Short Term Capital, Economic Transformation and EU Accession', *Economic Research Centre of the Deutsche Bundesbank Discussion Paper*, 2002(2).

Carlson, M. and L. Hernández (2002), 'Determinants and Repercussions of the Composition of Capital Inflows', *FRB International Finance Discussion Paper*, no. 717.

Effenberger, D. (2004), 'Institutional Vulnerability Indicators for Currency Crises in Central and Eastern European Countries', in M. Balling, F. Lierman, A. Mullineux (eds), *Financial Markets in Central and Eastern Europe: Stability and Efficiency Perspectives*, Routledge Studies in the European Economy.

Faria, A. and P. Mauro (2004), 'Institutions and the External Capital Structure of Countries', *IMF Working Paper*, WP/04/236.

Fernandez-Arias, E. (1996), 'The New Wave of Private Capital Inflows: Push or Pull?', *Journal of Development Economics*, **48**, 389-418.

Garibaldi, P., N. Mora, R. Sahay and J. Zettelmeyer (2001), 'What Moves Capital to Transition Economies?', *IMF Staff Papers*, **48**, 109-142.

International Monetary Fund (2009), 'Europe, Addressing the Crisis', *Regional Economic Outlook*, May 2009.

Kaufmann, D., A. Kraay and M. Mastruzzi (2009), 'Governance Matters VIII: Aggregate and Individual Governance Indicators, 1996-2008', *World Bank Policy Research Working Paper*, no. 4978.

Lee, J.Y. (1997), 'Sterilizing Capital Inflows', *Economic Issues*, IMF, no. 7.

López-Mejía, A. (1999), 'Large Capital Flows: a Survey of the Causes, the Consequences and Policy Responses', *IMF Working Paper*, WP/99/17.

Lozovy, O. and A. Kudina (2007), 'The Determinants of Portfolio Flows in the CIS Countries', *CASE Network Studies and Analysis*, no. 354.

Mohanti, M.S. and P. Turner (2006), 'Foreign Exchange Reserves Accumulation in Emerging Markets: What are the Domestic Implications?', *BIS Quarterly Review*, September 2006.

Montiel, P. and C.M. Reinhart (1999), 'Do Capital Controls and Macroeconomic Policies Influence the Volume and Composition of Capital Flows? Evidence from the 1990s', *Journal of International Money and Finance*, **18**, 619-635.

Montiel, P. and C.M. Reinhart (2000), 'The Dynamics of Capital Movements to Emerging Economies during the 1990s', in S. Griffith-Jones and M. Montes (eds), *Short-term Capital Movements and Balance of Payments Crises*, Oxford: Oxford University Press, 2000, pp. 3-28.

Taylor, M.P. and L. Sarno (1997), 'Capital Flows to Developing Countries: Long and Short-term Determinants', *World Bank Economic Review*, **11**, 451-470.

Verbeek, M. (2008), *A Guide to Modern Econometrics*, Chichester: Wiley.

13. Time-varying Diversification Benefits: the Impact of Capital Market Integration on European Portfolio Holdings

Alexandra Horobet and Sorin Dumitrescu

1. INTRODUCTION

International diversification of portfolio investments have intensified in the past years, as investors were seeking to reduce risk by globally spreading their holdings. The benefits of international diversification for international investors were first brought to the attention by Solnik (1974), who showed there is a limit to the risk reduction that may be achieved on a single domestic market, due to the same macroeconomic factors that influence domestic stock prices. Domestic diversification is capable of almost completely eliminating firm-specific risks but it leaves systematic risks untouched.

However, it is possible to attain further risk reduction by adding foreign securities to a domestic portfolio, building on the assumption that economic cycles are not fully synchronised between countries, which is reflected in less than positively correlated financial markets. Although several caveats have to be considered, such as exchange rate risk, the overall risk of an international portfolio, unhedged or hedged against currency risk, has been proven to be lower than that of a comparable domestic portfolio by various studies published afterwards (see, for example, Grauer and Hakansson, 1987; Jorion, 1989; Eaker and Grant, 1990). The main sources of diversification benefits are the low correlations between domestic capital markets, as shown by a vast literature in the field.

The benefits that internationally diversified holdings bring to an investor may be analysed from two perspectives: benefits arising from reduced volatility of international portfolios or benefits observed at the level of higher risk-adjusted returns as compared to a specific benchmark – here, international portfolios may be the minimum variance portfolios or the optimal portfolios, while the benchmark may be represented by a domestic portfolio or an equally or market capitalisation weighted international portfolio.

Our approach is to consider the benefits associated with holding internationally diversified portfolios from the perspective of their potential lower volatility and time-varying specificities. Therefore, we explore the time-varying benefits that Eurozone investors obtain from holding internationally diversified portfolios. From a theoretical perspective, the introduction of the Euro has an unclear effect on the portfolio decisions of Eurozone investors. We may expect indeed, on one hand, a reallocation of portfolios' weights in favour of EMU assets as a result of the complete elimination of currency risk, and, on the other hand, a higher weight for assets outside EU, as a direct consequence of increased financial market integration between European Union countries and the concomitant wish of EU investors therefore to diversify outside of the EU borders.

The chapter is structured as follows: Section 2 presents a review of the literature in the field, section 3 outlines the data and research methodology, Section 4 analyses the main results and section 5 concludes.

2. REVIEW OF RELEVANT LITERATURE

The increase in international economic integration in the past decades, fuelled by amplified cross-country trade and financial flows, raised the question of whether the benefits that international investors may obtain from holding internationally diversified portfolios did not diminish. International economic integration, translated in the integration of financial markets, is easily observable at the level of increased joint movements of financial markets around the world. In such circumstances, correlations between markets and assets traded in different domestic markets are expected to increase in time because the impediments to international investment are being progressively removed and countries are becoming more integrated, both from a political and economic point of view.

Roll (1992) argues that stronger economic integration may lead to lower correlation of asset returns if the integration process is associated with higher industrial specialisation, while Heston and Rouwenhorst (1994) identify country effects – fiscal, monetary, legal and cultural differences – as better explanatory factors for the co-movement of stock markets. Tavares (2009) analyses the impact of economic integration on cross-country co-movements of stock returns, in a large panel of developed and emerging countries, and finds that the correlation of returns is pushed up by bilateral trade intensity, while real exchange rate volatility, the asymmetry of output growth and export dissimilarity between countries tend to decrease it.

However, although studies generally confirm an upward trend of correlation coefficients among domestic capital markets, their trend over the last 30 to 40 years has been less abrupt than one might expect, because the enhanced competition between national economies has frequently led to specialisation. For example, Solnik et al. (1996) discovered a mean correlation of approximately 0.40 between US and foreign markets for the period between 1958 and 1995. These results were confirmed for the period between 1973 and 1982 by Eun and Resnick (1988). A slightly higher average correlation coefficient between US and foreign markets, of about 0.55, was calculated by Hunter and Coggin (1990) for the period from 1970 to 1986. More recent studies, such as Lee (2005), find that conditional correlations between the US, Japan, and the Hong Kong stock markets are positive and increasing in recent years. Overall, the set of evidence regarding the trend of correlations in time remains mixed: for example, Kaplanis (1988) and Ranter (1992) do not find consistent evidence in favour of increased cross-market correlations, but Longin and Solnik (1995) find that correlations have risen between 1960 and 1990. Bekaert and Hodrick (2006) use a risk-based factor model and conclude that no evidence of an upward trend in the correlation of returns across countries is observable, except in the case of European stock markets. Their findings are accompanied by research – see, for example, Ramchand and Susmel (1998), Goetzmann et al. (2001), Books and del Negro (2002), Heaney et al. (2002) and Larrain and Tavares (2003) – that shows that cross-country correlations in stock returns change over time and are generally higher in periods of accentuated integration and of high volatility of returns. But, as Fooladi and Rumsey (2006) point out, 'the differences among their results could be the artefact of the time period and need not apply to other times'.

Besides the findings referring to the value of correlation coefficients and their trend, a number of specificities of international capital markets are noteworthy (see Bracker et al., 1999): countries in proximate geographical areas tend to display greater co-movement than countries farther apart; pairs of national stock indices with similar industrial structure tend to experience more substantive co-movement; when the timing of movements is investigated, several different national markets display a significant relationship within the same 24-hour period, but beyond 24 hours they show few significant responses across markets. Nevertheless, empirical studies identified increased correlations and market interrelations as world capital markets evolved in the 1980s and 1990s, with a stronger tendency in the case of economically integrated markets such as European Union.

The extent of integration and its dynamics were investigated through the price differences or co-movements of markets, through the responses to information arrivals, or through the fit of models of capital flows and portfolio allocations. More sophisticated techniques, such as vector autoregression (VAR), Granger causality tests and co-integration are among the favourite tools in the more recent literature. Kasa (1992) estimates an error-correction VAR model and calculates a common stochastic trend for the equity markets of the United States, Japan, the United Kingdom, Germany and Canada. Jeon and Chiang (1991) examine the behaviour of stock prices in New York, Tokyo, London and Frankfurt stock markets based on univariate and multivariate co-integration techniques, while Chan et al. (1992) and Arshanapalli et al. (1993) study the links between the US and Asian equity markets. More recently, Chen et al. (2002) investigate the dynamic interdependence of the major stock markets in Latin America employing co-integration analysis and error-correction VAR techniques. Also, Hassan (2003) uses a multivariate co-integration analysis to test for the existence of a long-term relationship between share prices in the Persian Gulf. In case international capital markets would be co-integrated, this has interesting and concerning implications for international investors, as their efforts to improve the long-run risk-return profile of their investments would have to increase. The reasons of such long-term ties between markets are not easily identifiable, but one can think of the presence of strong economic links and coordination of macroeconomic policies between countries, deregulation and market liberalisation measures, and increasing activities of multinational corporations and institutional investors.

The European Union, as the most successful integration attempt so far, has been studied increasingly, with results indicating a significant increase of correlations among European markets, both at the geographical and industrial level. The introduction of the euro and the subsequent disappearance of exchange rate risk in the EMU area imply that investors should be concerned with the benefits of their diversification strategies, especially when before the introduction of the euro they held diversified portfolios at the European level. Recently, research on the European economic integration process and its impact on capital markets, including the introduction of the euro, has flourished. Fratzscher (2001) analyses the integration process of European equity markets since the 1980s, and demonstrates that these markets have become highly integrated only since 1998. This high level of integration between European equity markets is largely explained by the drive towards EMU through the elimination of exchange rate volatility. Reszat (2003) shows that the contribution of the common currency to financial integration has been stronger the more national markets have in common. On the other hand, Adjaouté and Danthine (2003) reassessed, in the light of modern financial theory, the recent evolution of capital markets in the euro area, and concluded that European capital markets are still segmented, which leads to higher costs for treasuries and taxpayers, urging for measures to be taken in favour of a higher integration of these markets. Garcia Pascual (2003) finds evidence of increasing integration of the French stock market, but not of the British and German markets, while Rangvid (2001) also identifies a rise in the degree of convergence among European stock markets in the last two decades. More recently, Kashefi (2006) studied the effect of the euro introduction on European equity markets and found a significant increase in correlations among stock returns between pre- and post-introduction periods, which shows that diversification opportunities within EMU, at least, have decreased at a country level in the post-introduction period.

In their search for improved portfolio performance, institutional investors' attention was drawn to emerging markets, beginning with the 1980s, as these countries were able to provide them with high returns and low correlations with developed markets. From the perspective of European investors in particular, Central and Eastern European markets are of interest at least for two reasons: the geographical proximity and their accession to the European Union. As a result, research on the links between this region's capital markets and EU markets has burgeoned, but the effective benefits of diversification received mixed results in the existing literature.

Gilmore and McManus (2002) found there is no long-term relationship between major markets in Central Europe, after conducting a co-integration test on stock returns from these markets, while the Granger causality test showed that no causality is present between these markets and the US markets. They found, however, evidence for causation between Hungary and Poland. Egert and Kocenda (2007) analyse co-movements among three stock markets in Central and Eastern Europe (Hungary, Poland and Czech Republic) and the interdependence between them and Western European markets (Germany, France and the United Kingdom), using intraday price data. They find no signs of robust co-integration relationships between stock indices in a bivariate or multivariate framework, but discover short-term spillover effects both in terms of stock returns and stock price volatility. Patev et al. (2006) evaluate the degree of market integration between the US stock market and Central and Eastern European markets, through the use of co-integration, Granger causality and variance decomposition tests, by studying the long-run and short-run convergence among stock prices in Hungarian, Polish, Russian, Czech and US markets. They find that Central and Eastern European markets are segmented, but during crisis times there is an increase in the comovements between markets, which leads to a sharp decrease in the diversification benefits for an American investor allocating his funds in the region's stocks. At the same time, the intensity of co-movements between markets decreased after the crisis, which restores the diversification opportunities in Central and Eastern European markets.

Our current research continues previous attempts to investigate capital market linkages between Central and Eastern European countries, including Romania, and between them and Western European countries (Horobet and Dumitrescu, 2009a, 2009b; Horobet and Lupu, 2009; Horobet et al., 2010). Horobet and Lupu (2009) analysed the stock markets of five emerging countries from the CEE region – the Czech Republic, Hungary, Poland, Romania and Russia – and contrasted them against four major EU markets – Austria, France, Germany and the United Kingdom – over the 2003-07 period, aiming at identifying the speed and significance of information transmission among them, as included in stock market returns. Using different return frequencies, after performing co-integration and Granger causality tests, their results indicate that these markets react rather quickly to information included in the returns on the other markets and that this flow of information takes place in both directions, from the developed markets to the emerging ones and vice versa. At the same time, investors on emerging markets seem to take into account information from other emerging markets in the region.

Nevertheless, the results cannot definitely indicate whether there is a direct transmission of information from one market to another or a common reaction of all markets to some other information relevant to them, either on a European or global level. Horobet and Dumitrescu (2009a, 2009b) explored the increase in correlations between three emerging markets from the European Union – the Czech Republic, Hungary and Poland – and three developed markets from the European Union, namely Austria, France and Germany, as well as the link between correlations and stock market volatilities in this sample of countries. They find that there is an observable and statistically significant positive trend in cross-market correlations after the euro introduction in 1999, which may indicate a higher integration of these capital markets. At the same time, they observe that movements in national stock markets are not fully synchronised, but correlations tend to be high in periods of high market volatility. Pursuing a different approach, Horobet et al. (2010) study the evolution of the financial integration process in Central and Eastern European emerging markets by analysing a wide range of factors that influence stock market returns in these countries. They find that regional factors have increased in importance, although local risk factors continue to play an important role in explaining the performance of the emerging capital markets. The differences between countries are significant, some of the markets showing a high degree of financial integration with developed markets, while other markets remain segmented.

Given these realities, it is not irrelevant to ask whether the benefits of international diversification have dramatically diminished in the past 30 years or so, particularly for European investors. Various methodological approaches and measures that show the extent of diversification benefits have been used in the literature so far. We explore a few of them and then point to the improvements that our methodology brings in terms of analysing the time-varying performance of an internationally diversified portfolio from the perspective of a European investor.

The simplest way to measure the extent of diversification benefits is to assess how much international diversification can reduce the variance of a domestic portfolio without changing its return, and to extend this to identify significant and persistent shifts at the level of the efficient frontier built with domestic assets only.

A number of studies have pursued this research direction (see, for example, Grauer and Hakansson, 1987; Levy and Lerman, 1988; Bailey and Stulz, 1992; Eun and Resnick, 1994). More recently, researchers began to address the question of whether diversification benefits have changed in time, by employing more advanced testing methodologies. Among the first studies in this line of research, Meric and Meric (1989) find evidence that diversification across countries results in higher risk reduction than diversification across industries, but the inter-temporal stability tests applied indicate that the longer the time period considered the better proxies ex-post patterns of co-movement can be for the ex-ante co-movements of international stock markets. De Santis and Gerard (1997) estimate that the expected gains from international diversification for a US investor average 2.11 percent per year and have not significantly declined over the last two decades, by employing a methodology that tests the conditional CAPM for the world's largest equity markets using a parsimonious GARCH parameterisation. Ang and Bekaert (2002) offer a solution for the dynamic portfolio choice problem of a US investor faced with a time-varying investment opportunity set which may be characterised by correlations and volatilities that increase in bad times. By using a regime-switching model, they find evidence for the existence of a high volatility regime, in which returns are more highly correlated and have lower means. They show that international diversification is still valuable with regime changes and currency hedging brings further benefit. Fooladi and Rumsey (2006) examine the benefits of international diversification between 1988 and 2000 using a variable constructed as a ratio between the standard deviation of return for an equally weighted internationally diversified portfolio and the average standard deviation of returns for all markets included in this portfolio. They show that despite the international capital markets integration process, the benefits of international diversification measured in US dollars persist because the increase in co-movements between equity market returns measured in local currencies has been counterbalanced by movements in exchange rates.

Another measure of diversification benefits has been proposed by Middleton et al. (2008), who examine the potential benefits from investing into eight stock markets of Central and Eastern Europe between 1998 and 2003. The authors examine the mean return per unit of risk (MRPUR) for a portfolio of CEE equities, estimated by calculating the ratio of the mean return of a portfolio to its standard deviation and reach the conclusion that investing in CEE offers substantial benefits for a European investor, accruing, however, more from the geographical spread than from the industrial equity mix.

3. DATA AND RESEARCH METHOLODOGY

We measure the benefits of diversification by considering the ratio γ of the standard deviation of the minimum variance portfolio (MVP) for a European investor to the average standard deviation of all markets included in the portfolio. The size of γ, which may vary between zero and one, is inversely correlated to the benefit a European investor derives from international diversification. The MVP includes equities from developed and emerging countries that we include in one of three categories: (1) EMU members – Austria, France, Germany, Italy, the Netherlands, Spain; (2) EU but not EMU members – the United Kingdom, the Czech Republic, Hungary, Poland, Romania; and (3) non-EU members – the United States, Japan, Brazil, Russia, India and China. The trend of benefits from international diversification is afterwards examined by studying the changes in γ over time. We use a period that spans over 135 months, from January 1999 to March 2010, and build a time series with daily values for γ.

We analyse the trends in γ in two ways. First, we regress γ against time. Second, we observe the difference between the means and volatilities of γ for three sub-periods: (1) January 1999 - April 2004; (2) May 2004 - September 2008; (2) October 2008 - March 2010. Each of these sub-periods is significant for the following reasons: May 2004 marks the entrance into the European Union of ten new countries and October 2008 represents the beginning of the current financial turmoil. Therefore, our time test of γ will offer insight not only on the impact of capital market integration on the benefits of internationally diversified portfolios, but also on the size of diversification benefits in normal versus turbulent times.

Understanding the nature of the time dependency of volatility is critical for macroeconomic and financial applications and models of conditional heteroskedasticity as return time series are used for making financial decisions, including portfolio choice decisions, on the basis of the observed asset price data in discrete time. ARCH models were proposed by Engle

(1982) and generalised as GARCH by Bollerslev (1986) and Taylor (1986), as these are better able at handling time-varying volatility.

If we let Z_n be a sequence of i.i.d. random variables such that $Z_n \sim N(0,1)$, then X_t is called a GARCH(q,p) process if

$$X_t = \sigma_t Z_t, \quad t \in Z \tag{13.1}$$

where σ_t is a nonnegative process with the following specification:

$$\sigma_t^2 = \alpha_0 + \alpha_1 X_{t-1}^2 + ... + \alpha_q X_{t-q}^2 + \beta_1 \sigma_{t-1}^2 + ... + \beta_p \sigma_{t-p}^2, \quad t \in Z \tag{13.2}$$

and $\alpha_i \geq 0, \quad i = 1,...,q, \quad \beta_i \geq 0, \quad i = 1,...,p$.

The simplest GARCH model of conditional variance, GARCH(1,1) may be written as

$$\sigma_t^2 = \omega + \alpha R_t^2 + \beta \sigma_{t-1}^2 \quad . \tag{13.3}$$

The RiskMetrics model is a special case of a GARCH(1,1) process if $\alpha = 1 - \lambda$ and $\beta = \lambda$, so that $\alpha + \beta = 1$. Also, $\omega = 0$ in this special case.

First, we estimated simple GARCH(1,1) models on the index return series (in EUR) and generated the series of conditional standard deviations for each country. Second, we applied the RiskMetrics model (using the value $\lambda = 0.94$, which is typical for this model) on the standardised returns $z_{it} = R_{it} / \sigma_{it}$, where σ_{it} is the conditional volatility of market index i obtained previously, to get the covariances of the standardised return pair $E(z_{it} z_{jt})$. Next, by multiplying the covariances of the standardised return pairs with the conditional volatilities of the respective market indices we obtained estimates of the conditional covariances $\text{cov}(R_{it}, R_{jt}) = \rho_{ij} \sigma_{it} \sigma_{jt}$. Using the standard approach (see, for example, Huang and Litzenberger, 1988), we computed the standard daily deviations of the minimum variance portfolio ($\sigma_{mvp,t}$) and the average daily standard deviation of an equally weighted portfolio $\sigma_{evp,t}$, assuming pairwise correlations to be 1. Afterwards, we obtained the daily γ series $\gamma_t = \sigma_{mvp,t} / \sigma_{evp,t}$.

In order to capture gamma trends we regress it on time using the following equation:

$$\gamma_T = \alpha_0 + \alpha_1 T + u_T \quad , \tag{13.4}$$

where, in order to allow for possible serial correlation of the residuals, the residual u_T is assumed to take the form

$$u_T = \theta u_{T-1} + \varepsilon_T, \quad \varepsilon_T \sim N(0,1) .\tag{13.5}$$

Regression (13.4) is run for three structures of the u_t: (1) a standard OLS, and (2) a generalised least squared regression with one lag.

4.   RESULTS

4.1. Descriptive Statistics

The stock market indices denominated in EUR for the entire sample of 17 countries used in our analysis show, with few exceptions, the same general evolution pattern between January 1999 and April 2010. In almost all countries one may observe the increase in indices until September 2008, followed by the subsequent dramatic decline induced by the current financial turmoil, and accompanied afterwards by some market recovery. The exceptions from this pattern are France, the United Kingdom, Italy, Japan, the Netherlands and the United States, in their cases the main explanation residing in the strong appreciation of the euro against the US dollar and other main currencies until the end of 2000, followed by the later swings of the euro exchange rates. Daily returns calculated from the same stock market indices allow one to notice the well-documented phenomenon of volatility clustering, particularly around the month of October 2008, which represents the culmination of the current financial crisis. From the perspective of any investor, regardless of his or her nationality, the increased volatility of all these markets does not bring good news, when we think of its impact on portfolio volatility (even in the case when the portfolio is well diversified).

   Table 13.1 shows the descriptive statistics for euro denominated daily returns for all countries included in our analysis, for the overall and also for the three periods that we considered relevant in terms of implications for international diversification benefits. The changing performances during 1999-2010 of all markets are easily observable and also the general behaviour of developed versus emerging markets. Over the entire period and over each of the three sub-periods, emerging countries would have provided euro-based investors with highest mean returns (Russia has the highest mean return over the entire period and the first sub-period, while China takes its place in the second and third sub-periods) and highest volatility (Russia displays the highest volatility of returns overall and during the first and third sub-periods, replaced by China during the second sub-period).

Table 13.1   Descriptive statistics for EUR-denominated daily returns, all countries, January 1999 - April 2010

	Austria	Brazil	China	Czech Rep.	Germany	Spain	France	UK	Hungary	India	Italy	Japan	Netherlands	Poland	Romania	Russia	US
Overall period: January 5, 1999 - April 22, 2010																	
Mean	0.0001	0.0006	0.0002	0.0006	0.0000	0.0000	0.0000	-0.0001	0.0003	0.0006	-0.0002	0.0000	-0.0001	0.0002	0.0005	0.0008	-0.0001
Median	0.0006	0.0014	0.0004	0.0007	0.0005	0.0004	0.0004	0.0003	0.0005	0.0010	0.0002	0.0001	0.0002	0.0005	0.0004	0.0013	0.0005
Maximum	0.1203	0.2340	0.1449	0.1779	0.0988	0.1061	0.0963	0.1028	0.1838	0.1904	0.1038	0.1124	0.0901	0.1230	0.1035	0.2309	0.0972
Minimum	-0.1218	-0.1800	-0.1202	-0.1540	-0.0956	-0.0981	-0.0950	-0.0908	-0.1913	-0.1313	-0.0883	-0.0972	-0.0945	-0.1342	-0.1502	-0.2353	-0.0830
Std. Dev.	0.0160	0.0280	0.0212	0.0179	0.0165	0.0154	0.0153	0.0144	0.0212	0.0196	0.0145	0.0155	0.0153	0.0206	0.0196	0.0289	0.0148
Skewness	-0.3261	0.0286	0.0126	-0.1422	-0.0214	-0.0472	-0.0579	-0.1109	-0.1549	-0.0235	-0.1211	-0.0704	-0.1744	-0.1866	-0.3230	-0.1771	-0.0571
Kurtosis	11.7428	9.1103	6.7045	11.9373	6.5302	7.6195	7.5014	8.2691	10.8287	8.7651	8.6532	6.1550	7.6902	6.1078	7.9882	10.7334	6.9215
Jarque-Bera	9441.11	4586.51	1685.80	9821.32	1531.04	2622.36	2490.61	3416.33	7540.03	4082.82	3932.78	1225.11	2717.02	1203.49	3107.66	7361.47	1890.57
First period: January 5 1999 - April 30 ,2004																	
Mean	0.0003	0.0001	-0.0003	0.0006	-0.0002	-0.0001	-0.0001	-0.0001	0.0003	0.0005	-0.0002	0.0000	-0.0003	0.0001	0.0006	0.0015	-0.0001
Median	0.0004	0.0010	-0.0005	0.0005	-0.0002	-0.0002	0.0000	-0.0001	0.0002	0.0005	-0.0001	-0.0001	-0.0002	-0.0001	0.0000	0.0013	0.0003
Maximum	0.0353	0.2340	0.1171	0.0746	0.0707	0.0648	0.0676	0.0719	0.0915	0.1007	0.0642	0.0723	0.0851	0.1035	0.0936	0.1901	0.0717
Minimum	-0.0511	-0.1354	-0.1062	-0.0716	-0.0956	-0.0812	-0.0812	-0.0705	-0.1191	-0.0788	-0.0777	-0.0634	-0.0817	-0.1342	-0.0984	-0.1979	-0.0720
Std. Dev.	0.0106	0.0293	0.0214	0.0163	0.0183	0.0157	0.0159	0.0140	0.0176	0.0182	0.0143	0.0154	0.0162	0.0202	0.0177	0.0307	0.0159
Skewness	-0.2808	0.2745	0.0254	-0.1216	-0.0187	0.0159	-0.0990	-0.0569	-0.1059	-0.1556	-0.1915	0.0037	-0.1234	-0.0619	0.1869	-0.1042	0.0942
Kurtosis	4.4016	7.9495	5.1548	4.3063	4.6759	4.6995	4.7012	4.6372	7.0391	4.9197	4.9963	3.8990	5.6994	5.4615	7.1169	7.0252	4.1390
Jarque-Bera	131.94	1435.25	268.86	102.18	162.62	167.22	169.77	155.88	946.77	218.89	239.13	46.78	425.26	351.55	989.02	940.24	77.13
Second period: May 1, 2004 - September 30, 2008																	
Mean	0.0001	0.0010	0.0005	0.0009	0.0009	0.0003	0.0001	-0.0001	0.0004	0.0005	-0.0001	-0.0001	0.0001	0.0005	0.0005	0.0003	-0.0001
Median	0.0011	0.0018	0.0013	0.0009	0.0010	0.0008	0.0007	0.0005	0.0011	0.0013	0.0006	0.0001	0.0005	0.0012	0.0006	0.0011	0.0005
Maximum	0.1181	0.1245	0.1201	0.1057	0.0591	0.0790	0.0784	0.0834	0.1128	0.0882	0.0777	0.0473	0.0631	0.0638	0.1021	0.2309	0.0743
Minimum	-0.0879	-0.1468	-0.1202	-0.0703	-0.0724	-0.0794	-0.0675	-0.0597	-0.0708	-0.1313	-0.0509	-0.0816	-0.0748	-0.0193	-0.1193	-0.1473	-0.0781
Std. Dev.	0.0135	0.0233	0.0186	0.0146	0.0109	0.0113	0.0112	0.0112	0.0175	0.0186	0.0101	0.0131	0.0110	0.0163	0.0184	0.0217	0.0111
Skewness	-0.2412	-0.4705	-0.1303	-0.0268	-0.3840	-0.1145	-0.0922	-0.0358	0.0267	-0.6450	-0.0809	-0.4058	-0.4313	-0.2431	-0.3758	0.3569	-0.3665
Kurtosis	11.5233	6.8046	7.9803	8.4406	6.4382	9.8002	7.6901	8.5356	5.1506	7.9433	8.2163	5.3409	8.6322	4.4885	7.1672	18.1373	9.3682
Jarque-Bera	3498.18	737.29	1193.82	1400.10	595.74	2222.19	1057.50	1471.11	222.13	1252.84	1307.31	294.65	1558.38	117.70	860.65	11023.11	1972.35
Third period: October 1, 2008 - April 22, 2010																	
Mean	-0.0005	0.0012	0.0010	-0.0003	-0.0001	0.0000	0.0000	0.0001	0.0002	0.0011	-0.0003	0.0002	0.0003	-0.0002	0.0005	0.0003	0.0002
Median	0.0001	0.0016	0.0002	0.0007	0.0003	0.0008	0.0003	0.0016	0.0012	0.0025	-0.0001	0.0010	0.0003	0.0009	0.0017	0.0027	0.0009
Maximum	0.1203	0.2069	0.1449	0.1779	0.0988	0.1061	0.0963	0.1028	0.1838	0.1904	0.1038	0.1124	0.0901	0.1230	0.1035	0.2050	0.0972
Minimum	-0.1218	-0.1800	-0.1158	-0.1540	-0.0758	-0.0981	-0.0950	-0.0908	-0.1913	-0.0927	-0.0883	-0.0972	-0.0945	-0.1180	-0.1502	-0.2353	-0.0830
Std. Dev.	0.0308	0.0348	0.0269	0.0285	0.0220	0.0226	0.0221	0.0221	0.0367	0.0262	0.0234	0.0210	0.0213	0.0306	0.0278	0.0390	0.0193
Skewness	-0.1854	-0.0344	0.1100	-0.0976	0.1493	-0.0614	0.0271	-0.1792	-0.1813	0.7326	-0.0321	0.0510	-0.1164	-0.2150	-0.6849	-0.5454	-0.1921
Kurtosis	4.7187	10.2185	6.6869	10.3074	6.0988	6.3775	6.9320	6.8108	6.8018	10.4703	6.1628	7.0436	6.5653	4.5792	6.5976	9.4650	7.9593
Jarque-Bera	52.43	883.72	231.34	906.18	164.36	193.71	262.23	248.45	247.35	982.77	169.71	277.46	216.49	45.43	251.31	728.96	419.59

On the other hand, EMU countries or other developed countries have the lowest mean returns and volatilities overall and during each of the three sub-periods, with the notable exception of the Czech Republic whose stock market shows the lowest return volatility during the third sub-period. Another noteworthy observation emerging from our results is that almost all return distributions are negatively skewed and leptokurtic, the Jarque-Berra test confirming non-normally distributed returns.

We present in Table 13.2 the average correlations between pairs of countries by taking into account the three categories of countries defined in Section 3: EMU countries, EU non-EMU countries and non-EU countries. All average correlations show increased values from the first to the third period, but the overall correlation coefficients are rather small, with the exception of correlations between EMU countries (0.762) and between EMU and EU non-EMU countries (0.5135). When interpreting the increased correlations from the first to the third sub-period one should be careful of not taking the higher correlation values for the third period as an indication of possible higher levels of market integration, but rather as the effect of financial turbulences that started at the end of 2008. At the same time, our results signify that Eurozone and EU investors benefit from diversification opportunities outside their regions, on one hand, and that, on the other hand, these benefits within their region have declined over time.

Table 13.2   Cross-country correlations of daily returns between groups of countries

	Overall period: January 5, 1999 - April 22, 2010	First period: January 5, 1999 - April 30, 2004	Second period: May 1, 2004 - September 30, 2008	Third period: October 1, 2008 - April 22, 2010
EMU / EMU	0.7621	0.6614	0.8423	0.8561
EU non-EMU / EU non-EMU	0.4453	0.2881	0.4622	0.6334
Outside EU	0.2973	0.2714	0.3134	0.3337
EMU / EU non-EMU	0.5135	0.3649	0.5561	0.6864
EMU / Outside EU	0.3441	0.2738	0.3956	0.4275
EU non-EMU / Outside EU	0.3033	0.2410	0.3111	0.4047

4.2. Analysis of Diversification Benefits

Figure 13.1 shows the evolution of γ in time and its trend over the three periods we analysed ((a) January 2001 - April 2004, (b) May 2004 - August 2008 and (c) September 2008 - April 2010), as well as γ's conditional volatility, while Table 13.3 presents its descriptive statistics. To generate the series for γ, we used 'rolling' expected returns for the market indices in the sample, computed as simple averages with increasing time span $e_T = (1/T)\sum_{t=1}^{T} r_t$ for $T = 1,...,N$, where N denotes the number of days in the entire period from 1999 to 2010 (2948 observations). We computed the results for γ starting in January 2001 to eliminate the high volatility present in the expected return series for low values of T.

Overall, γ values indicate that a Eurozone investor holding the minimum variance portfolio (MVP) obtains significant benefits in terms of volatility, but these benefits are highly variable from one day to the other. Over the entire period, γ has a mean of 0.316 and a standard deviation of 0.053, which suggests that MVP has a volatility that is approximately one third of an equally weighted portfolio constructed from the 17 countries assuming correlations of one among them. When we split the period over the three subperiods, we observe that γ means change in time, but the changes are rather small, maybe a more interesting observation referring to the changing volatility in γ over time. Moreover, gamma's volatility is lower and its means are higher during the first and the third period compared to the second period.

At least for what concerns the third period, we may interpret this result as showing that diversification benefits increase in turbulent times, although not dramatically, and are more concentrated, which may indicate higher incentives for portfolio rebalancing in such times. To some extent, the results for γ during the first period – which includes the turbulent years at the beginning of the 21st century marked by the dot-com bubble and corporate restructuring crisis – may confirm our findings for the third period.

The results of γ regressions on time are presented in Table 13.4. When using OLS γ has a slightly positive or negative statistically significant trend, for the overall period and for all of the sub-periods, but when the autocorrelation in residuals is taken into account by the use of GLS the trends become statistically insignificant (see the p-values for α_1 parameters and the high statistically significant values for θ). This means that from a European investor point of view the diversification benefits have not diminished or increased dramatically in time and when the trend is removed the γ series is mean-stationary.

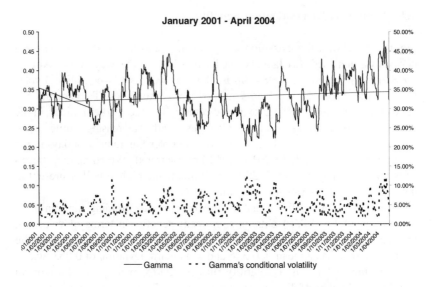

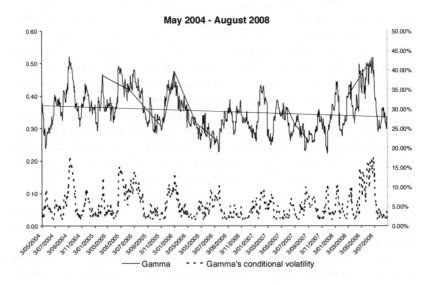

*Figure 13.1   Time-varying γ and conditional volatility estimated with a
GARCH(1,1) model for the three periods analysed*

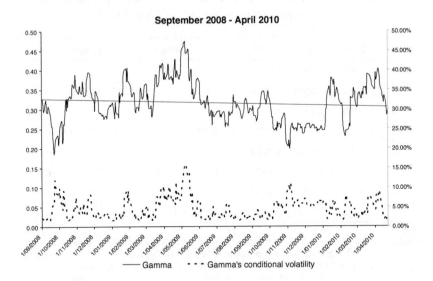

Figure 13.1 (continued)

Table 13.3   *Descriptive statistics for the γ series*

	γ		
	1st period	2nd period	3rd period
Mean	0.330	0.354	0.317
Median	0.330	0.347	0.315
Maximum	0.476	0.522	0.474
Minimum	0.203	0.223	0.187
Std. Dev.	0.051	0.061	0.053
Skewness	0.084	0.456	0.271
Kurtosis	2.502	2.652	2.878

Note: The 1st period starts in January 2001 and ends in April 2004, the 2nd period starts in May 2004 and ends in August 2008, and the 3rd period starts in September 2008 and ends in April 2010.

Table 13.4   Results of regression analysis for the overall period and the three sub-periods using standard OLS and GLS

	Model	α_0	p-value	α_1	p-value	θ	p-value	R^2
1st period	OLS	0.3014	0.0000	3.05E-05	0.0000			0.223
	GLS	0.2990	0.0000	3.19E-05	0.4115	0.9397	0.0000	0.218
2nd period	OLS	0.4147	0.0000	-3.13E-05	0.0000			0.279
	GLS	0.4275	0.0000	-3.72E-05	0.3310	0.9598	0.0000	0.265
3rd period	OLS	0.4510	0.0000	-4.92E-05	0.0165			0.134
	GLS	0.4578	0.1477	-5.19E-05	0.6515	0.9384	0.0000	0.132
Total period	OLS	0.3281	0.0000	4.00E-06	0.0001			0.005
	GLS	0.3350	0.0000	3.32E-05	0.8951	0.9493	0.0000	0.001

Note: Regression results for equation (13.4), where γ_T is the ratio of the standard deviation of the minimum variance portfolio to the average standard deviation of all markets included in the portfolio, estimated for day T. The residual u_t takes the form as in equation (13.5). The R^2 reported are for the OLS and GLS equations, respectively.

When judging the overall diversification benefit we need a measure of comparison not only for volatility, but also for returns. Therefore, we computed the daily MVP excess returns over the risk-free rate and plotted their values over the three sub-periods in Figure 13.2. The risk-free rate we used is the three-month interbank deposit rate in the Eurozone. Values above zero indicate higher MVP returns than the risk-free rate, while values below zero indicate a better performance in terms of returns for the risk-free securities.

We observe that excess returns are volatile and variable among the three sub-periods. Over the entire period, the MVP excess return has a monthly mean of −0.001095, but the mean is negative over the first and third sub-periods (−0.00254 and −0.00298, respectively) and positive over the second sub-period (0.000738).

Moreover, in the first and third sub-periods, 24.02% and 24.48% of excess returns are positive, while in the second sub-period more then 50% of excess returns (55.75%) are positive. These results imply that during the second sub-period investors will most likely have obtained higher Sharpe ratios for their optimal portfolios than in the other two sub-periods. This is not a surprising result, as the years between 2004 and 2008 saw high returns and lower volatility in all stock markets around the world, both having been corrected since October 2008.

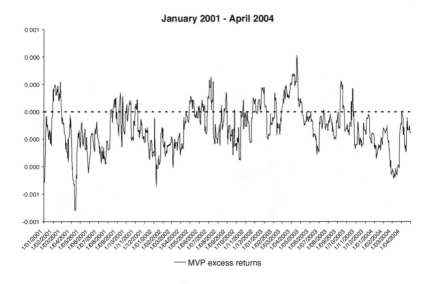

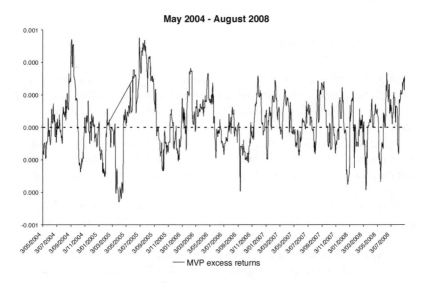

Figure 13.2   Minimum variance portfolio o excess returns

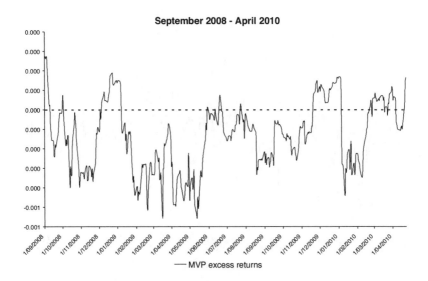

Figure 13.2 (continued)

5.   CONCLUSIONS

From a theoretical perspective, the introduction of the euro has an unclear effect on the portfolio decisions of Eurozone investors, as we may expect. On the one hand, we noted a reallocation of the portfolio weights in favour of EMU assets as a result of the complete elimination of currency risk, and, on the other hand, a higher weight for assets outside EU, as a direct consequence of increased financial market integration between European Union countries and the concomitant wish of EU investors therefore to diversify outside of the EU borders.

We measured the benefits of diversification by considering the ratio of the standard deviation of the minimum variance portfolio (MVP) for a European investor to the average standard deviation of all markets included in the portfolio, which we have called γ. The size of γ, which may vary between zero and one, is inversely correlated to the benefit a European investor derives from international diversification. The MVP includes equities from 17 developed and emerging countries that we include in one of three categories: EU and EMU members, EU but not EMU members, and non-EU members. The trend of benefits from international diversification was afterwards examined by studying the changes in γ over time and between three sub-periods: January 1999 - April 2004, May 2004 - September 2008 and October 2008 - April 2010. Each of these sub-periods is important for the following reasons: May 2004 marks the entrance into the European Union of ten new countries and October 2008 represents the beginning of the current financial turmoil. Therefore, our time test of γ offers insight not only on the impact of capital market integration on the benefits of internationally diversified portfolios, but also on the size of diversification benefits in normal versus turbulent times.

The behaviour of γ over time in the different periods indicates that a Eurozone investor holding the minimum variance portfolio obtains significant benefits in terms of volatility, but they are highly variable from one day to the other. We find that γ's volatility is lower and its means are higher during the first and the third period compared to the second period. At least for what concerns the third period, we may interpret this result as showing that diversification benefits increase in turbulent times, although not dramatically, and are more concentrated, which may indicate higher incentives for portfolio rebalancing in such times.

In order to better identify the overall diversification benefit we also computed the daily MVP excess returns over the risk-free rate. These excess returns are volatile and variable among the three sub-periods, but their value indicates that during the second of our three sub-periods investors will most likely obtain higher Sharpe ratios for their optimal portfolios than in the other two sub-periods. This is not a surprising result, as the years between 2004 and 2008 saw high returns and lower volatility in all stock markets around the world, both having been corrected since October 2008.

Our results show that diversification benefits are still high for a Eurozone investor and they have slightly increased after 2004. In times of financial crisis, such as the recent one, international diversification may bring attractive benefits in the form of low portfolio volatility, although these benefits are to some extent smaller than in normal times.

Our findings are important for international portfolio diversifiers despite the high correlations among markets typical for in crisis times, including the current one. As we showed above, the literature in the field acknowledged the (sometimes) dramatic increase in correlations in times of crisis, which raises the issue of diversification benefits compared to normal times. The severity of the current crisis may be largely due to the fact that market participants, including investors, banks, credit rating agencies and government authorities – who apparently supposed that returns on assets were largely uncorrelated, so that the Law of Large Numbers would apply – were indeed considerably underestimating risks and ignoring the size of risk exposures. Since our analysis covered the period underlying the current financial and economic crisis we may however conclude that diversification at a global level for Eurozone investors might have been valuable even in such harsh times.

To better understand the time-varying specificities of benefits derived from holding international portfolios, the analysis needs to further address the changes in countries' weights in the minimum variance portfolio, as well as the pervasive impact of exchange rate risk. We intend to continue our research in both directions.

REFERENCES

Adjaouté, K. and J.-P. Danthine (2003), 'European Financial Integration and Equity Returns : a Theory-Based Assessment', FAME Working paper, no. 84.

Ang, A. and G. Bekaert (2002), 'International Asset Allocation with Regime Shifts', *Review of Financial Studies*, **15**, 1137-1187.

Arshanapalli, A. and J. Doukas (1993), 'International Stock Market Linkages: Evidence from the Pre- and Post-October 1987 Period', *Journal of Banking and Finance*, **17**, 93-208.

Bailey, W. and R.M. Stulz (1992), 'Benefits of International Diversification: the Case of Pacific Basin Stock Markets', *Journal of Portfolio Management*, **16**, 57-61.

Bekaert, G. and R.J. Hodrick (2006), 'International Stock Return Comovements', *CEPR Discussion Paper* 5855.

Books, R. and M. del Negro (2002), 'International Stock Returns and Market Integration: a Regional Perspective', *IMF Working Paper*.

Bollerslev, T. (1986), 'Generalized Autoregressive Conditional Heteroskedasticity', *Journal of Econometrics*, **31**, 307-327.

Bracker, K., D.S. Docking and P.D. Koch (1999), 'Economic Determinants of Evolution in International Stock Market Integration', *Journal of Empirical Finance*, **6**, 1-27.

Chan, K.C., B.E. Gup and M.S. Pan (1992), 'An Empirical Analysis of Stock Prices in Major Asian Markets and the United States', *Financial Review*, **27**, 289-307.

Chen, G., M. Firth and O.M. Rui (2002), 'Stock Market Linkages: Evidence from Latin America', *Journal of Banking and Finance*, **26**, 1113-1141.

De Santis, G. and B. Gerard (1997), 'International Asset Pricing and Portfolio Diversification with Time-varying Risk', *Journal of Finance*, **52**, 1881-1912.

Eaker, M.R. and D. Grant (1990), 'Currency Hedging Strategies for Internationally Diversified Portfolios', *Journal of Portfolio Management*, **17**, 30-33.

Egert, B. and E. Kocenda (2007), 'Interdependence between Eastern and Western European Stock Markets: Evidence from Intraday Data', *Economic Systems*, **31**, 184-203.

Engle, R.F. (1982), 'Autoregressive Conditional Heteroskedasticity with Estimates of the Variance of United Kingdom Inflation', *Econometrica*, **50**, 987-1007.

Eun, C.S. and B. Resnick (1994), 'International Diversification of Investment Portfolios: U.S. and Japanese Perspectives', *Management Science*, **40**, 140-161.

Eun, C.S. and B. Resnick (1998), 'Exchange Rate Uncertainty, Forward Contracts, and International Portfolio Selection', *Journal of Finance*, **43**, 22-31.

Fooladi, I.J. and J. Rumsey (2006), 'Globalization and Portfolio Risk over Time: the Role of Exchange Rate', *Review of Financial Economics*, **15**, 223-236.

Fratzscher, M. (2001), 'Financial Market Integration in Europe: on the Effects of EMU on Stock Markets', *European Central Bank Working Paper*, no. 48.

Garcia Pascual, A. (2003), 'Assessing European Stock Markets (Co)integration', *Economics Letters*, **78**, 197-203.

Gilmore, C.G. and G.M. McManus (2002), 'International Portfolio Diversification: US and Central European Equity Markets', *Emerging Markets Review*, **3**, 69-83.

Goetzmann, W.N., L. Li and K.G. Rouwenhorst (2001), 'Long-term Global Market Correlations', *NBER Working Paper*, 8612.

Grauer, R.R. and N.H. Hakansson (1987), 'Gains from International Diversification: 1968-85 Returns on Portfolios of Stocks and Bonds', *Journal of Finance*, **42**, 721-738.

Hassan, A.M.H. (2003), 'Financial Integration of Stock Markets in the Gulf: a Multivariate Cointegration Analysis', *International Journal of Business*, **8**, 335-346.

Heaney, R., V. Hooper and M. Jaugietis (2002), 'Regional Integration of Stock Markets in Latin America', *Journal of Economic Integration*, **17**, 745-760.

Heston, S. and K.G. Rouwenhorst (1994), 'Does Industrial Structure Explain the Benefits of International Diversification?', *Journal of Financial Economics*, **36**, 111-157.

Horobet, A. and S. Dumitrescu (2009a), 'Correlation and Volatility in Central and Eastern European Stock Markets', 16th International Economic Conference – IECS 2009 'Industrial Revolutions from the Globalization and Post-Globalization Perspective', Sibiu, Romania.

Horobet, A. and S. Dumitrescu (2009b), 'Integration of Capital Markets in Central and Eastern Europe: Implications for EU Investors', Proceedings of the International Conference 'Economies of Central and Eastern Europe: Convergence, Opportunities and Challenges', Tallinn, Estonia.

Horobet, A., S. Dumitrescu and I. Tintea (2010), 'Risk Factors in Central and Eastern European Stock Market Returns', *Transformations in Business & Economics*, **9**, Supplement A, 339-360.

Horobet, A. and R. Lupu (2009), 'Are Capital Markets Integrated? A Test of Information Transmission within the European Union', *Romanian Journal of Economic Forecasting*, **10**, 64-80.

Huang, C.F. and R.H. Litzenberger (1988), *Foundations for Financial Economics*, Upper Saddle River, NJ: Prentice Hall.

Hunter, J.E. and T.D. Coggin (1990), 'An Analysis of the Diversification Benefits from International Equity Investments', *Journal of Portfolio Management*, **17**, 33-36.

Jeon, B.N. and T.C. Chiang (1991), 'A System of Stock Prices in World Stock Exchanges: Common Stochastic Trends for 1975-1990?', *Journal of Economics and Business*, **43**, 329-338.

Jorion, P. (1989), 'Asset Allocation with Hedged and Unhedged Foreign Stocks and Bonds', *Journal of Portfolio Management*, **15**, 49-54.

Kashefi, J. (2006), 'The Effect of the Euro on European Equity Markets and International Diversification', *Journal of International Business Research*, **5**, 1-21.

Kaplanis, E.C. (1988), 'Stability and Forecasting of the Co-movement Measures of International Stock Market Return', *Journal of International Money and Finance*, **8**, 63-95.

Kasa, K. (1992), 'Common Stochastic Trends in International Stock Markets', *Journal of Monetary Economics*, **29**, 95-124.

Larrain, F. and J. Tavares (2003), 'Regional Currencies versus Dollarization: Options for Asia and the Americas', *Journal of Policy Reform*, **6**, 35-49.

Lee, K.Y. (2005), 'The Contemporaneous Interactions between the U.S., Japan and Hong Kong Stock Markets', *Economics Letters*, **90**, 21-27.

Levy, H. and Z. Lerman (1988), 'The Benefits of International Diversification in Bonds', *Financial Analysts Journal*, **44**, 56-64.

Longin, F. and B. Solnik (1995), 'Is the Correlation in International Equity Returns Constant: 1960-1990?', *Journal of International Money and Finance*, **14**, 3-26.

Meric, I. and G. Meric (1989), 'Potential Gains from International Portfolio Diversification and Intertemporal Stability and Seasonality in International Stock Market Relationships', *Journal of Banking and Finance*, **13**, 627-640.

Middleton, C.A.J., S.G.M. Fifield and D.M. Power (2008), 'An Investigation of the Benefits of Portfolio Investment in Central and Eastern European Stock Markets', *Research in International Business and Finance*, **22**, 162-174.

Patev, P., N. Kanaryan and K. Lyroudi (2006), 'Stock Market Crises and Portfolio Diversification in Central and Eastern Europe', *Managerial Finance*, **32**, 415-432.

Ramchand, L. and R. Susmel (1998), 'Volatility and Cross Correlation across Major Stock Markets', *Journal of Empirical Finance*, **5**, 397-416.

Rangvid, J. (2001), 'Co-movements in National Stock Market Returns: Evidence of Predictability, but not Co-integration', *Journal of Monetary Economics*, **36**, 631-654.

Ranter, M. (1992), 'Portfolio Diversification and the Intertemporal Stability of International Indices', *Global Finance Journal*, **3**, 67-78.

Reszat, B. (2003), 'How the European Monetary Integration Process Contributed to Regional Financial Market Integration', HWWA Discussion Paper.

Roll, R. (1992), 'Industrial Structure and the Comparative Behavior of International Stock Market Indices', *Journal of Finance*, **47**, 3-41.

Solnik, B. (1974), 'Why Not Diversify Internationally Rather than Domestically?', *Financial Analysts Journal*, **30**, 48-54.

Solnik, B., C. Boucrelle and Y. Le Fur (1996), 'International Market Correlation and Volatility', *Financial Analysts Journal*, **52**, 17-34.

Tavares, J. (2009), 'Economic Integration and the Co-movement of Stock Returns', *Economics Letters*, **103**, 65-67.

Taylor, S.J. (1986), *Modelling Financial Time Series*, New York: Wiley.

Author Index

Subject Index